Critical Essays on
George W. Cable

Critical Essays on George W. Cable

Arlin Turner

G. K. Hall & Co. ● Boston, Massachusetts

Copyright © 1980 by Arlin Turner

Library of Congress Cataloging in Publication Data

Turner, Arlin.
 Critical essays on George W. Cable.

 (Critical essays on American literature)
 Includes index.
 1. Cable, George Washington, 1844-1925—Criticism and inter-
pretation—Addresses, essays, lectures.
I. Title. II. Series.
PS1246.T78   813'.4   79-17229
ISBN 0-8161-8256-6

This publication is printed on permanent/durable acid-free paper
MANUFACTURED IN THE UNITED STATES OF AMERICA

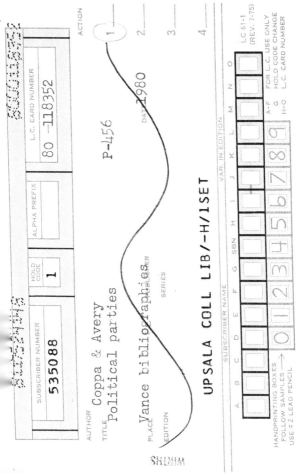

SUBSCRIBER NUMBER
535088

HOLD CODE
1

ALPHA PREFIX

L.C. CARD NUMBER
80 -118352

ACTION
1
2
3
4

AUTHOR Coppa & Avery
TITLE Political parties

DATE 1980

P-456

PLACE
EDITION

Vance bibliographies
SERIES
NUMBER

UPSALA COLL LIB/-H/1SET

VAR. IN EDITION

SUBSCRIBER NAME

A B C D E F G H SBN J K L M N O

0 1 2 3 4 5 6 7 8 9

HANDPRINTING BOXES →
FOLLOW SAMPLES →
USE #2 LEAD PENCIL

A-F FOR L.C. USE ONLY
G HOLD CODE CHANGE
H-O L.C. CARD NUMBER

LC 61-1
(REV. 7-75)

pls. fill up enough card to complete 3 sets

CRITICAL ESSAYS ON AMERICAN LITERATURE

This series seeks to publish the most important reprinted criticism on writers and topics in American literature along with, in various volumes, original essays, interviews, bibliographies, letters, manuscript sections, and other materials brought to public attention for the first time. Arlin Turner, a distinguished Cable scholar and former editor of *American Literature*, has compiled a collection of scholarship on George W. Cable which includes an important introduction assessing the history of scholarship on Cable along with several items from Cable's hand published here for the first time. In addition, the essays by Lafcadio Hearn, D. Warren Brickell, and S. Weir Mitchell are printed from manuscript and represent the first complete recording of these important critical works. We are confident that Professor Turner's volume will make a permanent and significant contribution to American literary scholarship.

James Nagel, GENERAL EDITOR

Northeastern University

CONTENTS

INTRODUCTION

George W. Cable began writing for a newspaper in 1870; he published his first story in 1873, and his last major work, a novel, in 1918. Most of his works are set in his native city of New Orleans and reflect the changing views on the issues of race, class and caste, and Creole-Américain relations from the close of the Civil War to the First World War. During that half-century there were wide shifts in attitudes on public questions, in both the South and the North, and vast changes in literary vogues and in the interests and the tolerances of editors and publishers. There were corresponding changes in Cable's outlook and in his literary aims and methods. Until about 1890, his writings were of two kinds: essays in social criticism and fiction in which he often embodied social comment; after that date, when his views on social matters, particularly on the race question, were no longer welcomed by editors and, presumably, readers, he wrote stories and novels showing little awareness of the current social scene. The criticism of Cable's works as they appeared took note of the changes in their nature and their purpose, and to a considerable extent the criticism shaped the course of his literary career.

The critical opinions of others were important to Cable. Favorable reception of his newspaper work encouraged him to write his first stories; approval by friends and editors kept him writing, even under most difficult circumstances, gave him courage to leave his clerkship and trust his pen for a livelihood, and introduced him to platform reading as a means of providing the income he must have. After he had launched into discussion of Negro rights, he found himself weighing the support against the opposition he encountered in reviews and editorials, as he decided what course to follow in his publications and in his lectures. He found that the widely diverse judgments on his social views carried over into criticism of his stories and novels. From 1885 onward, he could not avoid self-consciousness when writing either social essays or fiction.

The friends and neighbors of Cable's late years knew him as a man growing old quietly and supporting various efforts for social betterment, whether their aim was to spread culture, to improve public and private gardening, to simplify English spelling, to bolster public education, particularly among those he thought in greatest need (the immigrant factory workers in the New England towns and the Southern Negroes), or to enforce world peace through the League of Nations. Not many of them knew about the vigor and the perseverance and the cost to him of what was the greatest effort of his life, his campaign for Negro rights; for that issue had been settled with apparent finality three decades before his death—and settled on terms he had opposed by every means he could command. Those who read his last half-a-dozen books knew him as the author of careful and polished historical novels which showed his normal combination of realism and romance, and which bore unobtrusively but firmly in each plot a series of moral precepts. Few of those readers were aware of the great enthusiasm with which his first Creole stories were read, and the eagerness with which editors and readers awaited new contributions from what they considered his particular province, Creole New Orleans.

During the half-century following Cable's death in 1925, when the role of the Negro in American society was growing again into a topic of national concern, he was reread for the treatment he had given the topic in a score of essays and in much of his fictional writing; and he was reassessed, as it was discovered that he had dealt with the major aspects and the refinements of the subject with understanding far beyond his time—and that he had spoken on some elements of the subject with comprehension and clarity not often encountered in these later times. In this new reading of Cable, his achievement as a literary author has won increased respect, paralleling the greater value placed on his social and political judgment and approaching the critical approval his fiction had in the 1880s.

To an extent that is true of only a few American authors, Cable was self-educated and also self-taught as a writer. Leaving high school without graduating, he began work to support his widowed mother, two sisters, and a younger brother; while campaigning as a Confederate cavalryman and while working as a clerk in New Orleans after the war, he studied algebra and other high-school subjects and read American history. He wanted to write, and in February 1870 began contributing a column to the New Orleans *Picayune*. For a time he was a reporter and afterward he did editorial and feature writing for various newspapers. Encouraged by success with a series of historical sketches and fascinated with the history and the lore of early New Orleans he found in old newspapers and in the archives of the city—all unknown to literature, he said—he began writing stories and laying them away.

Edward King, traveling throughout the South to collect materials for a series of articles that were published first in *Scribner's Monthly Magazine* and later as a book entitled *The Great South*, went to Cable for local information. He took some of Cable's stories with him to New York in the spring of 1873, convinced of their worth and sure, he said, that Cable was a genius. He urged the stories on Richard Watson Gilder, the associate editor of *Scribner's Monthly*, and forwarded to other editors the ones rejected. Cable afterward called King his discoverer, but King said that Cable soon would have made himself known without a sponsor. King's enthusiasm for Cable's stories of Creole New Orleans was soon shared by editors and publishers in New York and Boston, who sought his writings, encouraged him to continue, and helped to shape his works. Although Gilder accepted the story "'Sieur George" only after King had read it aloud to him and had begged him to publish it, he wrote Cable afterward, "you have the makings of one of the best story-writers of the day. All you want is to appreciate yourself."[1]

The fact that Gilder nevertheless rejected several of Cable's early stories and within the next decade rejected some of his essays on the race question and also his novel *John March, Southerner* increased Cable's uncertainties and reminded him of the extent to which he depended on the appraisal of his work by others. Gilder gave him advice freely and had an earnest wish to help him toward the highest achievement possible. But he did not hesitate to insist on his own over Cable's views on realism and romance in fiction, on didacticism, on the allowable levels of the unpleasant and the indelicate in a family magazine, as he phrased it, and on the sectional and racial controversies.

Before sending his early stories away for publication, Cable had criticism and encouragement from friends in New Orleans, particularly from his newspaper associate and probably his closest friend in the city, Marion A. Baker. As the stories appeared, the local newspapers mentioned them with pride because their settings were local and they were written by a native son. The *Picayune* for October 5, 1873, called "'Sieur George" one of the best works in the current *Scribner's Monthly*. It said further that the story would be recognized locally "as a genuine story of New Orleans," that the individuality of the characters and their habits proved Cable's close study of his subject, and that the style had "an originality of thought and expression lifting it above the ordinary level of such contributions."

In February 1877, Cable had a letter from Hjalmar Hjorth Boyesen, a Cornell University professor, himself a novelist, who had read his Creole stories in the magazines and wanted "to hasten the day" when the whole public would recognize Cable's genius. In the correspondence that ensued, generous on each side, they discussed aspects of the novel, and Boyesen no doubt helped Cable to clarify his views on short fiction and encouraged him to undertake a novel.[2] Boyesen urged the Scribner firm to publish a collection of Cable's stories and himself contracted to make up any loss that might result. When *Old Creole Days* was out, the English-language newspapers of New Orleans were unreserved in their praise. The *Picayune* spoke of the "quaint delicacy of style," the "faithful delineation of Creole character," and the "careful rendering of the dialect." The New Orleans *Times* of June 1 said that Cable's writings could be "ranked with those of any other American prose writer, not excluding Nathaniel Hawthorne, which they in so many respects resemble, and in some respects excel." The writer of this review acknowledge the objection to Cable's portrayal of Creole characters voiced in the French-language newspaper, *L'Abeille:*

> He chooses his materials for his character sketches, like the real artist, and gives us the Creole, not perhaps as the upper crust think Creoles to be, nor as that upper crust would like them to be, but just as they are. . . . So true is the author to this idea that some of the pictures sting, and, with the sting, draw forth the critic's remonstrance, which remonstrance is the true criticism of the merits of the picture. . . . The author treads upon the Creole toe only accidentally, as it were, while on the road toward his subject . . . . he loses no opportunity to make due allowances for those same foibles of which he is speaking, and to bring out into as strong a light as possible all the noble and chivalrous traits for which the Creoles are distinguished.

Continuing in the obvious role of peacemaker between Cable and the Creoles, this reviewer remarks that "the Creoles cannot help being pleased" with the

Creole portrait in one story, that Cable shows both sides of the Creole character in another, and that Creole traits appear only slightly in yet another. The discomfort of the Creoles may not have been greater than other distinctive peoples have felt when portrayed in fiction; and there were Creoles who came forward to defend the authenticity of Cable's Creole portraits. When he became the advocate of Negro rights, many of the Creoles would have condemned him on that account alone, and some of them, the historian Charles Gayarré in particular, attached him bitterly for both his Creole stories and his stand on the race question.

Newspapers across the country took notice of *Old Creole Days*. The New York *Evening Post* found "the touch of a true artist" in "these half-pathetic, half-humorous, and altogether delicate sketches." The Detroit *Free Press* found the volume "full of a delicate pathetic humor which has rarely been equaled in American literature." The Boston *Courier* felt it "an imperative critical duty" to pronounce this new author "a genius with special and captivating endowments." In the words of the *Christian Intelligencer*, "The stories, themselves, display an inventive genius which ranks the author among the best of our modern writers." The author of such a slight volume as *Old Creole Days* could not ask for a fuller endorsement than that in the *Cincinnati Times:* "Here is true art work. Here is poetry, pathos, tragedy, humor. Here is an entrancing style. Here is a new field, one full of passion and beauty. Here is local color with strong drawing. Here, in this little volume, is life, breath, and blood. The author of this book is an artist, and over such a revelation one may be permitted strong words."[3]

Magazine reviewers showed themselves delighted with *Old Creole Days* and held out to this remarkable new author the challenge of writing long fiction. They agreed in commending his ability to suggest a charming woman and what the reviewer in the *Atlantic Monthly* for January 1880 termed his "mastery over mongrel dialects." No doubt reflecting his own writing of fiction, Edward Eggleston, the Indiana local colorist, spoke of "a little mistiness" now and then, and the reader's being left "guessing out a half-told riddle"; but he found the characters acting true to their natures. He mentioned the "gentle and joyous humor" of the tales, and other reviewers spoke of the lightness and airiness of the story "Madame Délicieuse."[4] Charles DeKay said in the July *Scribner's* that the man who could write "Jean-ah Poquelin" was "no mere talented writer," but "a genius in his way."

Cable wanted *Old Creole Days* to have a warm welcome in New Orleans, and was happy to see the local sales reach 250 copies early. But collections of stories do not sell, any publisher would say, especially When the contents have been published earlier, and Cable had been urged to write a novel. By the time *The Grandissimes* had finished its magazine serial run and appeared as a book late in 1880, readers and reviewers knew that it was an important novel. On September 27, just as the serial concluded, the New Orleans *Item* printed a review that opens by calling it a "strange, weird, powerful, and pathetic story, which is certainly the most remarkable work of fiction ever created in the South." The reviewer was Lafcadio Hearn (1850–1904), who had come from

Europe to America as a young man and, after a time as a journalist in Cincinnati, moved to New Orleans in 1877 and contributed voluminously to the local newspapers. He shared Cable's love for the semitropical city and his interest in its mixture of languages and peoples. The two of them planned to collaborate in publishing the songs and other lore they both collected on the streets and in the archives. Hearn's own writing in his review of *The Grandissimes* indicates that he knew from experience the richness of color and the sensuousness portrayed in the book, the half-real, half-remembered, dreamlike quality of both scene and action. He speaks of Cable's power of concentrated description, and concludes that as reviewer he can do no more than hint at "the peculiar impression" the novel makes on the reader. He doubts that the book will "become a favorite with residents of the Creole city; . . . its paintings are not always flattering to native eyes;—its evocation of dead memories will not be found pleasing." He questions the reality of Honoré Grandissime, asking, "Was there ever a Creole of Creoles, living in such an age, who could have entertained such ideas on social questions?"

In alluding to the Creoles' objection to *The Grandissimes*, Hearn said, "its spirit has already been severely criticized by a contemporary." His reference was to the pamphlet *Critical Dialogue Between Aboo and Caboo on a New Book; or a Grandissime Ascension*, published anonymously in New Orleans late in 1880. The author, the priest Adrien Rouquette, wrote for the newspapers and published dialect poems; he was a friend of Hearn's and an acquaintance of Cable's. The biographer of Rouquette can account for his writing this crudely scurrilous attack on *The Grandissimes* only by assuming that he wanted to voice the attitudes he knew to be common among the Creoles.[5] In the form of a dialogue between the spirit of a Creole character in the novel and one of his descendants in 1880, the pamphlet strikes most strongly at Cable's portrayal of the Creole ancestry and the injustices suffered by the Negroes and mulattoes. Since the friendship between Hearn and Rouquette seems to have ended in 1880, it may be supposed that this pamphlet was responsible.

The national magazines gave *The Grandissimes* full-scale reviews. In *Scribner's Monthly* for November, Boyesen wrote in language not much more restrained than that in his letters to Cable, in which he predicted that the novel would be, not a story of petty social affairs such as he found prevalent at the time, but a *Kulturroman*, tracing out the clash of opposing civilizations.[6] Unless Poe were counted as a novelist, Boyesen said in his review, Cable was the first Southern novelist to make "a contribution of permanent value to American literature." The reviewers in *Harper's*, the *Atlantic Monthly*, and the *Nation* (William C. Brownell) showed their respect for the novel and its author by touching on the narrative method, including the use of dialect, the historical and geographical orientation, and the social criticism, as well as the characters and the plot. They noted that Cable meant his picture of slavery to be applicable in the year 1880 no less than in the time covered by the novel. The reviewer in *Appletons' Journal* saw in the novel a treatment of the effects slavery had exerted on the slaveowners.[7]

There was agreement among most of the reviewers that the dialect is troublesome, although it may be at times delightful; that the character Frowenfeld is pale, if not simply a piece of machinery included for the convenience of the author; that the complex genealogies and the author's habit "of eddying about his point" leave the reader with unnecessary burdens in following the story. There was agreement also that Cable had based his work on careful research, had dealt with broad and important matters, and had taken full advantage of the fresh and distinctive materials at his disposal. They left no doubt that a major novelist had arrived on the scene.

Praise of *The Grandissimes* reached Cable from many quarters. One correspondent quoted Sidney Lanier as saying that Cable was the only author who had "mastered the sounds of dialect."[8] Robert Underwood Johnson, assistant editor of *Scribner's Monthly Magazine*, who saw the serial through the press while Gilder was abroad, wrote Cable, "This book, it may be almost said, restores the intellectual balance between North and South in fiction."[9] Cable's next book, the novelette *Madame Delphine*, came to the hands of critics who had been impressed already by the freshness of his material, his devotion to his art, and the success with which he had introduced to fiction Creole New Orleans and its varied population. Reviewers who had missed *Old Creole Days*, it can be supposed, went back to those stories and reinforced their admiration for the charm and the artistry of *Madame Delphine*. They found *Madame Delphine* worthy of comparison with acknowledged literary masters. One thought the novelette "direct evidence of genius," reminding one of nobody, "except for a rare whiff of Victor Hugo."[10] Another could not find "anything in American fiction outside of Hawthorne that exhibits so many of the literary qualities which go to make for a novelist an enduring reputation" as he found in *Madame Delphine*.[11] Still another continued his earlier puzzling over Cable's dialect and now concluded that it was written "with wonderful precision."[12] Edmund Gosse, writing for English readers who were being first introduced to Cable in a volume containing *Madame Delphine* and three stories, recommended this "master of a new field in fiction," "endowed with new powers and of brilliant promise." He declared that "no writer of modern times, except Flaubert," had displayed such skill in depicting riotous masses of people as Cable displayed in his story "Jean-ah Poquelin."[13] Another English reviewer said that Cable was doing for Louisiana what Nathaniel Hawthorne did for New England.[14]

Along with their warm enthusiasm for this third book of Cable's, the reviewers showed an increasing interest in the author. An essay by Charles M. Clay late in 1881 presents a short sketch of Cable's life and an anecdote about his service in the Confederate cavalry. Clay proceeds to a comparison of Cable and Hawthorne, with Cable standing up well at most points.[15] The editors of the *Century Magazine* (successor to *Scribner's Monthly* late in 1881) commissioned a biographical sketch of Cable by George E. Waring, an engineer with broad interests who had published widely in magazines and books. He engaged Cable to write the history of New Orleans and of the Acadian region west of the city for the Tenth United States Census. Waring's sketch proved particularly valuable for the purposes of the editors. He became fond of Cable, had great admiration for him and for his achievement, and, like others of Cable's friends, wanted to further the career he was making for himself. The reader of Waring's account has the feeling that he is receiving Cable's own explanation of his purposes and his achievements, with his statements, modest but firmly laid out, filtered through Waring's admiring and practical mind. This sketch did much for readers of the magazine to picture Cable against his background and in association with the people they encountered in his fiction.[16]

Readers of the essays by Clay and Waring learned the main features of Cable's life and were led to admire what he had achieved, coming from an unpromising background. His friends in the Scribner firm wanted to make sure that he was known favorably. *Old Creole Days* was reviewed in the magazine by Gilder's brother-in-law, Charles DeKay, *The Grandissimes* by Boyesen, *Madame Delphine* by one of the editors, Johnson; and, following Waring's sketch, they invited a major article by Cable's friend in New Orleans, Lafcadio Hearn. Under the title "The Scenes of Cable's Romances,"[17] Hearn related Cable's works to specific settings in New Orleans, adding to the richness and color and to the concrete reality along with the indefiniteness of a romantic past already present in the works themselves. Writing from his own love for the semitropical city and his own fascination with the vestiges of its past, Hearn could have been counted on to present a warm endorsement of Cable's re-creation of Creole New Orleans. To a degree, he and Cable collaborated on the article. Cable identified many of the scenes, no doubt, and Hearn states that Cable furnished him the words and the musical score of the song about Cayetano's circus included in the article.[18]

Among others who wanted to befriend Cable and further his career was Daniel Coit Gilman, president of Johns Hopkins University. At the instigation of Richard Watson Gilder, Gilman invited Cable to deliver a series of literary lectures at the university in March 1883, and asked him to give an additional program of readings from his own works. Gilman wrote for the *Critic* a highly favorable report on both the readings and the works from which the selections were taken.[19] Cable's friends at Hartford invited him soon afterward to a further test of platform reading. Chief among the sponsors at Hartford was Mark Twain, who had written William D. Howells after Cable had visited there earlier, late in 1882: "Cable has been here, creating worshipers on all hands. He is a marvelous talker on a deep subject. I do not see how even [Herbert] Spencer could unwind thought more smoothly or orderly, and do it in a cleaner, clearer, crisper English. He astounded Twichell with his faculty."[20] Charles Dudley Warner wrote for the *Century Magazine* a report on the readings which ends by saying that all who "have an opportunity to hear this author interpret his own fascinating creations have a great pleasure ready for them."[21] Thus Cable was launched into the readings which furnished his chief income for two decades and which brought him for four months in 1884–85 into associaion with Mark Twain on a joint reading tour. These readings—and those Cable gave afterward alone or in company with James Whitcomb Riley, Eugene Field, and others—were reported in the newspapers and kept Cable's name and his works before the public as he appeared in halls as far away as California, Canada, and England in 1898.[22]

George E. Waring encouraged Cable to adapt for commercial distribution the history of New Orleans he had written for the United States Census. As a result, *The Creoles of Louisiana* had magazine and book publication. The work was received as an important addition to Cable's portrait of the Creoles; and the illustrations by Joseph Pennell, like Hearn's article "The Scenes of Cable's Romances," illustrated also, served to enhance the reader's fascination with Creole New Orleans.[23]

In the *Revue des Deux Mondes* for January 15, 1884, French readers were introduced to Cable's works. Marie Thérèse Blanc, writing under the name Thomas Bentzon, had devoted one earlier article to William D. Howells and another to Henry James. In this article she includes a translation of "Jean-ah Poquelin" and a description and appraisal of Cable's other works. He stood above his contemporaries in America, she says, from the standpoint of newness of materials—except for Bret Harte. Whereas Howells, James, and Thomas Bailey Aldrich held to the portrayal of contemporary life, Cable offered the blasé appetite of his readers an almost fabulous earlier period, as Hawthorne did in his stories of the early Puritans in New England. Madame Blanc finds confusion in *The Grandissimes* but can commend the richness of the incoherent disorder. The reader, she concludes, finds himself following various interlocking paths across a virgin forest, "mais arrivé au sommet du labyrinthe, on est émerveillé d'avoir découvert un monde nouveau." The stories are better than the novel, she remarks, and in them the greatest charm lies in the original form in which the hand of a consummate artist reveals itself.[24]

Cable wrote *Dr. Sevier* while he was engaged in an extended and thoroughly successful effort to organize and lead a citizens' campaign for prison and asylum reform in New Orleans. He set the action in his own time and made prison reform and theories of charity prominent in the resolution of the plot. Lafcadio Hearn's review in the New Orleans *Times-Democrat*[25] called the novel "far more artistic" than *The Grandissimes*, and exclaimed, "But how fine the workmanship!" Hearn spoke of "unsteadiness" in the author's management of the plot, traceable perhaps to a lack of the force necessary for a large work. He noted that many readers, in the city and elsewhere, would be put off by the un-Southern tone, and he voiced the same general disappointment felt by reviews in other areas. The main characters, they thought, are not the Creoles Cable's readers expected; the auxiliary character Narcisse is a delightful young Creole, but not important enough in the story to keep his dialect speech from becoming tiresome. Nothing in *Dr. Sevier* gave them the delight they found in the Creole women of *The Grandissimes*, and nothing absorbed their interest as did the problems of slavery and race and the Creole-American rivalry presented in the earlier novel. Cable's experience with *Dr. Sevier* was the same that other authors have had who have written first about a distinct region and people and have turned later to less distinctive materials or have been unable to recapture the earlier freshness and attractiveness when they returned to the first materials.

For a decade after Cable's essay "The Freedman's Case in Equity" appeared in the *Century Magazine* for January 1885, the question of Negro rights entered almost every discussion of him or his writings, including his literary works. In New Orleans, he was attacked in lectures and newspaper pieces, with the historian Charles Gayarré and Page Baker, editor of the *Times-Democrat*, bitterest and most persistent. One who had inquired among the Creoles during a visit to New Orleans, W. S. Kennedy, reported in the *Literary World*[26] the Creole charges that Cable did not know the Creole culture of his time, that he misrepresented their speech, and that he portrayed low-class characters, largely to the exclusion of the noble and heroic figures in their history. But Kennedy added in a postscript to his essay that he had met afterward Creoles who thought Cable's dialect "marvelously correct" and said they were "delighted with the fidelity of his delineations of Creole life." Gayarré's writings make it clear that some of the Creoles had begun with resentment of Cable's Creole portraits and had readily added their voices to the clamor against Cable's stand on the race question.

The *Picayune* first took a moderate position, granting Cable's right to argue for better treatment of the Freedmen and remarking that, in reading *The Creoles of Louisiana*, "one cannot doubt the fondness and affection, whether returned or not, of Cable for the Creoles."[27] The *Times-Democrat* at first did not speak with one voice, for several members of its staff wrote favorably of him even after editorials by Page Baker and articles by Gayarré had begun. An article of January 19 entitled "Cable and the Creoles" included the following: "Many candid readers of *Old Creole Days* and *The Grandissimes* have borne witness that far from holding them up to ridicule, Mr. Cable has made the Creole sweet, lively and fascinating to the Northern men and women who delight in those books. It may be that he has not sketched them to the satisfaction of everyone, but it is certain that if he set out to caricature them he failed. To him is due the credit of dispelling from the minds of thousands most erroneous and unflattering ideas that prevailed throughout the North concerning the Creoles." Three days later an article with a title no doubt consciously chosen, "Cable and the Negroes," asserted that not a single person in the South had come out to defend Cable's views. After two days appeared another article entitled "Cable and the Creoles," which declared: "Now the truth is a reader would get as much of an idea of French or Creole ways by reading Elliott's [sic] Indian Bible and more sense from it than is contained in the trash, balderdash and nonsense" of Cable's writings. The article said further, Cable "is not a Creole, is not a representative Southern writer, does not know nor can he get into and associate with any of the Creole families of this region, and hence his essays are the most impudent specimens of fraud that can be imagined."

Cable and Gayarré had befriended each other in the past, and in two newspaper articles with the title "The Creoles of Louisiana"[28] Gayarré did not challenge Cable's writings directly; but in two articles on "The Freedman's

Case in Equity"[29] and in several lectures[30] he carried on a relentless direct attack. The newspapers in New Orleans and those elsewhere in the South quoted each other in refuting and disparaging Cable. The editors of the *Century Magazine* decided not to choose among the many rejoinders they received to "The Freedman's Case in Equity," but to ask Henry W. Grady, editor of the Atlanta *Constitution*, to write in behalf of the region. Grady had spoken for reconciliation between the North and the South and for generous treatment of the former slaves in the rebuilding of the South, but his belief in race superiority and white domination left him opposed to Cable's views on Negro rights. He kept his argument above the level of newspaper and political vilification, but he retained against Gilder's request the statement that Cable was born in the South of Northern parents and hence was out of sympathy with the outlook of his neighbors. Presumably Grady knew that Cable's father was a Virginian and owned slaves after moving to New Orleans. Grady probably would have shared the attitude of his colleague on the *Constitution*, Joel Chandler Harris, who on the editorial page of the paper attacked literary sectionalism and defended *The Grandissimes* against the objections of the Creoles.[31]

As long as Cable continued in the debate on the Southern question, as it was called, he provoked many replies, most of them from the South and in opposition. The notices of the two collections of essays he published in the controversy, *The Silent South* (1885) and *The Negro Question* (1890), could point to little or nothing in the books that had not been noted and discussed as the essays appeared.[32]

Cable's stories of the Cajuns (Acadians) on the bayous and prairies west of New Orleans had been in his plans since he visited the region in 1881 while writing the history of the region for the census. When *Bonaventure* came out in 1888, reviewers noted that the three separately published stories hardly became a novel when brought into one volume. They were delighted to have Cable again guiding them through a remote province that could be called his own, the primitive farms and villages occupied by these descendants of the French peasant farmers who were expelled from Nova Scotia in 1755. Some reviewers found in the book a reconciliation of realism and idealism; they found plausibly combined in the main character, Bonaventure, both goodness and strength. In *Strange True Stories of Louisiana* (1889), Cable illustrated his fondness for history and for the opinion he often stated that the best stories are found, not made. The volume contains such variety that those writing notices mentioned whatever pieces interested them. No one spoke of the book as more than a by-product of Cable's literary and historical interest.[33]

John March, Southerner brought to its climax and its close more than a decade of Cable's engagement with the Southern question. He wrote it while he was deeply and often frustratingly involved in lecturing, writing, and in other ways attempting to evoke a voice from what he called "the silent South" and to muster support for extending full civil rights to Negroes. The book was reviewed more widely than anything he had published since *The Grandissimes*. Reviewers referred with approval to the large subject, the American setting (rather than the foreign settings of James and others), the author's thoughtful study of the questions being treated, and his success with some of the characters, but they expected a better work than they found. One regretted that Cable had abandoned the field in which he had met such great success, and others clearly found the characters and the dialect less interesting than in the Creole stories. The greatest difficulty for the reviewers, however, was that they knew little about the problems of Southern Reconstruction which are central to the plot and felt no interest in them.[34] Richard Watson Gilder had rejected the novel for serial publication in the *Century Magazine* because he was tired and believed that readers were tired of the Southern question in its various facets. Charles Scribner published *John March, Southerner* (1894) in *Scribner's Magazine* and in book form, and Cable realized that neither essays nor fiction supporting Negro rights could any longer find a place in the literary market, since it had been accepted in both North and South that the segregated, nonvoting status being decreed for the Negroes was best for the country.

An essay published in 1897 by W. M. Baskervill, a professor at Vanderbilt University, traces Cable's literary career and evaluates his writings down to *John March*.[35] A student of literature with a special interest in the flourishing of a native literature, Baskervill had sponsored Cable in platform appearances in Nashville, and in 1888 and 1889 had joined Cable in organizing the Open Letter Club, which had as its purpose carrying on debates on various elements of the Southern question and publishing the sheaves of papers that would result. On a trip to lecture in Tennessee in 1889, Cable took a meal with a Negro family. After the matter was reported in a newspaper and Cable became the object of editorial attacks, Baskervill wrote him that of course he could not be invited back to Nashville to lecture. The Open Letter Club was soon disbanded. At about the same time, laws enacted in various states restricting the public rights of Negroes indicated that full rights could be denied them officially for at least a time. In his 1897 essay, Baskervill says that Cable possessed greater literary gifts than anyone since Hawthorne, with possibly one exception, but that his gifts were hampered by his devotion to "abstract truth and perfect ideals" at a time when in the South a "practical expediency" was a necessity. "This conflict between theory and actuality," Baskervill continues, "has so affected the sensitive nature of an extremely artistic temperament as to make this writer give a prejudiced, incorrect, unjust picture of southern life, character, and situation." Of Cable's portrayal of slavery in *The Grandissimes*, Baskervill says, "The man with a mission throttles the artist." *John March, Southerner* he labels "one of the most dismal failures ever made by a man of genius." If Cable had not concluded by 1897 that the time for discussing the Southern question had passed, reading the evidence of this essay on the change in Baskervill's thinking would have convinced him.

It can be assumed that before writing her essay "The Stories of George W. Cable" for the *Critic* for March 1889,[36] Cornelia Atwood Pratt had read Baskervill's essay. Her strictures are milder than his, as is her praise of Cable's literary talents. But like Baskervill, she regrets that Cable let other things interfere with the charm and the human interest in his work, particularly in *The Grandissimes* and *John March*. Whether she had the same reason for objecting to what Baskervill thought was a mistaken political view of the South in Cable's writings, she joined him in asking for stories told for their own sake.

After *John March, Southerner*, Cable published nine books. One of them, *The Amateur Garden*, received only such notices as had appeared in newspapers and magazines from time to time about his work with the Home Culture Clubs (later the People's Institute) and the garden club competition in Northampton. Three of the books—*Strong Hearts* (1899), *Posson Jone' and Père Raphael* (1909), and *The Flower of the Chapdelaines* (1918)—were fabricated from stories already published separately, and hence received only brief notices. The remaining five are novels which Cable often called, appropriately, romances. Reviewers of the first, *The Cavalier* (1900), compared it and *The Grandissimes*, to its disadvantage, but they agreed in finding it good reading and in commending its authenticity in re-creating the author's experiences in the Confederate cavalry. The reviewer in the *Atlantic Monthly*[37] said he knew of no one better fitted than Cable to stand "in the place next to Hawthorne's," but he was thinking less of *The Cavalier* than of the early stories and *The Grandissimes*. Comment on *Bylow Hill* (1902), as might have been expected, was mainly to express surprise that an author who had won fame writing about French Louisiana, and had written in *The Cavalier* a romance that became a best seller and a successful stage play, should write next a study of insanity set in a New England town.[38] In *Kincaid's Battery* (1908) and *Gideon's Band* (1914) Cable was credited with writing good romances based, respectively, on his experiences in the Civil War and on his knowledge of steamboat commerce on the Mississippi River.

Cable's last novel, *Lovers of Louisiana* (1918), took up again the questions that had engaged him thirty to forty years earlier: Creole-American relations in New Orleans, North-South business affairs, and the place of the Negro in American society. He wrote now as a historian and analyst, not as a novelist dramatizing his convictions on urgent matters and attempting to draw his readers to his position. Reviewers saw the book as an extended dialogue, as talk rather than action, as a book focused on topics of little interest and little importance when it appeared during World War I. Reviewers and readers of *Lovers of Louisiana* and others of Cable's late books would have known little about his early works and would have known little about the circumstances, personal and public, which had prompted his first stories, novels, and social essays. It remained for writers on history and literature some years after his death to see him in relation to his times.

Before Cable's death, however, some contemporaries, including friends of his, had offered appraisals of his total work. James M. Barrie visited Cable at Northampton in 1896 and traveled on to New Orleans to see the Creole city and its people that had fascinated him in *The Grandissimes*. Two years later in an essay that appeared in a magazine and also as the introduction to an English edition of the novel, he recorded impressions of the characters that he relished, particularly Aurora Nancanou, "the glory of the book," and impressions from visiting its setting, the "most picturesque city in America."[39] William D. Howells said of Cable, in introducing him to speak at the memorial service for Mark Twain in 1910: "If some finer and nobler novel than *The Grandissimes* has been written in this land, any time, I have not read it. From Mark Twain himself I learned to love the literature of the delightful master who wrote that book."[40] In more than one of Howells's books he restated his high regard for Cable's work. In placing the characters Aurora and Clotilde of *The Grandissimes* among those from world literature included in *Heroines of Fiction* (1901), he seems to be refuting W. M. Baskervill and others who had said that Cable's art had been destroyed by his mission as a reformer. Howells says firmly that the author's chief interests reflected in *The Grandissimes* are social and personal, not political.[41] In a commemorative tribute read before the American Academy of Arts and Sciences after Cable's death, one of his editors and long-time friends, Robert Underwood Johnson, declared, in tones appropriate to the occasion and apparently with conviction, that Cable was, "with the possible exception of Hawthorne and Poe . . . the greatest figure in American fiction." He added, "I believe the final verdict of criticism will be that *The Grandissimes* is not only the greatest novel to date but that it stands in the front rank of the fiction of the world."[42] Howells and Johnson spoke out of strong personal regard and from recollections extending back to the climax of Cable's literary career, in the early 1880s. Fred Lewis Pattee, belonging to a later generation and writing from the perspective of a historian of the total American literary achievement, called *The Grandissimes* "the most powerful American novel" written since the Civil War, and said that with *Madame Delphine* and *Dr. Sevier* it forms "a trilogy that has been rarely surpassed in American literature." In later writings on American literature, Pattee dealt more in detail with Cable's works, including his later novels, but no less favorably with his best work. Some of the stories in *Old Creole Days* he thought "among the most perfect of American short stories"; he said that *The Grandissimes* in "unsparing realism" surpasses "anything indeed in the Russian realists," and that *Dr. Sevier* is a specimen of Howellsian realism. Like Baskervill, he lamented that Cable spent so much effort in reform work in the decade beginning in 1885, but he seems to have realized that much of the strength in the earlier work derived from the earnestness of Cable's devotion to reform.[43]

In a review-essay on *Lovers of Louisiana*, Randolph Bourne shows himself tolerant of the social criticism in this book and of Cable's whole career as a reformer. To Bourne's "Northern mind," as he remarks, there is nothing unjust in Cable's criticism of the South's handling of the Negroes and other elements of the Southern problem. He mentions the same faults others have noted— puzzlingly intricate plots, confusing indirection of statement, and dialects that cost the reader more than they are worth. But instead of following Gilder, Johnson, Baskervill, and Pattee in regretting that Cable did not return to the matter and the manner of his early stories, he considers *John March, Southerner* one of Cable's best novels, and he applauds Cable's courage and his conscience in attacking the social problems of his time, saying, "He has felt deeply enough about his land to be its sound and bravely passionate counselor."[44]

Publication of The *Life and Letters* of George W. Cable by his daughter Lucy L. C. Biklé in 1928 prompted reviewers, Edmund Wilson among them, to evaluate Cable's strictly literary work and also his career as social critic and reformer.[45] Wilson considered writing more on Cable than this review, as did others in the decade after Mrs. Biklé's book appeared, but he did not until he wrote in 1957 a long review article in the *New Yorker* on Arlin Turner's biography of Cable, and published a revision of it in the book *Patriotic Gore* in 1962.[46] Among others who wrote on Cable from the reformist or leftist position in the 1930s is Granville Hicks, who could commend Cable for breaking with the Southern tradition at some points, chiefly in *John March, Southerner*, but who left him hazily condemned because he continued to respect some of the values of his native region.[47]

Scholarly studies of Cable began to appear about 1930, no doubt in part because Mrs. Biklé had published The *Life and Letters*, but in part also because American literature was beginning to gain a place in the curricula of some colleges and universities. In 1929 George S. Wykoff published his findings on Cable's parents in Indiana before they moved to New Orleans in 1837.[48] Edward Larocque Tinker had brought Cable into his *Lafcadio Hearn's American Days* (1924) and in 1934 he published an article, "Cable and the Creoles,"[49] which is not accurate in all details but served to invite further study of an important element in Cable's literary career. The fruits of research have appeared in half-a-dozen book-length works: Kjell Ekström, *George Washington Cable: A Study of His Early Life and Work* (1950); Arlin Turner, *George W. Cable: A Biography* (1956);[50] Philip Butcher, *George W. Cable: The Northampton Years* (1959) and *George W. Cable* (the Twayne Series, 1962); and Louis D. Rubin, Jr., *George W. Cable: The Life and Times of a Southern Heretic* (1969). These works have drawn on extensive holdings of letters, literary manuscripts, and other documents, located mainly in the Cable collection at Tulane University.

From time to time additions have been made to the available works by Cable, including some of his early writings for the New Orleans newspapers,[51] the commencement address he delivered at the University of Mississippi in 1882,[52] and his autobiographical essay "My Politics."[53] New editions of different works of Cable's have included important factual and critical materials, among them Newton Arvin's edition of The *Grandissimes*,[54] and three volumes edited by Arlin Turner: Cable's essays on Negro rights, his stories,[55] and *The Silent South*.[56]

Scholars have in recent years pursued several matters that puzzled Cable's contemporaries. Cable and the Creoles is an important consideration in writings by Kjell Ekström.[57] One recent article by J. John Perret, "Ethnic and Religious Prejudices of G. W. Cable,"[58] shows that Catholics and Louisianians of French descent may still object to the portraits drawn by Cable; an article by Elmo Howell, "George Washington Cable's Creoles: Art and Reform in *The*

Grandissimes,"[59] views the Creoles in a fuller context and reaches much the same conclusions as does Perret. On Cable and the race question Philip Butcher has written valuable articles,[60] and Cable has entered into such works as Sterling Brown's *The Negro in American Fiction*;[61] the topic is so important as to appear in every work of any scope dealing with Cable. Among the historians of the postbellum South, including prominently C. Vann Woodward,[62]Cable is an important figure, for he dealt with major issues of the era, was an earnest student of both the history and the theories involved in the issues, and carried on his campaign in the North as well as the South. The fabulous platform-reading tour by Cable and Mark Twain in the winter of 1884–1885 has been presented in full detail in several works, some of which report the friendship of the two authors extending over thirty years.[63] These works also furnish important information on the vogue of platform readings in the second half of the ninetenth century.

Cable's wide friendships among authors and editors over several decades are reflected in a number of memorial statements of his and other tributes which would make, if published together, a valuable record of personal and literary relations. The letters exchanged between Cable and several contemporaries have been published, including his correspondence with Booker T. Washington,[64] William D. Howells,[65] Mark Twain, as indicated above, and Hjalmar H. Boyesen.[66] His correspondence with editors and publishers, particularly with Richard Watson Gilder, Robert Underwood Johnson, Roswell Smith, and Charles Scribner, has a good deal to reveal about editing and publishing in America during his time. Although they are primarily of social rather than literary interest, Cable's activities in the Home Culture Clubs, in the garden competiion, in church organizations, and in various civic affairs might profitably receive more attention than they have had. In an area closer to literature are Cable's experiences as editor of the *Letter* of the Home Culture Clubs, the *Symposium*, and *Current Literature*.

As fuller information on Cable and his times has become available and as his works have been better understood, scholars have undertaken to view him in the development of the national literature. Howard W. Fulweiler has made an interesting study of the story "Belles Demoiselles Plantation" in the context of Vernon L. Parrington's "main currents of American thought."[67] Louis D. Rubin, Jr., has advanced the idea that in *John March, Southerner* Cable anticipated William Faulkner and others in picturing a Southern community torn by conflicting forces and violence, and that, whether Cable influenced Faulkner directly or not, he set an example and prepared publishers and readers for the later Southern writers.[68] In his study of the Civil War in literature entitled *The Unwritten War*,[69] Daniel Aaron places Cable in his literary and social scene as observed from our vantage point. A student of American jazz, Hugh L. Smith, has summed up the influence Cable exerted on the growth of jazz through his publication of the words and musical scores of songs he heard in New Orleans.[70] William P. Randel has published a full account of Frederick Delius's interest in Cable's Creole stories and *The Grandissimes* for musical purposes and the composition and performance of *Koanga,* the opera Delius based on those materials.[71]

Notes

1. R. W. Gilder to G. W. Cable, August 29, 1873, in L. L. C. Biklé, *George W. Cable: His Life and Letters* (New York: Charles Scribner's Sons, 1928), p. 49.

2. See Arlin Turner, "A Novelist Discovers a Novelist: The Correspondence of H. H. Boyesen and George W. Cable," *Western Humanities Review,* 5 (Autumn, 1951), 343–72.

3. The quotations in this paragraph are taken from excerpts of newspaper reviews printed as advertising matter in the Scribner edition of Frances Hodgson Burnett's *Louisiana* in 1880.

4. Edward Eggleston, "Some Recent Works of Fiction," *North American Review,* 129 (November, 1879), 510–17; pp. 00 in this volume.

5. Dagmar Renshaw LeBreton, *Chahta-Ima: The Life of Adrien-Emmanuel Rouquette* (Baton Rouge: Louisiana State University Press, 1947), pp. 319 ff.

6. See Arlin Turner, "A Novelist Discovers a Novelist," p. 346. In a letter of December 28, 1878, Cable declared that his hopes for the novel he was writing were no less than Boyesen's expectations. He had "grasped at so much"; he must break up "the wild, virgin soil" of "a field never plowed before," enclosing "the Creole character, the Creole society, the philosophy of these things, Creole errors and defects and how to mend them, all clamoring to be treated." He would finish the book someday, and prayed that it would "not only be good in an artistic sense, but do good in a moral sense." His townspeople were watching for the first magazine installment. It would disappoint all of them who did not "love truth above all things else." In the Houghton Library, Harvard University.

7. *Harper's Magazine,* 62 (December, 1880), 153; *Atlantic Monthly,* 46 (December, 1880), 829–31; W. C. Brownell in the *Nation,* 31 (December 9, 1880), 415–16; pp. 00 in this volume.

8. A. C. Redwood to G. W. Cable, September 14, 1880; in the Cable Collection, Tulane University Library.

9. R. U. Johnson to G. W. Cable, October 1, 1880; in the Cable Collection, Tulane University Library.

10. R. U. Johnson, *Scribner's Monthly,* 12 (September, 1881), 791; pp. 00 in this volume.

11. *Critic,* 1 (July 16, 1881), 190; pp. 00 in this volume.

12. *Literary World,* 16 (July 30, 1881), 259; pp. 00 in this volume.

13. *Saturday Review* (London), 52 (August 30, 1881), 238; pp. 00 in this volume.

14. *Quarterly Review* (London), 155 (January, 1883), 223; pp. 00 in this volume.

15. "George W. Cable," *Critic,* 1 (October 8, 1881), 270–71; pp. 00 in this volume.

16. George E. Waring, "George W. Cable," *Century Magazine,* 23 (February, 1882), 602–05; pp. 00 in this volume.

17. *Century Magazine,* 27 (November, 1883), 40–47; pp. 00 in this volume.

18. Cable later printed the song, with some variations in the words, in his article "Creole Slave Songs" in the *Century Magazine,* 31 (April, 1886), 807–28. This article is included in *Creoles and Cajuns,* ed. Arlin Turner (Garden City, N.Y.: Doubleday, 1959), pp. 394–432.

19. *Critic,* 3 (March 24, 1883), 130–31; pp. 00 in this volume.

20. Mark Twain to W. D. Howells, November 4, 1882, in *Selected Mark Twain–Howells Letters 1872–1910,* ed. Frederick Anderson and others (Cambridge, Mass.: Harvard University Press, 1967), p. 204.

21. *Century Magazine,* 26 (June, 1883), 311–12; pp. 00 in this volume.

22. See Guy A. Cardwell, "George W. Cable Becomes a Professional Reader," *American Literature,* 23 (January, 1952), 467–70, and *Twins of Genius* (East Lansing: Michigan State University Press, 1953); Arlin Turner, *Mark Twain and George W. Cable* (East Lansing: Michigan

State University Press, 1960); Fred W. Lorch, "Cable and His Reading Tour with Mark Twain in 1884–1885," *American Literature*, 23 (January, 1952), 471–86.

23. See G. P. Lathrop, "Mr. Cable's History of the Creoles," *Book Buyer*, 1 (December, 1884), 277–79; pp. 00 in this volume.

24. Bentzon, "Les Nouveaux Romanciers Américains," No. III, Cable, *Revue des Deux Mondes*, 61 (January 15, 1884), 402–39; also *Les Nouveaux Romanciers Américains* (Paris, 1885), pp. 159–226.

25. October 5, 1884; pp. 00 in this volume.

26. 16 (January, 1885), 29–31; pp. 00 in this volume.

27. New Orleans *Picayune*, January 6, 11, 1885.

28. New Orleans *Times-Democrat*, December 28, 1884; January 4, 1885.

29. New Orleans *Times-Democrat*, January 11, 18, 1885.

30. See New Orleans *Times-Democrat*, January 28, March 8, 22, April 25, 1885.

31. Grady, "In Plain Black and White," *Century Magazine*, 29 (April, 1885), 909–17. For Harris's editorials, see *Joel Chandler Harris: Editor and Essayist*, ed. Julia Collier Harris (Chapel Hill: University of North Carolina Press, 1931).

32. See a review of *The Silent South* in the *Critic*, 6 (January 9, 1886), 14–15; pp. 00 in this volume.

33. See the review in the *Literary World*, 20 (December 21, 1889), 473–74; pp. 00 in this volume.

34. Paul van Dyke in the *Book Buyer*, 12 (April, 1894), 118–20, and a review in the *Nation*, 60 (March 14, 1895), 206; pp. 00 in this volume.

35. W. M. Baskervill, "George W. Cable," *Chautauquan*, 25 (May, 1897), 179–84; pp. 00 in this volume. See also his *Southern Writers*, 2 vols. (Nashville, Tenn.: Barbee & Smith, 1897), I, 299–356.

36. See pp. 00 in this volume.

37. 83 (December, 1901), 847–48; pp. 00 in this volume.

38. See Francis W. Halsey's review, *Book Buyer*, 24 (July, 1902), 469–70; pp. 00 in this volume.

39. James M. Barrie, "A Note on Mr. Cable's *The Grandissimes*," *Bookman*, 7 (July, 1898), 401–03; pp. 00 in this volume.

40. This speech appears in the *Proceedings* of the American Academy and National Institute, III (1911), 21–24.

41. See pp. 00 in this volume.

42. *Commemorative Tributes of the American Academy of Arts and Letters* (New York, 1942), pp. 178–80.

43. Fred Lewis Pattee, *A History of American Literature Since 1870* (New York: Century Company, 1915), pp. 246–253; pp. 00 in this volume.

44. Randolph Bourne, "From an Older Time," *Dial*, 65 (November 2, 1918), 363–65; pp. 00 in this volume.

45. Edmund Wilson, "Citizen of the World," *New Republic*, 57 (February 13, 1929), 353–53; pp. 00 in this volume.

46. Edmund Wilson, *Patriotic Gore* (New York: Oxford University Press, 1962), pp. 548–604; first published in the *New Yorker*, 33 (November 9, 1957), 172–216.

47. Granville Hicks, *The Great Tradition: An Interpretation of American Literature* (New York: Macmillan, 1933), pp. 52–55.

48. George S. Wykoff, "The Cable Family in Indiana," *American Literature*, I (May, 1929), 183–95.

49. *American Literature*, 5 (January, 1934), 313–26.

50. See also the pamphlet *George W. Cable* by the same author (Austin, Texas: Steck-Vaughn, 1969).

51. Arlin Turner, "George Washington Cable's Literary Apprenticeship," *Louisiana Historical Quarterly*, 24 (January, 1941), 168–86.

52. Arlin Turner, "George W. Cable's Revolt Against Literary Sectionalism," *Tulane Studies in English*, 5 (1955), 5–27.

53. In Arlin Turner, ed., *The Negro Question: A Selection of Writings on Civil Rights in the South* (Garden City, N.Y.: Doubleday, 1958), pp. 1–27.

54. New York: Sagamore Press, 1957, pp. v–xi; pp. 00 in this volume.

55. *Creoles and Cajuns: Stories of Old Louisiana by George W. Cable* (Garden City, N.Y.: Doubleday, 1959).

56. *The Silent South, Together with . . . Eight Uncollected Essays on Prison and Asylum Reform* (Montclair, N.J.: Patterson Smith, 1969). In a projected complete edition of Cable's works, six volumes were published by the Garrett Press (New York, 1970), with a biographical introduction by Arlin Turner repeated in each volume.

57. "Cable's Grandissimes and the Creoles," *Studia Neophilologica*, 21 (1949), 190–94, and *George Washington Cable: A Study of His Early Life and Work* (Uppsala, Sweden, and Cambridge, Mass.: Harvard University Press, 1950).

58. *Louisiana Studies*, 11 (Winter, 1972), 263–73.

59. *Mississippi Quarterly*, 26 (Winter, 1972–73), 42–53; pp. 00 in this volume. William Evans's essay, "French-English Literary Dialect in *The Grandissimes*," *American Speech*, 46 (Fall-Winter, 1971), 210–22, throws scholarly light on a matter long in need of clarification; pp. 00 in this volume.

60. "George W. Cable and Negro Education," *Journal of Negro History*, 34 (April, 1949), 119–34; "George W. Cable: History and Politics," *Phylon*, 9 (Second Quarter, 1948), 119–34; pp. 00 of this volume.

61. Washington: Associates in Negro Folk Education, 1937.

62. See especially *Origins of the New South 1877–1913* (Baton Rouge: Louisiana State University Press, 1951).

63. See n. 22 above.

64. Philip Butcher, "George W. Cable and Booker T. Washington," *Journal of Negro Education*, 17 (Fall, 1948), 462–68; pp. 00 in this volume.

65. Kjell Ekström, "The Cable–Howells Correspondence," *Studia Neophilologica*, 22 (1950), 48–61.

66. Arlin Turner, "A Novelist Discovers a Novelist: The Correspondence of H. H. Boyesen and George W. Cable," *Western Humanities Review*, 5 (Autumn, 1951), 343–72.

67. "Of Time and the River: 'Ancestral Nonsense' vs. Inherited Guilt in Cable's 'Belles Demoiselles Plantation,'" *Midcontinent American Studies Journal*, 7 (Fall, 1966), 53–59; pp. 00 in this volume.

68. "The Road to Yoknapatapha: George W. Cable and *John March, Southerner*," *Virginia Quarterly Review*, 35 (Winter, 1959), 119–31.

69. New York: Alfred A. Knopf, 1973, pp. 272–82; pp. 00 in this volume.

70. "George W. Cable and Two Sources of Jazz," *The Second Line*, 11 (January-February, 1960), 1, 3–5, 19; pp. 00 in this volume.

71. "*Koanga* and Its Libretto," *Music and Letters*, 52 (April, 1971), 141–56; "Frederick Delius in America," *Virginia Magazine of History and Biography*, 79 (July, 1971), 349–66.

REVIEWS AND ESSAYS

Cable's *Old Creole Days*

Charles DeKay°

It would be hard to pick out the most charming from these Creole tales. We might make a beginning by eliminating that called "Café des Exilés;" not because it does not show us an entirely new and most piquant phase of New Orleans life, but because, relatively to the others, its plot is less clearly drawn, and its dialogue—the peculiar English of the Louisiana Frenchman and Spaniard—is less intelligible. Yet, even in this, how delightfully Mr. Cable introduces us to his heroine, the daughter of an exile of noble family, who, having escaped the insurrections in the West India Islands, is forced to keep a cafe at New Orleans! "Posson Jone'," which appeared originally in *Appletons' Journal,* brings before one the curious contrasts of race that were and are still found at New Orleans. There is the herculean Parson Jones from West Florida, with his strange English,—half Bible, half poor white; and there is the devil-may-care, happy-go-lucky Jules de St. Ange, with whom Parson Jones forms a street acquaintance. The hangers-on and satellites of these two, one a mulatto, the other a coal-black negro, are as good as their masters. It seems a pity not to use the story, or rather let us say, not to use the talents of its writer, for the drama. In "'Sieur George" the mystery of the life of the hero is well kept to the end; "'Tite Poulette," however, turns out rather tamely. 'Tite Poulette is supposed to have a tinge of African blood; but the author makes her a pure white before marrying her to Kristian Koppig, the rosy young Dutchman. Mr. Cable is quite inimitable in the way he suggests a charming, delightful woman: witness the young girls of the De Charleu family in "Belles Demoiselles Plantation," and the heroine of "Madame Délicieuse." But he reaches his greatest height in "Jean-ah Poquelin," the story of an old slave-trader who adores his younger brother, and at last consents, at the urgent request of the latter, to take him with him on a voyage. Jean Poquelin comes home alone and shuts himself up with a deaf and dumb slave in a great dilapidated house which stands in a marsh. Gradually, to his reputation of a slaver people add the suspicion of being a murderer, the infamy of being a wizard. A mob that comes to serenade him discovers that he has lived a terrible life of self-sacrifice and isolation. The man who can write such a story is no mere talented writer; he is a genius in his way.

°Reprinted from *Scribner's Monthly Magazine,* 18 (July, 1879), 472–73.

[Review of *Old Creole Days*]

Edward Eggleston[*]

... Very admirably have Mr. Howells and Mr. James helped us to national self-knowledge by their international stories, but we shall not have an American literature in the large sense until we learn to rejoice in the widely differing forms of human development shown on our own ground, and until we cease to apologize for our life, and proceed to refine it by the direct reaction of literature upon it. It is impossible to prognosticate the future of literary art; but, if richness and diversity of material were the only things needed, the American Republic ought to produce presently—when the copyright law shall have been changed, perhaps—an aesthetic literature of the most picturesque and catholic sort.

And one may hold it to be a pretty sure mark in a new writer of the individuality and robustness which endure in art, that he does not seek some country already hallowed by literary association, but resolutely undertakes to break a path for his art through the untrodden thicket of the life that immediately environs him. Such a writer, if we may judge from work so slight as his first collection of stories, is Mr. George W. Cable, of New Orleans. That he knows New Orleans thoroughly, and is to the manner born, one perceives at the first dash. That he knows something else than New Orleans, and so has that very necessary requisite, the fulcrum of an outside standpoint, is equally certain from the entire absence of local prejudice, and the gentle and joyous humor with which creole life is revealed to the outside world. These short stories have some of the faults of inexperience: there are a few rather improbable happenings in some of them, such as would be rejected by a more practiced writer, because an improbable incident, even though it be but the transcript of a fact, disturbs the reader's illusion. But in a world so new as that which is here revealed to literature—a world so rich in new elements of romance, with its contact of a Saxon with a Latin and of both with a black race; its families annihilated in epidemics, its children of lost parentage, its old aristocracy, and its wild and picturesque forms of moral degradation—in such a world who shall say from without what is probable and what lacking in verisimilitude? And, in the important point of motive, the stories are never lacking, and never once strike a false note. Next to the correct and picturesque conception and delineation of character, the chief thing in story-writing is that the personages shall never break the law of their several natures, shall be evidently moved in all that

[*]Reprinted from *North American Review*, 129, pt. 2 (November, 1879), 516–17.

they do by the natural action of adequate motive on their proper characters. It is here that the beginner in fiction most easily fails; it is here that Mr. Cable never falters. We have to complain of a little mistiness sometimes—the reader does not quite perceive how certain things have come to pass. This befogging of the reader by hiatuses is not a very worthy expedient, nor does it produce the most legitimate result. In "Posson Jone' " and "'Sieur George" the reader is like one guessing out a half-told riddle. But the life is finely idealized, the aristic spirit is through all distinctly dominant, the moral tone is thoroughly sane, there is a tropical richness of color, a Southern enjoyment of female beauty, a masterful handling of dialects with wonderful strokes of description. The "Café des Exilés," for instance, makes a commonplace subject picturesque, and leaves an ineffaceable impression of place and character. All the stories have that indefinable something called charm. But they are all light—mere trials of the wing before flight. If the constructive power needed to organize a full-length composition exists in Mr. Cable, we shall have at his hands some day novels that will give a wholly new sort of life to American literature. One feels irresistibly that, where scenery, character, motive, and dialect are touched with so sure a hand, there is promise of important achievement.

[Review of *Old Creole Days*]

Anonymous[*]

The fugitive sketches of George Cable, collected under the attractive title of *Old Creole Days*, are as fresh in matter, as vivacious in treatment, and as full of wit as were "The Luck of Roaring Camp" and its audacious fellows when they came, while they are much more humane and delicate in feeling. The scene of all these seven sketches is laid in New Orleans; and certainly no other city on this continent ever began to exhibit such bizarre conjunctions of race and lively clashings of race prejudice as did the Gulf city during the earlier half of the present century,—for a generation or so after the cession of Louisiana. Mr. Cable has availed himself specially of these contrasts to give animation to his legends and reminiscences. French and Spanish creoles, negroes, half-breed Indians, and *Américains* of every grade circulate gayly through his pages, meet and part with immense evolution of electricity; and "we hear them speak each in his own tongue," for the author's mastery over mongrel dialects is something marvelous. Surely never before were such novel and varied vocal effects represented by the twenty-six letters of the English alphabet and a few italics and apostrophes. Mr. Cable draws powerfully upon his readers' emotions also, touching rapidly and surely the stops of laughter and of tears. Some of his plots are better made than others, and occasionally he is almost over-dramatic, relying solely upon the action of his puppets, and hardly pausing or condescending to explain sufficiently, in his own person, to make his motive intelligible. But again, as in the smiling tale of Madame Délicieuse, the construction is perfect,—airy as gossamer, and yet firm as steel. The "Belles Demoiselles Plantation" is the most pathetic of the seven legends. "Jean-ah Poquelin" is darker and grimmer in its tragedy, but singularly impressive. "Posson Jone' " is exquisitely droll. One and all have an ardor, a spontaneity, a grace of movement, a touch of fire, which are severally present as elements and summed up in that rarest of endowments, an original and delightful *style*. Mr. Cable's dialogues are so concise and complete that quotation cannot illustrate them. Each one is a dramatic whole, which to break is to mutilate. A short extract may, however, convey some slight notion of the energy and effectiveness of his descriptive style. . . .

[*]Reprinted from *Atlantic Monthly*, 45 (January, 1880), 44–45.

Not even Mr. Cable, however, can be held to have won his double-first until he has acquitted himself of a long romance, and shown that he can suspend his reader's attention, and sustain through at least three hundred pages the same sort of exhilarating interest with which he has so easily invested his detached pieces. . . .

The Grandissimes

[Lafcadio Hearn]*

At last it has come out in book form, this strange, weird, powerful, and pathetic story, which is certainly the most remarkable work of fiction ever created in the South.

It is difficult to render any idea of what this book is without making copious extracts. It is a dream which is not all a dream, a tale which is but half a tale, a series of pictures which, although in a certain sense created by the pencil of an Impressionist, wear a terrible resemblance to terrible realities. There are chapters which affect the imagination like those evil dreams in which dead faces reappear with traits more accentuated than the living originals ever possessed.

Is this strange New Orleans which grows up under Mr. Cable's wand our own New Orleans? It is; and yet it is something more. It is such a city as a wanderer sees by night in his dreams, who has left the shores of the Father of Waters for the icy winds and snow-shrouded scenes of some far-Northern winter;—a Southern metropolis, her streets paved with the gold of summer suns, her shadowy trees whose leaves never fall, her flowers that never die, her streets quaintly constructed like the Latin cities of the older continent, and all the motley clamor of a semi-tropical land in which even the sharp accents of European tongues lose their firmness, and old languages obtain a new softness and sweetness and languor. And there is all this inexpressible glamour, and yet more, in the familiar and yet unfamiliar New Orleans of *The Grandissimes*.

If it be so with the scenes, with the characters it is also so. We have seen these characters, and yet we have not seen them. Or, to describe our own impression still more correctly, we believe that we have seen them somewhere, and yet are not quite sure—like one greeted by some stranger whose features are not unfamiliar but whose name is forgotten.

There is, therefore, a certain vagueness about the work. But it is an artistic vagueness, like the golden haze of an Indian summer softening outlines and beautifying all it touches. The old streets seemed clouded with a summer mist; the voices of the people speaking in many tongues came to the reader as from a great distance. Yet why not? Is he not looking back and listening to the speaking shadows of another era, when Claiborne first came to Louisiana?

Yet the vagueness is never too vague. Sometimes the scenes are dimmed,

*Reprinted from New Orleans *Item*, September 27, 1880. This essay appears in Lafcadio Hearn, *Creole Sketches*, ed. Charles Woodward Hutson (Boston: Houghton Mifflin, 1924), pp. 115–23.

but it is when the reader's eyes are dimmed by that moisture which it is the artist's triumph to evoke. Sometimes the scenes become terribly vivid, however, as in the death of Bras-Coupé, or the tragic end of Clémence. There is no dreaminess in those powerful pictures. Nor is there any in that painful incident when the apothecary reads the letter to Palmyre. This scene, not even excepting the execution of Clémence, seems to us the most vividly truthful in the book. It is less tragic, less exciting, less terrible than others; but it is a genre study of inimitable verisimilitude.

If there be one special characteristic of Mr. Cable's style that is specially striking, we believe it is his power of concentrated description. What could be more pithily forcible, more briefly comprehensive, more intensely impressive than the following description of an interior furnished in the old-fashioned Creole style? One must have seen such, however, to appreciate the power of these few lines. . . .

We doubt whether this book, in spite of its delicate merit, will become a favorite with residents of the Creole city;—its spirit has already been severely criticized by a contemporary;—its paintings are not always flattering to native eyes;—its evocation of dead memories will not be found pleasing. We cannot perceive that the merit of the romance is at all marred, nevertheless, by Mr. Cable's own peculiar views; and if we were inclined to criticize anything unfavorably in it, we should only question the reality of Honoré Grandissime. Was there ever a Creole of Creoles, living in such an age, who could have entertained such ideas on social questions?

There are very curious chapters upon Voudooism in this book; and we cannot share the opinion of many that it is a mere "absurd superstition." We believe it to be, or at least to have been, a serious and horrible reality; and we know of most intelligent families among our French-speaking population who share this opinion. Those who have really given serious attention to the subject have doubtless found that the traditions of Voudooism in Louisiana and elsewhere have at least as much claim to belief as the history of the aqua Tofana or of the secret poisoners of the Middle Ages.

We must specially call the attention of our readers to the Creole songs and refrains, published with the music, throughout the work. They are very curious, and possess a special philologic value. One, in particular, an African chant, sung by the negroes in cutting down the cane, deserves special notice.

But we cannot attempt to criticize Mr. Cable's book further. It must be read to be appreciated. We have not even attempted to tell the public what it is. We have only undertaken to express in a few words the peculiar impression which, as a work of art, it produces upon the reader.

Cable's *Grandissimes*

[Hjalmar H. Boyesen]°

Mr. Cable is a literary pioneer. He has broken a path for the daylight into the cane-brakes and everglades, and into the heart of Creole civilization. He is the first Southern novelist (unless we count Poe a novelist) who has made a contribution of permanent value to American literature. The old-fashioned romances of chivalry, which by a strange anachronism of feeling are still surviving among the Southern people, and the terrifically lurid and feverish productions of the author of *Beulah,* are, of course, not to be mentioned in the same breath with Mr. Cable's dignified and wholesome work. Even compared to such novels as J. W. DeForest's *Kate Beaumont,* which was typical of a class representing, with a fair degree of insight and literary skill, the outside Northern view of Southern society, *The Grandissimes* not only holds its own but easily casts its predecessors into the shade. Although obviously the result of years of reflection and acute observation, it has the beautiful spontaneity of an improvisation, and all the slow and laborious processes of thought, from which it has gradually grown to its present completeness of stature, are not even remotely felt by the reader. For all that, it is patent to any one skilled in aesthetic analysis that the author's attitude toward his work is primarily that of a philosopher; we are inclined to think that he saw his problem before he saw its possibilities for a story. And his problem is nothing less than the conflict of two irreconcilable civilizations. To grapple with so large a theme requires courage, but Mr. Cable has shown that he has not overestimated his powers. At any rate, it would have been nobler to fail in an attempt to describe a battle of civilization than to succeed in describing a lady's foot or a charming conglomeration of laces and satins. We are well aware that these fascinating trivialities have not been without influence upon the fate of nations; but if we were to judge by a certain school of novelists which has eminent representatives on both sides of the Atlantic, it would be safe to conclude that nothing happens in the world which has not its origin in a *boudoir* intrigue. It is refreshing to escape from the tepid and perfumed atmosphere of this artificial over-refinement into the healthy semi-barbarism of Mr. Cable's Louisiana during the years immediately following the cession to the United States. In fact, the state of affairs in Louisiana in 1804 is so nearly parallel with the state of affairs to-day, or at all events

°Reprinted from *Scribner's Monthly Magazine,* 20 (November, 1880), 159–61.

previous to 1876, that to all intents and purposes the book is a study (and a very profound and striking one) of Southern society during the period of reconstruction. Accordingly, we cannot help suspecting Mr. Cable of a benevolent intention to teach his Southern countrymen some fundamental lessons of society and government, while ostensibly he is merely their dispassionate historian. Whether the Creole gentlemen whom Mr. Cable characterizes with such admirable vigor and distinctness are capable of accepting a lesson, even though it involves the very problem of their existence, is a question which we dare not decide. But if our inferences from the story are correct, that little strip of France, which by an unfortunate accident was deposited on the delta of the Mississippi, represents a civilization that is doomed, and which already bears in its bosom the germ of decay. Whether single individuals like Honoré Grandissime, who break with the traditions of their people, and whom their kinsmen, with the instinct of self-preservation, hate and would like to trample upon, can do more than prolong the period of decay and the final death-struggle, is another problem which the reader is left to solve in accordance with the logic of the story. Nevertheless, we venture to say that M. Grandissime shows a marvelous depth of insight or of instinct when he attaches himself to the plain and honorable apothecary; for the apothecary, though he has no antiquity to boast of in the way of pedigrees, carries the future in his pocket, while M. Grandissime's grandeur lies chiefly in the past, and his only chance of survival (not individually but generically) is determined by his ability to identify himself with the Anglo-American civilization, and his readiness to adopt its codes of law and honor. Opposed to him, as the champion of the Gallic tradition and the *ancien régime*, stands his uncle Agricola Fusilier—an admirably conceived type of the shallow but magniloquent Southerner who bewilders and overwhelms you with his sonorous rhetoric, and while patronizing, humiliates you by his exaggerated and insincere flatteries. In the title "citizen," which is so strenuously insisted upon, and in a great deal of Fusilier's self-exalting and didactic talk, we find a subtle allusion to a fact which we have nowhere else seen commented upon—viz., that the South clothes itself in the worn-out intellectual garments of Europe, and glories in its provincial attitude toward the nations of Latin blood. It is no rare thing in the Creole South to hear social theories and doctrines which were exploded half a century ago in France, propounded with a recklessly progressive air, as if they were the latest novelties in the world of thought.

The influence of the pure and high-minded hero, Frowenfeld, upon Honoré, Palmyre, Doctor Keene, and in fact every one with whom he comes in contact, was evidently a central *motif* with the author, and as such is properly emphasized. It strikes the reader, however, that Frowenfeld's influence is unduly passive; it is by being what he is, and not by any pronounced deed, that he lifts and exalts the lives which intersect his own. As with the sweet Pippa in Browning's dramatic poem "Pippa Passes," the exhaled purity and loveliness of his character become, as it were, a palpable influence for good and give an upward impulse to many a wavering life. For all that, it is not to be denied that

Frowenfeld's character is very pale, in its approximate perfection, when compared to that of the vividly individualized Creoles by whom he is surrounded. Again, if we are to persist in minute fault-finding, we perceive that Mr. Cable has not followed the dramatic rule (which is, indeed, applicable to all fiction) requiring, as it were, an acceleration of *tempo*, and a proportionate accumulation of interest toward the end. His last chapters, though they deal out poetic justice, and gather up most satisfactorily all the suspended threads of the plot, seem to be a little lagging, and, on the whole, impress one less strongly than many of their predecessors. This may in part be owing to the fact that the *denouncement* becomes after the forty-third chapter a foregone conclusion, and its anticipation necessarily distracts one's attention. The interest of the book really culminates in the terrible story of Bras-Coupé, which is very skillfully interwoven with the fates of the principal characters in the book, and incorporeally pursues them to the end.

We would fain go into a still further analysis of Mr. Cable's excellent novel; but as our space compels us to be brief, we will pass by the many tempting passages we had marked for comment, and merely add a concluding remark regarding his style. We believe it is the opinion of the average reader that it is too luxuriant, that it is full of allusions which are hard to trace. We have heard this judgment frequently expressed, but we have always combatted it. To us Mr. Cable's style is that of a highly imaginative man, in whose mind every fresh thought opens up a long vista of alluring suggestions. An author who is in this manner actually embarrassed by his wealth has to exercise severe self-denial when the temptation to imaginative disgression presents itself; and if occasionally he grants himself the luxury of a striking metaphor or paradox, it is because he knows its value to be too great to justify the sacrifice. Who would, indeed, miss those inimitable little touches which in *The Grandissimes* are scattered through the soberer narrative like blazing poppies through a field of wheat? We shall not quote (though we can hardly refrain from calling attention to the "worthless berries, whose spendor the combined contempt of man and beast could not dim"), but would rather leave to the reader the pleasure of chuckling to himself at each fresh discovery.

[Review of *The Grandissimes*]

Anonymous°

We can hardly expect the readers of these last-named books [which create false notions of the South] to take up *The Grandissimes*, but if they would and could give heed to it they would find a novel wholly Southern in *locale*, yet entirely serious in workmanship and historically truthful. We say this with no more special knowledge of New Orleans and creoles than such as the book gives, but the internal evidence of conscientious labor is unmistakable. Mr. Cable has chosen for his story a place and time hitherto quite untouched by other novelists than himself. The scene is laid in New Orleans at the beginning of the present century, just at the time of the cession of Louisiana to the United States by France, and the change of sovereignty is made the background upon which the picture of life is drawn. Governor Claiborne scarcely appears on the scene, and the few "Yankees" about him are known only by their shadows; the entire story is wrought by creoles, quadroons, and blacks, with the important addition of a young solitary German immigrant, and as regards history one is given rather the culmination of an old order of things than the beginning of a new. The antiquarian details seem carefully studied, and the author certainly succeeds in presenting the New Orleans of 1803 without requiring the reader to make frequent comparisons with the city which he may happen to know to-day. Nevertheless, he is not unmindful of the posterior relation which he holds to the story, and thus the narrator establishes a sympathy with the reader. These things were, he plainly says, but let us draw near enough to them in imagination to see them distinctly and minutely. As a historical composition, therefore, *The Grandissimes* has a frank and natural treatment.

There is, however, something more than this. The author has taken not merely a picturesque theme and treated it with freshness and veracity; he has had a profound sense of the larger laws of history underlying the change in which his scenes are laid. He has read to admirable advantage the occult pathology of slavery, and has perceived the nature of the problem which confronted Governor Claiborne and all sagacious statesmen, when a province so foreign from the customary traditions of the United States passed under the control of the government at Washington. A surprise awaits the novel-reader in this book. He is drawn into a strong interest in the characters displayed and

°Reprinted from *Atlantic Monthly*, 46 (December, 1880), 829–31.

their personal fortunes, but discovers that the novelist has offered also a parable. The questions, in a word, which agitated so much of the new nation as regarded Louisiana are, with only slight variations, such as have perplexed the entire body of thoughtful men in the nation ever since the downfall of the Confederacy. Mr. Cable is too sincere an artist to push this parallel, but the reader will make it for himself out of the excellent materials offered. There can be no mistaking the undercurrent of thought in the short interview which is given between Honoré Grandissime and Claiborne. It is introduced very cleverly by the spectacle of the two men riding together through the Place d'Armes. . . .

We have taken the liberty to give the creole's words in intelligible English, not to confuse the reader unaccustomed to the singular *cacobepy* of the English-speaking French of the book. A more tragic interest attaches to Mr. Cable's presentation of African slavery. He has, with excellent judgment, made the conscience regarding slavery to reside chiefly in the person of Joseph Frowenfeld, a young German immigrant, who is stripped of his entire family by yellow fever shortly after coming to New Orleans, and, setting himself up as apothecary, becomes in many ways the central figure of the story. To speak more exactly, he is the chorus; for though his action occasionally affects the story, his chief function is to ask the questions and bring out the prior conditions, and especially, as we have hinted, to be the external conscience. His presence in the community is historically more likely than that, for example, of an upright, over-sensitive New Englander, and his relation to the people about him is more natural, because he is a foreigner, than it would have been in the case of a Northern man. Still, we suspect Mr. Cable has not made Joseph Frowenfeld as good a character as he is a useful part of the machinery of the novel, and his importance in the development of the ideas of the story is out of proportion to his value as one of the *dramatis personae*. His chorus function has somewhat interfered with his personal existence. It is not always Frowenfeld, however, who lays bare the tragedy of slavery. The author himself does this with some very trenchant words, and the various characters in their several ways lift the covering now and then from that hideous evil. But the story itself is more effective than any denunciation of the evil could be: the incident of Bras-Coupé is not an episode, but an integral part of the structure of the novel; it is magnificently told, for the author's fault of eddying about his point has been forgotten in this instance, and he has marched straight forward in a dramatic recital. Bras-Coupé, Palmyre, Clemence, and the *other* Honoré,—these in their separate ways are marks by which to measure the power of slavery to effect wrong, and the strength of the book is in the masterly tracing of the several threads by which their lives and the lives of their social superiors are interwoven.

It would be a mistake to suppose that the book is simply a clever historical novel, or that it is a philosophical exposition of society in New Orleans under the influence of a dread cause,—the "shadow of the Ethiopian," as Frowenfeld well names it. Mr. Cable, with all his insight into history and society, is an artist and a man of large imagination. Indeed, the defects of the book may be traced generally to the struggle after adequate expression of commanding conceptions. It is built upon a large pattern. The author has conceived, with a classic sense, the immense reach of a proud family; he has constructed a House of Grandissimes, and never loses hold of the idea of this dominating clan. The very names given to the members of the family remind one of the Greek drama, and the turn of the story upon the opportunity of the head of the family to make or mar the fortunes of all is finely intended. Finely intended, we say, for we cannot help feeling that the author has missed a fundamental law of the novel, and has omitted to make Honoré's decision, admirably as it is described, the significant climax of the story. In the great number of details and half-followed clews, he fails to lead his reader straight on to the moral turning-point with breathless interest. Why, for instance, should we be asked to take so much interest in Dr. Keene? His actual part in the drama is unimportant, and the figure which he cuts as disappointed lover is not very noble; yet the author seems to have a consideration for him, based, as it were, upon what he has done or might do outside of the story. The chronology, too, of the tale is confusing, and it is not easy to say how long an interval elapses between the opening and the close, while the reminiscences and the retrocessions in the story add to the reader's confusion. One hardly succeeds in mastering the ramification of the Grandissime family until he has closed the book; but that is rather the fault of the family, and the details seem necessary to fill out the conception of the *gens*.

The patois and the creole English are evidently given with care. One can amuse himself a little with them if he does not read the book aloud. We do not know why we should not accept this local burr in literature with as much complacency as we do Scotticism. We own to a reluctance to read books where "Hoot, mon!" catches our eye on the printed page, and it certainly would take a novel of the power of *The Grandissimes* to reconcile us to Honoré's "my-de'-seh" and his reckless use of *h* in impossible combinations. The broken English of the De Grapion ladies, however, is often delicious. If we had not already said so much we should be tempted now to present more carefully to the reader these charming creatures. Mr. Cable has shown himself possessed of a strong imagination and a power to do serious work in fiction. If now he will consider that his public is sufficiently instructed in the superstitions of the creoles, and will order his narrative more perfectly, he may be assured of an increasing attention. His story is not to be read by a languid reader, but it will repay study, even though we think the author has sometimes set unnecessary tasks.

The Grandissimes shows how fine a field there is for the American novelist who will give us a local story with national relations.

[Review of *The Grandissimes*]

Anonymous*

The Grandissimes, by George W. Cable, is a spririted reproduction of the manners, customs, social life, and institutions of the early French colonists and their descendants at New Orleans, just prior to and at the time of the Louisiana purchase. The narrative brings out in strong relief the characteristic traits of the French creoles, and in particular the social groupings and exclusiveness which were the fruit of their relationship to the mother country, and of their attachment to its memories and institutions, as modified by the new country into which they had been transplanted, and in whose soil they had taken root. Out of the composite and peculiar material afforded by these artificial surroundings, Mr. Cable has woven a romance congenial to the atmosphere in which his actors live and to their temperaments, in which he depicts with considerable skill the play of passion and prejudice, of self-interest and lofty principle, and the power of love to triumph over barriers that had been considered insurmountable. The action of the story generally is spirited, but its interest is diluted and its movement retarded by the undue space allotted to the reproduction of the peculiarities of intonation and pronunciation of the Anglo-Gallican dialect that prevailed in Lousiana at the time of the events described. The dialect dialogues with which the story is profusely garnished have often little to commend them beyond their singularity, and although sufficiently novel and curious to amuse the reader at first, finally become tedious by their excess.

*Reprinted from *Harper's Magazine*, 62 (December, 1880), 153.

Cable's *The Grandissimes*

[W. C. Brownell]*

The author of *The Grandissimes*, instead of following in the beaten track of character-analysis trod by the latest and youngest of our magazine writers even, makes a diversion in favor of the old romance. Nevertheless, in painting the Creole life of New Orleans at the beginning of the century he has in effect broken new ground, and, as the soil is rich, one's first impression is that he has contented himself with merely overturning it. But, rich as it is, it needs an artist to exploit it with the success shown in *The Grandissimes*, and Mr. Cable is a literary artist of unusual powers. Indeed, considering his sensitive appreciation and executive skill, and considering too his nativity, his appearance just now is almost to be called sensational. The peculiarities of Southern men of letters are so well known that to advert to them pointedly is not only to wound an *amour-propre* singularly alive to criticism, but is to be guilty of platitude. Yet the appearance among them of a literary artist is surely not to be lightly passed over, Southern art having hitherto appeared nowhere but in oratory, and modern oratory, if art at all, being in any but the most highly humanized societies so debased as to be perilously near parody. Mr. Cable not only has the artist's aim of producing an effect rather than of giving vent to personal emotions, but he has the artist's sense of the importance to that end of good workmanship, and one is equally impressed by his absorption in his subject and his contained, concise, and unrhetorical manner of setting its attractions before the reader. The result is inevitably the happy one that the reader shares his enthusiasm before he suspects its existence, and—as we have admitted—is led into referring the merit of the book to its material. On the whole, one finally reflects, however, this is the homage a work of talent always exacts, and it is entirely probable that the actual Creole *milieu* in 1803 was as prosaic as actuality always appears till the chronicler arrives with his magic lenses. The poetic vein in Mr. Cable is well developed and defined, and the picture he conjures up from the old Louisiana levees and swamps is steeped in sentiment. It has an atmosphere and fragrance quite its own through which it communicates itself and its meaning palpably to the senses. Long ago, in the twilight of the Louisiana day, the ancestors of the Grandissimes and the De Grapions came from France and

*Reprinted from *Nation*, 31 (December 9, 1880), 415–16.

founded their families and the rivalry between them; the seed of the former became as the sands of the sea-shore, while the latter, after a brief period of prosperity in numbers, dwindled steadily till but two women were left. One of these, a widow, marries the head of the Grandissimes, her daughter a stranger who is not even a Creole, and thus the De Grapion name dies out completely. The two who unite at last the families so long hostile are the hero and heroine of the book. Aurora is pure Creole; Honoré, by force of intellect and character, rises out of the Creole stratum of sloth and lays firm hold on the things of the modern world. Intimacy with an ardent German-American just come to New Orleans, plain-spoken and inelastic as his parentage and having the intolerance of inexperience for Creole prejudices, assists him; he uses Frowenfeld as a flagellant, his goad, and probably cares little if the other fancies himself a successful missionary. Frowenfeld is so regarded, at all events, by the rest of the *dramatis personae,* though he manages to win their Creole hearts before the last chapter to an extraordinary extent. Over the action and characters of the story hangs the pall of slavery, and the picturesqueness at once and the impossibility of a society founded upon absurd but heroic devotion to an exaggerated notion of the wisdom and necessity of caste, form the theme of the novel.

What a clever writer to whom it is familiar ground can make of this may be easily imagined. Those who followed it as a serial we heartly advise to reread it consecutively lest they miss some of its excellences. If this discloses a suspicion of the vicious serial fault of ending chapters with suspense, on the other hand the singleness and totality of its impression are naturally greatly emphasized. For one thing, the genealogies, which may have seemed confused heretofore, not only clear up but add an important element to the general effect; you feel the ancient and honorable character of the Grandissime and De Grapion ancestry, appreciate the strength of the family feeling better, excuse its concomitant excesses more readily, and, perhaps more than all, through the appeal of this hazy past to the imagination get a quicker sense of the reality of the different persons who have emerged from it. The pedigree business is beautifully done, too. It recalls the similar portion of *Henry Esmond;* though, since it does recall Thackeray, that is enough to suggest that it is a trifle too beautifully done, and to remind us that Mr. Cable at times displays a rhetorical over-refinement, consisting in a rather playful assumption of the reader's information on some point to be elucidated further on. Everything is cleared up in due time, and you don't mind being mystified, of course, but the uncertainty is annoying; the narrator comes to have the air of caressing what he has to tell, of fondling it and letting you get glimpses of it, but retaining it long and handing it over wholly to your inspection at last with wistful regret. This shows respect for what he is engaged upon, but it is a kind of *espièglerie* that is essentially not admirable and is plainly something to be outgrown. It is proof of the care which Mr. Cable has bestowed upon his work; but it is a needless one, since there is nowhere a negligent touch to be noted, and other faults of a similar kind testify to an excess of finish, grateful enough if one thinks of its rarity in Mr. Cable's literary *entourage*, but a blemish in itself like any other. On the other hand, it is obvious that in general its results must be good; Mr. Cable has in such measure the gift of language, is so felicitous in point of pure exression, moreover is so clearly a born story-teller and is so evidently in love with his subject here, that one rightly attributes to his scrupulousness in execution the happy impression the book leaves of more than justifying by its material the affectionate sympathy with which it is written. The Louisiana landscape, the warm New Orleans late afternoon when the Creole world is airing its courtliness and pride in the plazas, the Nancanou and Frowenfeld interiors, and the dozen situations which develop the "laughable, pathetic jumble" of Creole character, are suffered to make the reader's acquaintance quite of their own accord, apparently; and so nice is the author's art that we hardly notice his several introductions, which means, of course, that they have been in the best taste.

It would be doing *The Grandissimes* an injustice, however, to imply that it is only a charming picture cleverly painted. It deals with graver elements of social existence than mere picturesqueness; and though the society it depicts no longer exists, and its problems have been solved by time, it is none the less a serious and important work for that. The effect upon a tropical society habituated to the substitution of impulse, good or bad, for reasoning, loose or exact, of an institution whose maintenance involved an inversion of the mental processes of the modern world, is a theme worthy the powers of any expositor. It, or the neatly identical situation presented for so many years by the *Américain* successors of the Louisiana Creoles, has been often enough depicted from a moral standpoint; that is to say, from *Uncle Tom's Cabin* down, there have been many sermons preached from this text. As a situation which when adequately described suggests its own sermon it has nevertheless been left for Mr. Cable, who has, in the main, made the most of his extraordinary opportunity. Wherever the effect of slavery upon the Creole society or the individual Creole is concerned it is admirably painted; it is suggested or shown by the writer in true dramatic manner, illustrated in the action and betrayed by the characters themselves. The author does not asseverate in *proepria persona*. On the contrary, when the effect upon the slave or the free Pariah is in question Mr. Cable is apt to appear upon the scene. He makes sententious comments, characterized by great good sense and right feeling, but nevertheless palpable intrusions. He says there are some Southerners who still believe the negro slaves were the "happiest people under the sun." But—except for Mr. Carlyle—no one else does, and clearly preaching to Ephraim is breath wasted. The audience Mr. Cable really addresses needs neither instruction for itself nor a protest from him as to his own position in the matter. And if it did it would not be Mr. Cable's fault or alter his literary duty. Nearly the same thing may be said and nearly the same explanation hazarded concerning the Bras-Coupé story and the episode of the murder of Clémence. The reader's withers are wrung in behalf of a cause already won. Neither incident is improbable, nor is either probably exaggerated, considered even as a type. The fact of Clémence's fate is perhaps necessary in order to show vividly the extent to which the master shared the superstition of the slave; but, in treatment, both are distressing and appeal distinctly to the nerves. Clémence's piteous plea for her life is good enough to compensate in a measure, but not wholly, for the shock, and one's feeling is that only readers too impervious to suffer from it ought to be visited with the sequel. It is, we think, clear that Mr. Cable's nice instinct is here at fault, and that what used to be called "politics" by sensitive conservatives is responsible for it. It should not be understood that we object to the darkest shadows in a picture of this kind, or to melodrama à outrance, or that we incline to the Greek fashion of killing the victim off the stage; only, that when the intellect and even the emotions are passed over, and the nerves are sought for the purpose not of thrilling but of shocking them, a mistake is made in point of art. In point of art melodrama is never so effective as when it is managed by a cynic with an eye constantly on the peril from bathos, however subtly disguised in contained writing; and we are tempted, by way of illustration, to ask Mr. Cable to compare his narrative of Bras-Coupé with Mérimée's somewhat similar story of 'Tamango,' which is to the full as tragic and pathetic, and far superior in permanence of effect.

It is not, however, owing to any positive blemish—and the character of its melodrama is after all a slight one compared with the positive merits of the book—but rather to its omissions that *The Grandissimes* is not a great novel as well as a charming one. We own to finding the fact agreeable, not because of cherished prejudices or of innate hostility to the way in which the world is going in fiction, but partly on account of the change, which is a little in the nature of relief, and partly because pure charm is none the less charming for being unadulterated with anything of greater strength. Nevertheless this is selfishness, and does not alter the fact that what prevents *The Grandissimes* from taking the front rank in contemporary fiction is its weakness in portraiture of an intellectual interest. The best contemporary fiction is wholly given over to the study of subtleties of character, and the entertainment it provides is almost exclusively of an intellectual variety. The old romance amused in a totally different way; it had not the faintest notion of psychology. Each has its advantages, and, no doubt, the fiction of the future will combine them. Meantime, to succeed, Mr. Cable needs, one may almost say, modernizing. His Aurora Nancanou is admirably characterized, and takes her place at once as a delightful addition to the prize portraits of fiction; Honoré is well-nigh as distinct and fully as admirable; Raoul is a creation of genius. The over-astute reader may ascribe this, perhaps, to their seductive dialect, which will be a mistake. But beyond these we have types. Even Palmyre and Agricola are not sharply enough characterized to seem individuals. Froenfeld is a lay figure. The company in general are enshrouded in the poetic and many-tinted Louisiana haze, and one hardly makes out their features. It may be said of the story, as the author remarks of a narrative of one of his characters: "There shone a light of romance upon it that filled it with color and populated it with phantoms." There is, however, indefinite promise in such acute sentences as these: "There are understandings that expand, not imperceptibly hour by hour, but as certain flowers do, by little explosive ruptures, with periods of quiescence between" (p. 130), and: "The one as fond of the abstract as the other two were ignorant of the concrete" (p. 180); and it is possible to expect more incisive power in Mr. Cable's next work. One's last word, however, is that it would be vain to look forward to anything more captivating.

Madame Delphine

Anonymous[*]

So long as the vein of literary ore which Mr. Cable has opened up for English readers continues to make so good an assay as in the present work, the public is in no danger of losing its interest in the mine. The homogeneity of the subject-matter of his Creole stories would, in a less imaginative writer, have imparted a flavor of provinciality to the whole—such a flavor as attaches to much of Mrs. Stowe's New England stories or Col. Johnston's Georgia sketches—some sense of "loss of larger in the less," however faithfully the lesser theme might have been treated from a local point of view. That Mr. Cable's work has, to an unusual extent for American fiction, a national significance, is not so much owing to his experience of other sections of the country, for he had had almost none when his book was written, but to the fact that the imagination—"that antiseptic of all literature"—has lifted his themes and characters out of their remote and foreign interest into a vital human companionship. He has, so to speak, acclimatized Creole life in our literature, and demonstrated anew that what is chiefly interesting in a novel is that portion which the author, and not somebody else with the same "facilities," might have written. To be sure, the interest of Creole life is more than usually piquant and alluring, but it would be hard to convince those who have read Mr. Cable's books that its magic would rise as quickly at the conjuring of another pen. What is interesting is Creole life *plus* Mr. Cable.

It is a little curious to note how he proceeds in this novel to make the reader believe that Mons. Lemaitre was capable in Louisiana, in the first quarter of this century, of marrying an octoroon. To be sure, it was an exceptional case, and instead of attempting to prove it otherwise, Mr. Cable has taken the bull by the horns and proved the rule by insisting on the fact that this was an exception. It is the candor of a lawyer before a jury, and it has a similar effect. The mind leaps the improbable events in the life of the pirate and the illusion is complete. Some of the most interesting events in *The Grandissimes* arise out of Mr. Cable's conviction that the improbable is also in a certain proportion probable. By his hands the elements are kindly mixed.

The story is quickly told; but Mr. Cable's sensibility is of so delicate a quality that he would be as alert as any reader to the incongruities of the plot he

[*]Reprinted from *Critic*, 1 (July 16, 1881), 190.

has chosen, and he softens the descent with gentle steps. While he nowhere rises to the tragic height of the Bras Coupé episode in *The Grandissimes*—a tension that could not be endured in a short story—he has shown in this novelette a firmer hold of his art. There are no disgressions or extravagances, and no such disproportion of the picturesque as that which in *The Grandissimes* occasionally gave an air of bad perspective to the drawing. The action progresses rapidly and agreeably, and every character is here of human mould. The least consistent is perhaps Lemaitre, whose wilfulness in engaging himself to Olive is only related, and finds hardly the expression one would expect of a man capable of piracy. A chastened touch of original sin in him would not have been unwelcome. *The Grandissimes* is a novel of great parts; a novel of such uniform literary fibre as *Madame Delphine* would be a great novel. As far as it goes, we do not recall anything in American fiction outside of Hawthorne that exhibits so many of the literary qualities which go to make for a novelist an enduring reputation.

[Review of *Madame Delphine*]

Anonymous*

We yield to none of Mr. Howells's admirers in admiring him so much that we would not have him different, and it may be said without invidiousness that the reading of *Madame Delphine* after his stories has the effect of deepening one's impression of Mr. Cable's warmth and color. In the degree in which Mr. Cable possesses them these are properly Southern qualities, and it is agreeable to find that they lose nothing in intensity from the high literary standard to which their exhibition is made to conform. *Madame Delphine* is by no means the work that *The Grandissimes* is, but it does not lay the least claim to be so considered, though it deals with the same subject. The study of the social results of slavery offers a large field to the romancer, as Mr. Cable has already shown us, and it may continue his special subject for some time yet, we should say, before it becomes exhausted. In *Madame Delphine*, as in *The Grandissimes*, we have a mother and daughter for heroines, only here "dey's quadroons," and the dramatic centre of the story is the falsehood of the mother, who denies her child that the latter may wed a white without offence to the laws prohibiting the intermarriage of races. Olive is apparently a pure Caucasian, and Madame Delphine's perjury is credited; but her own sacrifice has cost her so much that she expires at the confessional after admitting her guilt to the kind Père Jerome. The scene of the perjury is very dramatically set forth, gaining much from Mr. Cable's eminent faculty for subdued intensity; and that of the confession is deeply affecting. Short and even episodical as the story is, it contains some of the remarkable portraiture of *The Grandissimes*—portraiture which owes its success to the power of intuitive sympathy rather than to experience and close observation, and which, therefore, though it may be a trifle less graphic, is wonderfully true and real. Père Jerome is a prize portrait, and the keynote of sweetness and gentleness set by his character seems to have governed the narrative, which is throughout related with charmingly poetic feeling. Besides being less comprehensive it is also less powerful than *The Grandissimes*, but it is even more winning in the sustained warmth and color, as we say, of its diction than our memory at least of the more important work. One criticism suggests itself, though we are in two minds about offering it. The Creole patois is introduced with an ingenuity perhaps a little evident. It is difficult to see how it could be better managed, and to consent to the loss of any of it is quite out of the

*Reprinted from *Nation*, No. 838 (July 21, 1881), 54–55.

question, but the problem is one for Mr. Cable's own solution. Possibly he would do well on occasion to disregard the proprieties altogether, and make his Creoles speak as he chooses; it would be a very literal taste that this would offend, whereas at present only a literal taste can be quite satisfied with the apologetic makeshifts resorted to to compass the natural introduction of the dialect. Finally, we may remark of *Madame Delphine* that its pathetic interest is broadly human, and would be felt with equal keenness by readers who thoroughly believe in the peculiar institution as well as by those who have never reflected upon its inherent enormities, and are surprised into indignation by accounts of them. *The Grandissimes* was a tractate as well as a romance, and so too is *Madame Delphine*, but its interest as a romance does not at all depend upon its tractarian character, and would be as great if the tragic element of it proceeded from any law, just or unjust, instead of from the Louisiana statute against miscegenation.

Madame Delphine

*Anonymous**

An ungrammatical sentence on page 1, an incomplete sentence on page 2, and an arithmetical inaccuracy on page 3, did not predispose us to a favorable opinion of the carefulness in style of Mr. Cable's last story, *Madame Delphine*, which we have read for the first time in its book form. Nor on finishing it can we say that we have any very clear idea of what it is all about; nor, on asking our very intelligent next-door neighbor, who had likewise read it at a sitting, could we get much light from him. But its workmanship is curious, and it will bear study, as it certainly cost study. As nearly as we can make out, Madame Delphine, a New Orleans creole, disowns her daughter to enable her to marry; but we give this interpretation with great diffidence, lest we should be knocked over the head at once by some more penetrating critic with the charge of inexplicable stupidity. The book is very much marked with what the critics call "local color," the strongest touches of which come out in the creole dialect, which is certainly reported with inimitable skill. A good illustration of this is Madame Delphine's interview with Monsieur Vignevielle, in which she asks that mysterious banker to become the guardian of her child.

> "Miché." "Wad you wand?" asked he gently. "If it arrive to me to die"—
> "Yez?" Her words were scarcely audible: "I wand you teg kyar my lill' girl." "You
> 'ave one lill gal? Madame Carraze?" She nodded with her face down. "An' you godd
> some mo' chillen?" "No." "I nevva know dad, Madame Carraze. She's a lill' small
> gal?" Mothers forget their daughters' stature. Madame Delphine said: "Yez." For a
> few moments neither of them spoke, and then Monsieur Vignevielle said: "I will do
> dad." "Lag she been you' h-own?" asked the mother, suffering from her own bold-
> ness. "She's a good lill' chile, eh?" "Miché, she's a lill' hangel!" exclaimed Madame
> Delphine, with a look of distress. "Yez; I teg kyah 'v'er, lag my h-own. I mague you
> dad promise."

On first looking over this passage it would seem impossible to read it; but a close enunciation of the words as spelled will be found to bring out the dialect with wonderful precision, and to set the mongrel-blooded speakers before the imagination with almost the reality of life. In this, it seems to us, is Mr. Cable's strong point, though we should be sorry to be understood as limiting his powers

*Reprinted from *Literary World*, 16 (July 30, 1881), 259.

to a mere repetition of strange talk. He does more than that, and the pages of his story, while not nearly so broad as those of *The Grandissimes*, are wrought with great artistic expression, and leave the reader in a large degree possessed by the beauty, the languor, the quaintness, the wholly un-northerly and almost wholly un-American aspects of an early period in the life of that city by the Gulf among whose romances his pen is finding such choice and fresh material.

Madame Delphine

Edmund Gosse[°]

In this remarkable story an American novelist, who has already achieved a reputation in his native country, for the first time brings his name before the English public. As the author of a collection called *Old Creole Days*, and of an interesting novel entitled *The Grandissimes*, Mr. Cable has already shown himself to be master of a new field in fiction—namely, the curious Creole and Quadroon population of the city and environs of New Orleans. In *Madame Delphine* he takes a series of idyllic scenes from the same unexhausted source, and delights us with pictures of a strange, old-world, timid civilization of which it is safe to say that English readers know nothing. Those who have read *The Grandissimes* must not expect to find in *Madame Delphine* any situation so tragically pathetic as the death of the old, indomitable African King; in his latest story Mr. Cable has given himself up to the warmth and perfume of the tropical city, to the romance rather than to the tragedy of its population, and to the pathos of its divided races. At the same time, a certain dimness of style that gave a hazy effect to some of the pages of the earlier novel gives place in *Madame Delphine* to a more incisive and exact manner of writing. It should be said at once that Mr. Cable writes exceedingly well, with a rich and musical prose that suits his subject; his fault as a stylist is that he introduces too incessantly a profusion of ingenious detail, and is not content to let enough simplicity divide his "purple patches" from one another. But this severity is "what Nature never gives the young," and its absence is not to be very sternly reprimanded in the present dearth of novelists who take any thought whatever about their style.

It will give at once an idea of Mr. Cable's manner of writing, and of the scene to which he introduces us, if we quote from his pages a description of that part of New Orleans in which, some sixty years ago, the incidents related in *Madame Delphine* took place. . . . In the midst of this moss-grown suburb, a low brick house in the middle of a square preserves a close and discreet aspect which is noticeable even in so retired a neighbourhood; sixty years ago the wall of this house enclosed an ill-kept, shapeless garden, full of untrimmed roses and tangled vines, where, in the walks of pounded shell, the coco-grass and the crab-grass had successfully asserted their right to exist. The little house itself was muffled in jasmine and crape-myrtle, and deeply overshadowed by branching orange-trees, the whole forming an odorous and umbrageous retreat in the

[°]Reprinted from *Saturday Review* (London), 52 (August 20, 1881), 237–38.

midst of the tropical city. And in this sequestered place lived Mme. Delphine
Carraze, a little quadroon woman with faded eyes. In those days there existed in
New Orleans a class which had sprung up between the Creoles and the negroes,
and which belonged to neither. This was the free quadroon caste, a race il-
lustrious for the extreme beauty and grace of the women, often almost absolutely white, with massive regular features, lustrous eyes and hair, and manners
of the most bewitching grace and refinement. Yet, by the whim of that cruel
law which forbade marriage with a white man until the ninth departure from
the negro had been reached, these lovely quadroons and still lovelier octoroons
were unable to form any legitimate attachments with men scarcely their equals
in social standing. Out of this evil state of legislation there arose a condition of
things which encouraged a universal laxity of manners, and which entailed, at
the best, shame and embarrassment on the next generation. Mme. Delphine was
euphemistically called the widow of an American with whom she had long
lived happily in this house of perfumes and shadows; but he had been dead
nearly twenty years, and she was still living on the property which, in defiance
of the law, he had left her. Their one child had been brought up in the North by
his mother and sisters; but, after being separated for sixteen years, the mother's
heart had yearned for her daughter, and Olive was now on her way back to
New Orleans to live with Mme. Delphine.

We are next introduced to a quartette of very oddly-assorted friends. Père
Jerome, a little fat priest; Evariste Varrillat, a doctor; and Jean Thompson, an
attorney, are characters which Mr. Cable draws rapidly, but with a firm hand.
These three are united in adoring and in lamenting a fourth, who should
complete their number, but who has unfortunately adopted the profession of
pirate and smuggler, and upon whose head the American Government has set a
price. This is Capitaine Ursin Lemaitre, a weather-beaten young man of thirty,
with noticeable eyes, who has been trained, rather against his nature, to remember "that none of your family line ever kept the laws of any Government or
creed." He is doing a brisk, but highly illegal, trade between Cuba and Louisiana, darting occasionally over to New Orleans with the spoils he has taken
along the northern coasts of the Antilles. It greatly shocks and grieves Père
Jerome that his Ursin, who is the very pink of courtesy and gallantry, should
have taken to such a life, but he cannot persuade the other two friends to see
anything but a rare good joke in the whole matter. At last a wonderful story
reaches the Creole suburb—namely, that a ship sailing from the North to New
Orleans was boarded by pirates, and would have been ransacked, had not a
beautiful girl stepped up to the captain, with a missal in her hand, and, pointing
to the Apostles' Creed, commanded him to read it. Upon which he drew off his
men, and left the vessel to make her way to New Orleans unmolested. This story
creates a great sensation, and there is much speculation as to who this freebooter
can be who was so suddenly converted by a passage in a missal. Varrillat and
Thompson guess that it is their friend Lemaitre, and decide that he must have
fallen in love with the beautiful heroine of the adventure. But the simple-
hearted little priest will not hear of this worldly interpretation, and determines,

on the other hand, to make this edifying circumstance the theme of his next sermon in the cathedral.

Among his auditors are Mme. Delphine and her lovely daughter, lately arrived from the North, and also, as the reader gradually perceives, the pirate himself. But something in the audience, a face or a movement, suddenly changes the current of the dear little priest's mind, and just as he is coming to the point of his story, and about to tell how the missal in the hands of a beautiful girl converted that desperate freebooter, he falters and stops, turning the anecdote into a less personal tale of how the fine order and exquisite appropriateness of nature so affected the pirate's mind in solitude, he being himself a very orderly person, that he determined to quit a mode of life so contrary to the design of nature. The audience is perhaps a little disappointed, but edified upon the whole, and Mme. Delphine is so much touched by the benevolent air of Père Jerome, that she determines to make him her confessor, and obtain his help and counsel in the terrible responsibility of her newly found daughter. Meanwhile Capitaine Ursin Lemaitre has not been miraculously converted by the missal, but he has fallen hopelessly in love with the girl who presented it to him, and in order to find her out he has given up his ship, said farewell to his men, and come back to live at New Orleans. But to do this is to endanger his head, and he is obliged, therefore, to adopt a disguise. He opens a bank in the Rue Toulouse, under the name of Vignevielle, it being known only to his three friends that the banker Vignevielle is one and the same man with their old comrade Ursin Lemaitre. But neither Varrillat nor Thompson suspects for a moment that the returned prodigal is in love, and if Jerome guesses it, it is more by an intuition than anything else; for Vignevielle, who used to be so frank, has become excessively reserved, neglects his business markedly, even for a Creole, and spends so much of his time wandering around the city, and peeping into windows and doorways, that he gradually gets a reputation for being crazed. Of course it is the beautiful octoroon for whom he is searching, but she is so carefully hidden in the shadows of that discreet garden full of orange-trees and crape-myrtle, that he never catches a glimpse of her. At last, one moonlight night, in a scene which is the gem of the book, and described with an exquisite charm of style, he pushes a gate open in his usual way, glancing and searching, and there, listening to the mocking-bird, with her face lit up by the moonlight against the rich darkness of the orange-tree, is the girl that he has been looking for so long, and he learns, what the reader has long ago found out, that it was Mme. Delphine's daughter Olive who faced him on the ship.

It would not be fair to Mr. Cable to tell the plot any further. How the hero contrives to become acquainted with Mme. Delphine, how the unsurmountable barrier between him and Olive is honourably removed, how roughly the course of their true love runs, and what a sublime sacrifice is made at the last by poor old Mme. Delphine, for all this we must recommend the reader to the pages of the novel itself. He is not likely to put the book down until he has finished it.

We think that a novelist's quality is often best shown in his conduct of a short story. *Madame Delphine* is followed by three tales, which really form part of the same study of old Creole life. The first of these, "Belles Demoiselles Plantation," would be more striking if the reader were not irresistibly reminded by its conclusion of Edgar Poe's "The Fall of the House of Usher." It might very well have been written by a man who had never read the earlier story, but for readers of Poe the similarity destroys the necessary shudder of surprise. "Madame Délicieuse," on the other hand, is one of Mr. Cable's perfectly original pictures of the glittering, lazy, graceful life of the Creole population in its palmy days. But we recommend any one who is still unconvinced that in Mr. Cable we have gained a novelist with new powers and of brilliant promise to read the last story, "Posson Jone' "; we have every confidence in the result. For, unless we are greatly mistaken, he will recognize in the treatment of this short tale a skill in depicting riotous Southern masses of people, in full sunlight, moved by sudden passion to the exercise of whimsical and cruel revenge, combined with a sense of the gentleness and placability which make these races a paradox to Northerners, such as no writer of modern times, except Flaubert, has displayed. The destruction of the circus, and the horrible game played with the tiger and the buffalo, in this story of "Posson Jone'," may be recommended as certain to give the jaded reader that *frisson nouveau* of which he is so much in need. We must add a word on the dialect which Mr. Cable uses. It is new, and must be learned; but it is simple, and easy to learn. It is merely an alternation of French corrupted by English, and English directly translated from French; a soft and languid speech, invented by the easy Creole for his needs.

Cable's *Madame Delphine*

[Robert Underwood Johnson]°

It is a marked evidence of Mr. Cable's range and general force as a writer that he has constructed in this novelette an impressive tragedy without the use of the element of humor, which in the highest examples of fictitious writing, whether dramatic or narrative, has been the handmaid of tragedy. A reader, making acquaintance with this book, would have no basis from which to infer that fine sense of the incongruities which permeates his other work, and which overflows in the rolicking fun of "Posson Jone'." Conversely, one who should read "Posson Jone' "—a story without the sentiment of love,—indeed, without a female personage—would never know with what delicacy and refined suggestion of femininity Mr. Cable depicts a woman, and especially a beautiful woman, in love. However, though without a humorous character, scene, paragraph, or line, *Madame Delphine* is not a *tour de force* of somber plotting, but a readable and picturesque setting of a naturally acted drama on the theme of the inductive or vicarious responsibility for sin. Mr. Cable does not assume the burden of this theme to be proved as a proposition—he is too true an artist for that—but has left it where it ought to rest—upon the characters, and has subdued it to a distinct undertone of a story which owes its main interest to characterization and action. The moral is lightly carried, and not heavily dragged by the movement of the plot: there are no *détours*, no superfluities, and the close construction of the story gives it a buoyancy as a book which its compactness may have led one to overlook in the always exacting and often exasperating slowness of a serial.

Considered from a literary point of view, *Madame Delphine* is an advance on any one of Mr. Cable's previous short stories and on much of *The Grandissimes*, in which the scene gave more opportunities for excess of writing as background to the heroic action and large drawing. Here every word is directly in the drift of the story. The style is polished but not ornate—rather like the furniture of Père Jerome's room, "carved just enough to give the notion of wrinkling pleasantry." There are more uniformly elegant writers of contemporary fiction than Mr. Cable, but we can think of none more vital, none who gives more direct evidence of genius. He reminds one of nobody. Except for a rare whiff of Victor Hugo, he has an uninvaded individuality. It would be hard to find in current literature scenes to exceed in freshness, force, and charm

°Reprinted from *Scribner's Monthly Magazine*, 22 (September, 1881), 791.

Madame Delphine's disavowal of her daughter, or Lemaitre's discovery of Olive in the moonlit garden—where the ground seemed to him "an unsteady sea and he to stand once more upon a deck." How aptly, too, these words heighten the situation by recalling the first meeting of the two on shipboard! The book is full of such passages appealing to the imagination and preparing the way for some telling scene. It is more than good reading—it is good art.

The story is also an advance along the line of the weakest, or rather the least strong, of Mr. Cable's qualities as a writer—his sense of proportion. In *The Grandissimes,* the casual reader once in a while was puzzled by the emphasis laid upon minor scenes and people. This is the fault of *Gabriel Conroy,* and of most other first novels. The atmosphere is rarer than in a short story: one is deceived as to distances and forces are miscalculated. Doubtless something similar is the experience of a brigadier-general who is called for the first time to handle a corps in action. There are but slender traces of this fault in *Madame Delphine,* and it is so surely a fault merely of inexperience that we may confidently look for its disappearance in Mr. Cable's (or Mr. Harte's) next novel. It is even now compensated for by the extreme vigor and clarity of his characterization—which is the most evident excellence of this book. There is, properly speaking, no hero and no heroine, but four evenly sustained characters, unmistakably human and all unmistakably different. Indeed, take any two characters created by Mr. Cable, select the two most alike, and the likeness will only be the likeness of the genus, while there will still be wide individual differences, mental and physical. This can be said of very few other writers of the day; it is much to say of any writer at a time when English character-drawing is largely vague and metaphysical, when characters often stand for single forces instead of for men and women, and when the tendencies of criticism and of creative art are to exalt the contemplative above the dramatic. Mr. Cable's work is free from the malaria of dilettanteism; it has a strong backbone of popular interest, and it may be commended to the American reader or the foreign critic as a portion of that too small body of current writing which is likely to last and be referred to as American literature.

George W. Cable

Charles M. Clay[°]

In Broadway, yesterday, I met two charming women. You ask, "What has that to do with your subject?" Something—a little—wait, and we will see. One of these ladies was a Spaniard, the other French—"tout ce qu'il y a de plus faubourg. . . ." I had in my hand the photograph from which was made the engraving upon the first page of this number of *The Critic*. Two pairs of bright eyes flashed recognition of me, and inquiry at the secret-telling envelope. "Une photographie—c'est la vôtre?" "Non, mesdames; c'est la photographie d'un grand écrivain Américain." I drew it from the envelope. There was a fluttering of lace and ribbons, two dainty bonnets touched each other, and two lovely heads bent over the "counterfeit presentment." After a prolonged study, *la belle Espagnole* said softly: "C'est une très jolie figure, spirituelle, romanesque; une vrai figure de poète." Another pause; then the *Parisienne* returned me the picture, saying, with smiling lips and eyes, "Il est bien moqueur, celui-là!" I bowed my acquiescence, with my adieux, to both, and walked on to my office, considering their verdict. The fine feminine instinct had not failed in its divination of quality. The pictured face was measured at its worth; what was lacking in their judgment was the fault of photographic art.

George W. Cable was born in New Orleans, December 12th, 1844. His father died when he was quite young; and at fourteen years of age the boy entered the office of a cotton factor. In 1863 he joined a cavalry regiment in General Smith's division of the Confederate army, and served in Louisiana until the war ended. One incident of his campaigning that Cable tells with irresistible humor, framing it in slow, deliberate speech, will be the best personal introduction to him that we can give our readers.

A squadron of Federals were out on a raid south of the Red River. The company to which our cavalryman belonged had for hours followed fast in the track of the raiders, stopping only to question the negroes they found in the swamps, or others who were clustered together near the road at the end of the long furrows of the sugar-cane. At one point the hot pursuit promised quick success. This time the information was definite. The Yankees were at Mr.———'s plantation. Over the ditches, through the cane-fields the Confederate cavalry spurred their panting horses to fresh effort. Again too late! The

°Reprinted from *Critic*, 1 (October 8, 1881), 270–71.

planter stood under a live oak on his trampled lawn, gazing with an air of bewilderment at a raw-boned, blind, broken-winded horse, upon which was seated an old gray-headed negro who blankly returned his master's expressionless stare. This equestrian statue of ruin was quickly surrounded by eager avengers. The officer in command questioned the planter as to the number and probable route of the enemy. Mr.——— only shook his head mournfully, repeating in a mechanical manner an enumeration of his losses, ending with, "Not a horse or a hoof left, except that broken-winded old racer," and the index-finger pointed fixedly at the blindly-blinking eyes of the motionless animal. Fresh questioning brought the same answer, with its pitiful refrain, "Only that broken-winded old racer," until the planter caught sight of Cable. His eyes seemed magnetically fastened, and his voice fell to an abysmal depth, as he asked, "My son, do *you* belong to the army?" "Come on," called the captain, "Mr.———'s losses have upset his mind." Down the avenue of live-oak, over the broken fences, filed the cavalry, closing the ranks as they crossed the ditch and got up in the dirt road, urging on their tired horses with hand and spur, till a lagging soldier called, "Here comes Mr.——— after us, on the old racer. He's waked the old hoss up, and they're a-booming along like a steam injine. Maybe he's come to himself and 's going to tell us whar we can ketch the Yankees." Gallantly came the racer, breaking into the ranks like a thunderbolt, and scattering the cavalry to right and left, until, tugging at the reins, his rider succeeded in stopping him beside Cable. There was a husky, grieved tone in his voice as he repeated his former question, "My little son, do *you* belong to the army?" Proudly the youth raised himself in his stirrups, straightening out the very last quarter of an inch of his height; then bowed assent. The planter dropped his reins, threw up his arms and with a despairing look exclaimed, "Great Heavens! Abe Lincoln told the truth—We *are* robbing the cradle and the grave."

In 1869 Mr. Cable was married, and soon after obtained a position on the staff of the *Picayune*. Then commenced the training that rapidly developed the ability of the writer. I wish to qualify that statement: his training did not begin then. It began when the boy of fourteen devoted his spare hours to his books—when the young cavalryman, the long march over and his horse cared for, diligently studied the Latin grammar, which he carried in his haversack—when the clerk recovered his place in the cotton factor's office, where his diligence, and patient carefulness were distinctive marks of his work, and the artist hand found its delicate perception in the subtle touch that defined the quality of cotton and its market value in New York or Manchester. In such schools he was trained. His degrees were taken in the university of journalism. Mr. Cable's life has been exceptionally full of work; his domestic life exceptionally happy; the inter-action of these conditions has made a great author. One other condition of his life was the more immediate *motif* of his success. He was born in New Orleans before the social customs, the usages, the unwritten laws of old Creole days were quite buried out of sight. There were living memorials he must have known in his boyhood of that strangely picturesque past that he has brought to us "in its very habit as it lived." He found rare material for his work—material which is his by right of discovery, and which would fail of the effect that charms and delights us if handled by an artist who had fainter perception of its value, and less skill in the usage.

Mr. Cable's method is peculiarly his own, though he works from models. This I must believe, because I have his word for it. Doubtingly I asked him, "But where did you find Honoré Grandissime?" The quick, bright smile answered before the deliberate speech had set the answer in words: "I have known him for years. I met him only last week in Canal Street." "And Madame Nancanou?" "Oh, she is the closest study I have made—my very best portrait." How I, how all men, must envy him that privilege! With that loveliest of his lovely creations, or portraits, in view, we think not so much of Cable the novelist as of Cable the poet, for has he not written the sweetest and tenderest of prose poems? Or have you read *Madame Delphine?* But we must go back of that date. There is the ballad of "Jean-ah Poquelin." And then *The Grandissimes*, that perfect painting of the quaint, picturesque old city by the Gulf, which will surely win one of the first prizes in the literary exhibit of this century.

Scribner's Monthly should mark with a white stone the day it gave the first of those early stories of Cable a place in its pages. It was a new revelation to American readers—this discovery of a Southern writer, who, to the nervous force and power of the English tongue, added the grace, the airy lightness, the fervor and the passion he had caught from the Creole modification of the Latin race. The three first and the three last sketches in *Old Creole Days* are beautiful bits of word painting—*genre* pictures, exquisitely clear, delicately tender. In each is revealed the hand of a master. There is nothing forced, yet nothing crude or unfinished; neither touch nor hint of the amateur. Evidently Cable's trial efforts—the inevitable partial failures, for even genius fails until eye and wing are trained for flight—found their grave in the waste-basket. Taste sat in judgment upon effort. There is the shading of a pure pathos; of a rare humor, as delicate as it is spontaneous. There is richness of color, and tenderness of tone; but nothing garish, nothing untrue to nature in Cable's art. Above all are we thankful that he has escaped the cramping and the trammels of a certain school of writers, who, in their blind worship of an impostor they call art, would fain dethrone nature. We are glad and thankful that he gives us feeling, and passion, and spares us the minutiae of atomic analysis. He has not confounded the art of the romancer, of the poet, with the skill of the scientist or the art of the critic. To feel a passion and to paint it is the gift of genius. To show where some cord is twisted awry, some feature is distorted, is the province of criticism. It may be urged that a great painter's first study is anatomy. True; but the studies made in the dissecting-room are only outlined under coverings of flesh and color—they are a part of the mechanism which is hidden under the curtain with the lay figure and the drapery. The true artist respects the tools of his art; but he never places them on exhibition. Anatomy is useful, indispensable in figure painting; but the section of a muscle belongs more properly to a museum of science than to a picture gallery. We repeat, we are glad and thankful that the greatest of living American novelists is a disciple of nature; glad that he has studied the hearts of men and women; that he belongs to the school of the great masters, and not to the fashionables of the "Internationals"; glad that he recognizes plot and action as legitimate adjuncts of the romancer's art. Thankful that we find in his pages picturesque description, depth of feeling, and even dramatic bursts of passion; thankful that we do not find merely a "prolonged analysis of a psychical condition," or "studies of the patient renewals of life, the slow gatherings of wasted forces, the gradual restoration of landmarks and symptoms of content, the gravely rebuilt firesides, by which forever ears must listen for the footsteps of the flood"—whatever all this may be! Most thankful that he was born in New Orleans, not in recently aesthetic New England; born in that semi-tropical clime, where rich, luxuriant nature is the lender and not the borrower of art. Cable found light and passion on the surface of the earth; he had not, like Hawthorne, to uncover the fires by digging beneath the ashes of Puritanism.

"Jean-ah Poquelin" was the first of Cable's sketches that suggested, to the critics, comparison with Hawthorne; since that appeared, we find such comparison floating through the book-notices of nearly all the leading journals; and this is not strange or wonderful. The tragic story of the old slave-trader, in its pathos, its imagery, and its dramatic power, is suggestive of *The Scarlet Letter*. Beneath the hard exterior, the prosaic present of New England life, Hawthorne found the hidden possibilities of romance which were buried in its past. It is a perfect but a ghostly revival, this reclothed spirit of Puritanism. The design, the finish show the work of a master. It is the melancholy study of the slow martyrdom of a life painted, as it needs must be, in gloomy shadows—a Salvator Rosa in literature.

In the old Creole life which Cable has reproduced there are wider contrasts and richer color. It is not so far removed in time that the coloring has faded. The incongruous mingling of squalor and splendor is not altogether a thing of the past. He found a broad deep basis of realism upon which to build the structures of his imagination. There were differences of race, bitterness of caste prejudice, restiveness under imposed rule, jealousy of alien rulers, in the New Orleans he knew. These were lessons in effects; they taught him how to give light and shade to the passionate loves and hatreds of the old Creole city.

Hawthorne's characters are creations, placed in a world he has exhumed. Cable's are antedated portraits of living people. He is inferior to Hawthorne in creative power, and consequently at times lacks clearness. In a gallery of portraits, individuality is confused; one or two lovely female heads, a few strong faces, will impress themselves upon the memory, but the many fade into a panoramic indistinctness. Yet the few vivid likenesses are so perfect that we are reluctant to find fault. We are willing to believe Cable's occasional obscurity only an *embarras de richesses*—only the multiplied shadows of many-sided genius. Having admitted the one inferiority to Hawthorne, we claim that in color Cable is the better artist. In "Jean-ah Poquelin," in the episode of Bras Coupé, in the subjective sketch of the Free Man of Color, the shading is as sombre, the light as lurid as Hawthorne's; but the finer colorist gives us lovelier contrasts. Cable delights in sunshine. He catches the flash and sparkle on the crest of the waves of the unfathomable sea upon which he is afloat. His clouds are broken into purple rifts, and when most deeply massed are edged with rosy tints. In subtlety of perception, Cable is quite the equal of Hawthorne. To quote from an able critic, "He has penetrated to the very marrow of Creole character; and in his patient painstaking investigation, he never lets his imagination blind him to the actual—to the salient points of the period he has reproduced. He has given us a faithful picture of Louisiana in the early years of this century."

But this brings us to *The Grandissimes*, at the moment I am reminded that the limit of my critique is reached. To take up that masterpiece of Cable, I must wait "for a more convenient season."

George W. Cable

[George E. Waring]°

The charge that we have no characteristic American literature has hardly been a just one, both because there always has been much that was characteristic in our best writings, and because our writers, with a few notable exceptions, have necessarily been, first of all, English—in language, in tradition, and in habit of thought—and, as writers, American only because of certain accidental surroundings. These surroundings themselves, in spite of an American origin and character, were still marked with a strong English quality. "America," as we know it at the North and East, is mainly a newer England, where the social and mental qualities of the older have been modified and adapted to new conditions without losing their original impulse and stamp.

Far away in the South-west, born of purely French enterprise, strongly modified by Spanish association and control, heated with the glow of a subtropical sky, lulled and intoxicated with the delusive curse of slavery, secluded behind the defenses of restricted speech which slavery built for itself everywhere, and allied to the American family of States by ties which long failed to touch its real heart, there has grown up at our side a community in which English influence has found no place, and which has hitherto been subjected to only a distant and purely external study. A keen and sympathetic eye has studied it at last, and the wealth of its material is being laid before us, warm with the touch of the Southern sun, and throbbing with a life that is new to our colder zone. If we had had no characteristic literature before, we surely have one now; and if it were ever safe to predict permanent favor for a writer, we should claim it for the author who has so allied himself to all the varied humanity he has depicted that his name must live as long as interest in the picturesque and plaintive creole survives.

Were we to ask the source of such skill and success, it would be an easy begging of the question to say that Mr. Cable is a genius, and that genius is its own creator. A somewhat intimate study of the man himself, and of the methods of his work as well as its results, shows that while he unquestionably is a genius, his genius has been trained to walk in a very strait path, and to submit to very rigid discipline. The God-given quality is there, and its mettle and freak and force are always felt, yet we feel almost equally the wholesome subjection

°Reprinted from *Century Magazine*, 23 (February, 1882), 602–05.

in which it is held. It is like a weanling race-horse trained to serious work and made to lead a useful life,—the native spirit and vim always evident, but always controlled by wisely accepted restraints. Given the divine spark, without which no friction can produce light, we find the remaining factors of Mr. Cable's success in his surroundings and necessities, and in the spirit in which he has met them. Not a little of his peculiar quality, and very much of his peculiar development, may be traced to the Puritan element in his composition—a Puritanism inherited, cultivated, and stalwart, but a Puritanism mellowed by the sunny sky under which he has grown, humanized by the open and cordial habit of Southern life, and made wise and forbearing and discreet—almost made not to be Puritanism at all—by an all-embracing and ever-vigilant sense of humor, which is as quick to check his own act as to catch his neighbor's lapse; a sense of humor which ripples at every shoaling of the serious stream of his life and work.

Resolute, earnest, laborious to the last degree, and so trained to toil that no detail of research or execution deters him; with a mind schooled to the minuter systems of the counting-room; with an ear ever alert for characteristic expression or dialect; with a quick eye for shades of manner, and with an unfailing memory for what he sees and hears, he has passed his life among the people of New Orleans, gleaning, as he went his busy way, for the sheaves he now presents us. While thus equipped for his calling, he evidently recognizes his own limitations, and works well within his powers. He has made a special study of the creole population in and about his native city, and of the conditions under which that city has grown,—finding in its later colonial and earlier territorial life his most congenial field of work—a field he has made so much his own that another writer poaching upon it would probably be warned off by the public as an imitator.

Personally, Mr. Cable is a small, slight, fragile-looking man, thirty-seven years old. He is erect, bright and frank, with a strong head, and a refined, gentle face. His hair and beard are dark, and his large hazel eyes are expressive,—happily more often of merriment than of sadness, though they are capable of becoming sad eyes, too.

A young author should be accorded the privilege of having his more intimate biography withheld until his career is finished, but it can be no unwelcome invasion of Mr. Cable's privacy to say that he is happily married, that he has four charming little girls, and that he lives in a high-porched, broad-verandahed house, somewhat after the manner of the Grandissimes' mansions we know so well, and situated far up in the "Garden District" of New Orleans.

What is of more legitimate interest to the public, and more important as a study of character, is the combination of inheritances and of circumstances which have helped to make him what he is. He is descended on the father's side from a colonial Virginia family, and on the mother's from the old New England stock. The two branches came together in Indiana, where his father and mother were married in 1834, and whence they moved to New Orleans after the financial crisis of 1837. In New Orleans, Mr. Cable prospered in commercial pursuits until some time after the birth of the subject of this sketch. In 1859, after a second disastrous failure, the father died, leaving the family so reduced in their circumstances that young Cable was obliged to leave school at the age of fourteen to aid in their support. From this time until 1863 he was usually employed as a clerk. Although then in his nineteenth year, he was such a tiny and youthful-looking lad that his sisters, when sent beyond the lines for refusing to take the oath of allegiance, had no difficulty in obtaining permission to take their "little brother" with them. Once within the Confederacy, the valiant youth soon volunteered, and was mustered into Colonel Wilburn's Fourth Mississippi Cavalry, of General Wirt Adams's brigade. The experiences of the field and the rude life of the camp produced a marked change in the hitherto gay disposition of the young recruit. He is described as having been a good soldier, scrupulously observant of discipline, always at his post, and always courageous and daring. During days of inactivity, he employed his leisure hours in making a critical study of the Bible, in working out problems in the higher branches of mathematics, and in keeping up his knowledge of Latin grammar. In one of his engagements he received a serious wound in the left armpit, making a narrow escape with his life.

At the end of the war, like most of his comrades, he returned penniless to New Orleans, a city then overflowing with young men, clamorous for employment. He began his career as errand-boy in a mercantile house. Subsequently, for a time, he found employment at Kosciusko, Mississippi. Returning to New Orleans several months later, he took up the study of civil engineering, and joined a State surveying expedition for the reëstablishment of the lines and levels of levees along the banks of the Atchafalaya River. The most important outcome of this enterprise, so far as Mr. Cable was concerned, was a very serious attack of malarial fever, from which he did not fully recover for two years. During his convalescence, he became an enthusiastic student of natural history, and laid the foundation for those close descriptions of bayou and prairie and swamp life, and still-life, which are such a marked feature of his writings.

Mr. Cable's first attempt at literary work was in the capacity of a contributor, over the signature of "Drop-Shot," to a special column of the New Orleans *Picayune*, devoted to critical and humorous papers, with an occasional poem. These contributions, which at first appeared but once a week, became, later on, a daily feature of the paper, and Mr. Cable was regularly attached to its editorial staff. In this field he developed originality, and vigor and delicacy of expression. His newspaper career was, however, destined to be brief. In accepting the position, he had stipulated that he should not be called upon to write theatrical notices, as attendance at places of dramatic entertainment involved a moral question which he had not investigated, and which was condemned by the stricter rules of the Presbyterian church, of which he was and is an active member. On an urgent occasion it was considered necessary to instruct him to take charge of the theatrical column of the paper. This he positively refused to do, and as soon as his services could be spared, he was informed that they were no longer required.

Soon after this, he accepted the position of accountant and corresponding clerk of the firm of William C. Black & Co., cotton factors, a successful and conservative house, which he continued to serve for several years, and of which he became the trusted representative. He retained this position until the sudden death of the head of the firm, in 1879. In addition to his office duties, he acted as secretary to Mr. Black in various offices of trust, especially in the treasurership of the New Orleans Cotton Exchange, and as secretary of its finance committee.

The success achieved by the sketches which first appeared in this magazine and which are now collected in *Old Creole Days*, made Mr. Cable decide to depend thenceforth mainly on his pen for his future career. Thus far, literature had been to him only a stolen industry. The earlier sketches, and much of *The Grandissimes*, were written as with the left hand, while the right was busy with the invoices and the correspondence of the cotton firm. In the odd moments of his busy life he jotted down, on odd scraps of paper, the conceits that grew out of his passing intercourse with creole men of business of all grades, and with the stray bits of creole life with which he was thrown in contact. With a good gift of language, and a very rare one for dialect, he has made a systematic study of creole French, of which he may be regarded as the first thorough exponent. He has been no less successful in acquiring the patois of the New Orleans negro, and the music of the curious old slave-songs. In singing these, as in rendering the speech of the creole and the negro, he evinces a talent which is at somewhat strange variance with his former prejudice against the dramatic art.

His work in this direction, as in others, has been carried on with a direct purpose, and with a success which is now yielding him good fruit. He is, and he will, probably, remain, the first authority in all matters, light or grave, relating to the people and the history of Louisiana. He would be a bold man and a resolute one who, with Cable's precedence assured, would now attempt that mastery of a slightly known dialect, without which no true portrayal of the character of this people could be possible. Probably, also, the true spirit of the creole could never be gained by one not born among them, and whose life had not been passed in close observation of their characteristics. His work has by no means been confined to speech and personal traits. It has penetrated every remote corner of the whole history of the colony, and he has gained a hard-earned familiarity with his subject, such as few writers ever consider it worth their while to achieve. For more than a year past he has devoted himself almost exclusively to the preparation of a history of New Orleans, which is now being published by the Census Office in connection with the social statistics of that city, and except so far as relates to the mere enumeration, he has collated the statistical information himself. He might well rest his reputation for thorough and judicious historical and descriptive work on this production alone. He has gathered also the material for a census report on that curious and romantic people of the Têche and Attakapas country, who, exiled from Acadia, found a home only in far Louisiana, where, as 'Cadjiens, they still retain their original peculiarities. Charmed as he is with the brilliant color and picturesque effects that this study has developed, there is ground for the hope that a novel which he is to write before long may be laid in the land of Evangeline.

Mr. Cable has said, in *The Grandissimes*, "a creole never forgives a public mention," and his work has hitherto been received by the race it has delineated in no such cordial spirit as has marked its welcome elsewhere. Much resentment has been expressed; the correctness of the portrayal has been denied, and the suspicion was aroused that a strange and unkind critic had been making free with the sacred traditions of a proud and over-sensitive people. Happily this condition is now changing, and the creoles themselves are beginning to recognize the kindly and appreciative spirit which has actuated all his dealings with them. Indeed, the better men among them, who at first resented *The Grandissimes* as an intrusion and an impertinence, realizing, at last, that it was written by a native of New Orleans and by an ex-Confederate soldier, have been penetrated by its true meaning, have seen that it was written in a spirit of reform rather than of criticism, and have expressed their hopeful satisfaction that it was written.

As was natural in the case of one exploring such an unfamiliar field, Mr. Cable has been charged by more than one of his critics with inaccuracy and exaggeration. His methods of work and his methods of thought, if not indeed his inherent character, are a perfect answer to this charge. He has carried into his study the habits and processes of the counting-room, making sure that his day-book and cash-book are quite correct before they are posted into his literary ledger, which is a complete index to his material. He works slowly and carefully, with his authorities at his elbow; mastering the details of every subject and making himself familiar with all its bearings before accepting it for his work. Nor does he stop here. Any one who has seen the earlier drafts of his writing must recognize in his frequent erasures and interlineations, not only a search for the best methods of expression, but a desire for exact statement.

Mr. Cable's reading has been thorough rather than general. For a long time he cherished scruples against novel-reading, but this prejudice is now laid, his convictions having been completely changed by reading George Mac-Donald's *Annals of a Quiet Neighborhood*. He is still innocent of the modern French novel. Victor Hugo, Thackeray, Tourguéneff, and Hawthorne he holds in the highest estimation. He is fond of music, and has a more than ordinary knowledge of it, and is especially given to working out the score of the songs of his favorite birds, having succeeded after many efforts, in recording the roulade of an oriole that sings in his orange-tree.

His frank and manly treatment of the peculiar social problems of his native city has not failed to cause a certain feeling of antagonism. This, however, is yielding to a recognition of the real drift of his purpose. Although a Southerner, bred to the prejudices of his community, and although he has rarely been subjected to other influences, he has been able, by the sheer force of his own genius, to lift himself above his immediate surroundings and to view them with the eye of a man of the world. A friend has written of him: "What he hopes to accomplish is the amelioration of the colored race in every possible way. To this end, he would incite them to greater ambition, extend to them, through the State, every educational advantage, afford them opportunities for a fuller religious instruction, give them a more exalted idea of the sanctity of the marriage relation, and so widen their sphere of action that they may become useful, intelligent, and contented members of the community." He has shown, as in *Madame Delphine*, a special tenderness for the quadroons and octoroons, who have hardly a place in the social economy. The careful reader of his works, looking beyond their humor and their dramatic and pathetic elements, must recognize a deep-lying purpose, not only to elevate these lower orders of the community, but even more to humanize and civilize the dominant race which has suffered so deeply from its false relation to its dependents.

It is not possible, in a brief sketch like this, to give an adequate idea of the force and delicacy of Mr. Cable's writing; of his close study of creole character, of his appreciation, remarkable in a Southerner, of the underlying principles involved in the question of slavery, or of his great cleverness in handling the creole dialect. Indeed, the difficulty with which any rendering of this dialect is caught by those not familiar with French, or rather with Louisiana French, is the only serious limitation to the general popularity of his work. His rendering of creole English is perfect, and once its key is found, it becomes entirely familiar.

[Review of *Madame Delphine*]

Anonymous*

Another writer who has gained a great and well-deserved reputation in the United States, although he is comparatively little known in this country, is Mr. George W. Cable, who is doing for the State of Louisiana what Nathaniel Hawthorne did for New England—reproducing for us the people and customs of an age which, though not remote, has passed away. The French and the Spaniards of the last century, who held Louisiana, left the impress of their civilization upon its people, and it will be long before it entirely disappears. Until 1803, when Napoleon ceded the State to the American Government, partly in consideration of receiving fifteen millions of dollars, but chiefly to prevent the control of the Mississippi falling into the hands of the English— until then, the City of New Orleans was almost as French as any city in France itself. The population was then, as it largely is now, composed of people of French descent or of Creoles. It is this mixed and singular community which Mr. Cable has studied with so much care—not from a distance, but on the spot. He has revived, or imagined, many strange and touching stories of days when the French were doing great work on the Mississippi, and he has thrown the charm of romance round the old streets, whose very names still tell of the departed glories of the colonial epoch. The time is probably not far distant, when the only visible remains of the French and Spanish domination will have to be sought in the curious cemeteries, where the dead are put to rest in sealed tombs above ground; for New Orleans stands from two to four feet below the level of the Mississippi, and it would be impossible to dig a grave without coming to water. On the monuments which are preserved in the French and Spanish cemeteries, many a quaint inscription is to be seen, dating back to the period when Bienville was governor of the State. The people retain to this day some of their old peculiarities, but Mr. Cable has dealt chiefly with the Louisiana of from fifty to thirty years ago, and this was entirely unknown to the majority of Americans prior to his labours. In *The Grandissimes* he has presented a vigorous series of pictures of a somewhat earlier date—the period when Louisiana had just been sold, and her people were indignant at the unceremonious way in which they had been turned over to the United States. The colonists were faithful to the mother country, although the mother country was not faithful to them. Mr. Cable has given many illustrations of the bitter-

*Reprinted from *Quarterly Review* (London), 155 (January, 1883), 223–26.

ness which was at first caused by their compulsory transfer to the United States, and in *The Grandissimes* he makes one of his principal characters die with the declaration on his lips, that 'old Louisiana will rise again. She will get back her trampled rights.' And doubtless the Louisianians wished sincerely for the fulfilment of some such prediction as that in the days when General Butler ruled over them with a rod of iron; or in the still darker days when they were delivered over, bound hand and foot, to be governed by the negroes. Many, who had the means to go, fled into Texas; others remained, only to be ruined. There was no 'vindictiveness' on the part of the United States Government; but a generation was destroyed.

The Grandissimes is the most carefully wrought-out of Mr. Cable's stories, but the most finished is, we think, *Madame Delphine*, and some of his shorter sketches in *Old Creole Days* are scarcely inferior to it. Madame Delphine is supposed to be one of the quadroons whose beauty made New Orleans famous, and whose descendants still attract the admiration of every traveller who visits the Crescent City. "Old travellers," as Mr. Cable tells us, "spare no terms to tell their praises, their faultlessness of feature, their perfection of form, their varied styles of beauty—for there were even pure Caucasian blondes among them— their fascinating manners, their sparkling vivacity, their chaste and pretty wit, their grace in the dance, their modest propriety, their taste and elegance in dress. In the gentlest and most poetic sense, they were indeed the sirens of this land, where it seemed 'always afternoon.'" To this class belongs Madame Delphine, she and her daughter Olive, a beautiful girl, but bitterly oppressed by the law of the State, which forbad the marriage of a white man with a woman of the coloured race, no matter how fair she might be. The daughter falls in love, and with a man whom she cannot marry. There is no way of escape for her but one—and that one her mother alone can open up. Madame Delphine does not hesitate. She goes before a magistrate and swears that Olive is not her daughter; that her parents were of the white race, and committed the child to her charge to be brought up as her own. There is no longer any impediment to the marriage, and Madame Delphine is present at the ceremony, and bears bravely up, but afterwards she desires to see the priest, and makes confession:—

> "Olive *is* my child. The picture I showed to Jean Thompson is the half sister of my daughter's father, dead before my child was born. She is the image of her and of him; but, O God! Thou knowest! Oh, Olive, my own daughter!"
>
> She ceased and was still. Père Jerome waited, but no sound came. He looked through the window. She was kneeling, with her forehead resting on her arms— motionless.
>
> He repeated the words of absolution. Still she did not stir.
>
> "My daughter," he said, "go to thy home in peace." But she did not move.
>
> He rose hastily, stepped from the box, raised her in his arms, and called her by name.
>
> "Madame Delphine!" Her head fell back in his elbow; for an instant there was life in the eyes—it glimmered—it vanished, and tears gushed from his own and fell upon the gentle face of the dead, as he looked up to Heaven and cried:
>
> "Lord, lay not this sin to her charge!"

In all these stories of Mr. Cable's there is one disadvantage which may, we fear, tend to diminish the pleasure of the ordinary reader in them. It is the free use which he is obliged to make of the Creole *patois*. If this difficulty can be patiently endured for a few pages, it will afterwards be easily surmounted, and it is not greater, after all, than that which must be faced in any novel which sets before us in true colours the local life of various States in America. For although we are often told that 'dialect' is peculiar to England, and that identically the same language is spoken all over the United States, the fact is that the local peculiarities of speech are as mysterious as those which still remain in the different counties of England. The New England dialect itself—the only place, as we are assured, where we may draw from the "well of English undefiled"—is not without the "provincialisms" which some American writers dwell so much upon as characteristic of old England alone. . . .

Mr. Cable's Lectures in Baltimore

[Daniel Coit Gilman]°

George W. Cable, the novelist, has been giving a course of lectures on the Relations of Literature to Modern Society before the Johns Hopkins University. At their close, by request of the President, he devoted an hour to the reading of extracts from *Old Creole Days* and *The Grandissimes*, before a crowded assembly made up of college-professors and students, and some of the most cultivated ladies and gentlemen of Baltimore. His lectures had been of a serious philosophical cast, good and sensible, but affording no opportunity for the manifestation of his particular characteristics. On the other hand, in the interpretation of his own writings, he was "every inch a king." He selected a scene from "Posson Jone'," where Colossus of Rhodes and Jules are conspicuous, and made his audience merry with his vivid portrayal of these two persons; and then from *The Grandissimes* he selected that ghastly and pitiful story of Bras Coupé's death, and afterward that admirable scene in which Raoul Innerarity presents himself and his painting to Frowenfeld. The author's exact reproduction of the various dialects with which he has made us familiar, his simple, unaffected and yet truly dramatic gestures, his pithy illustrative sentences, and his own keen enjoyment of the scenes he was portraying, were delightful. He was as natural, modest, and free as if he were talking upon his own balcony to a company of familiar friends. Occasionally he turned to the blackboard in order to show by a diagram the site of the places referred to. His comments on the historical and actual Creole society were so appreciative and commendatory that the most sensitive Creole could not take offense at his photographic pictures. Indeed, the charm of the entertainment was the tone of verity which pervaded it,—the truth of the portraiture and the truth of the enunciation. Besides that, there was wit and poetry, pathos and history.

°Reprinted from *Critic*, 3 (March 24, 1883), 130–31.

On Mr. Cable's Readings

Charles Dudley Warner°

Mr. George W. Cable has been giving some readings from his own books in Hartford, one in public, and two in private parlors. An ordinary "reading" is one of the entertainments that reconcile us to the brevity of life and beget a longing to go to the land where there will be no more sighing and no more reading. But Mr. Cable is not an elocutionist, and has none of the smart bravery of the professional which we admire, and praise, and shun. He is just an interpreter of his own writings, and by a method so simple and so without pretence that it seems to lack all art—until we attempt to account for the effect produced. This effect was not so satisfactory before a large and miscellaneous audience as in presence of a small, compact, and more sympathetic one, partly because the selections were not so judiciously made for the public performance, and partly because of the limitations in the writer himself and in his material.

Mr. Cable's work is delicate and subtle, and his interpretations of it must be the same. The love scene between Aurora and Honoré Grandissime is a fascinating model for all apprentices in the art of fiction, full of tenderness, witchery, and the utmost archness and finesse of a woman about to capitulate. To broaden and exaggerate this refined and delicate scene so as to satisfy the spectators and listeners in the back seats of a large hall, to substitute for the bashful, half-broken utterances of love the loud tones of the eloquent elocutionist, is to lose a certain charm of the proceeding. If you have ever tried to make love through an ear-trumpet, you will understand what I mean. The public reading of this was delightful, but it lacked the subtle shading which the author gave it in private.

That which thoroughly captivated his hearers in the private readings was "Posson Jone'," the last sketch in *Old Creole Days*. In originality of creation, in exquisite moral distinctions, in distinct dramatic force, this seems to be the most important addition that American literature has received in many years. It has refinement, breadth, and humor; it gives us two new types; it is as complete as a miniature portrait, and yet it is so freely and largely placed upon the canvas that we feel no limitations. The author has not given us a study of two men only, but a wide picture of human life.

Mr. Cable is a master of the Creole dialect, and in his mouth the broken English of Jules St. Ange, delicious in its elisions and accent, interpreted to us

°Reprinted from *Century Magazine*, 26 (June, 1883), 311–12.

perfectly the character of the insouciant, conscienceless, kind-hearted, volatile Creole. The writer does not describe him nor analyze him; he simply places Jules before us with a dramatic skill that is very rare. And the reader brings him out from the page in all his airy substantiality and elusive, non-moral gayety.

> "What a man thing right *is right;* 'tis all 'abit. A man muz nod go again' his conscien'. My faith, do you thing I would go again' my conscien'?"
> It is not the drinking of coffee, but the buying it on the Sabbath that troubles the parson.
> "Ah! *c'est* very true. For you it would be a sin, *mais* for me it is only 'abit. Rilligion is a very strange; I know a man one time, he thing it was wrong to go to cock-fight Sunday evening."
> "Ah!" continued St. Ange, as they descended the stairs, "I thing every man muz have the rilligion he like' the bez—me, I like the *Cattolique* rilligion the bez—for me it is the bez. Every man will sure go to heaven if he like his rilligion the bez."
> "Jools," said the West-Floridian, laying his great hand tenderly upon the Creole's shoulder, "do you think you have any shore hopes of heaven?"
> "Yass!" replied St. Ange, "I am sure-sure. I thing everybody will go to heaven. I thing you will go, *et* I thing Miguel will go, *et* Joe—everybody, I thing,—*mais,* hof course, not if they not have been christen'. Even I thing some niggers will go."

While the author was unfolding to his audience a life and society unfamiliar to them and entrancing them with pictures the reality of which none doubted and the spell of which none cared to escape, it occurred to me that here was the solution of all the pother we have recently got into about the realistic and the ideal schools in fiction. In "Posson Jone'," an awkward, camp-meeting, country preacher is the victim of a vulgar confidence game; the scenes are the street, a drinking place, a gambling saloon, a bull-ring, and a calaboose; there is not a "respectable" character in it. Where shall we look for a more faithful picture of low life? Where shall we find another so vividly set forth in all its sordid details? And yet see how art steps in, with the wand of genius, to make literature! Over the whole the author has cast an ideal light; over a picture that, in the hands of a bungling realist, would have been coarse and repellant he has thrown the idealizing grace that makes it one of the most charming sketches in the world. Here is nature, as nature only ought to be in literature, elevated but never departed from. For me it is a good deal truer than a police report, and it adds something to life that I would not part with.

This is not the place for a discussion of Mr. Cable's genius. I only took up my pen to say that those who are so fortunate as to have an opportunity to hear this author interpret his own fascinating creations have a great pleasure ready for them.

[The Native Element in Cable's Fiction]

James Herbert Morse°

What Eggleston was for the coarse, crude, but strong animal life of Indiana, Cable was for the proud, fast-lodged, diluvian drift of Louisiana. It was Cable's merit, as has been said, to have discovered the Creole element. In a series of striking sketches, culminating in *The Grandissimes* and *Madame Delphine*, we find a most unique people, treated in a thoroughly unique manner. The treatment is worthy of the theme. It is delicate, poetical, imaginative in a high degree. In all those details of art that go to the creating of atmosphere, Cable was strong; nor did Hawthorne succeed better in producing a Puritan *aura* for the setting of Hester Prynne and Dimmesdale than Cable succeeded in getting a Creole *aura* for the working out of the impotent pride of the Grandissimes. The confused intermingling of elements in the ball-room was the natural prelude to the confusion of family relations, of family passions, and of race peculiarities. The pride of Agricola, the implacable spirit of Palmyre, the animal passion of Bras-Coupé, are shown in fine relief. They are all human passions, but with a touch of the Grandissime impotency, which was not one of cold latitudes, like that in Lowell's "New Priest," but one of race decay. The finest part of the artist's work, however, is in the nice shading of character between Aurore and her daughter Clothilde. Both women are beautiful. The elements of similarity between mother and daughter are many, as they should be, but the differences are clear. Both are children in feeling and knowledge of the world. Both have a shy, natural coquetry, to which is added, in the mother, the innocent finesse born of widowhood. They have some pride and very considerable poverty, and while the latter has something to do in overcoming the former, the part played by innocent, shy love is so deftly managed that we do not miss any lady-like quality of refinement. The dialect is another excellence in Cable's work. We find in it the piquant charm of a lapse from the French rather than the lazy drawl of deteriorated English. The vocabulary is small and well utilized; a few dozen words do a good deal of service, and in the end we might tire of them; but it is a grace of the author to hold back dialect conversation except when it can be made telling. To all these artistic gifts Cable adds a stronger grasp on the fate of the story than Eggleston gets. But his poetic and antiquarian

°Reprinted from *Century Magazine*, 26 (July, 1883), 368.

spirit leads him too often to step aside to illustrate graces of manner and fantasticalness of customs; he pauses sometimes too long to give fullness to his picture of a passing race. Like Eggleston, he lingers fondly over the novel features of his theme, perhaps with a view to their present value. This is a danger which all original discoverers must encounter. When their wealth becomes common property, they will be called to account for their management of the grand passions of human nature, which may get a hint of quaintness from deciduous fashions, but are, after all, essentially the same the world over. By their work in this enduring stuff they will be judged as novelists. *The Grandissimes* will always have the beauty of local color, the tint of a poetical conception; but perhaps it will be said that the development of dramatic action was made subordinate.

The Scenes of Cable's Romances

Lafcadio Hearn[*]

When I first viewed New Orleans from the deck of the great steam-boat that had carried me from gray northwestern mists into the tepid and orange-scented air of the South, my impressions of the quaint city, drowsing under the violet and gold of a November morning, were oddly connected with memories of "Jean-ah Poquelin." That strange little tale had appeared in *Scribner's Magazine* a few months previously; and its exotic picturesqueness had considerably influenced my anticipations of the Southern metropolis, and prepared me to idealize everything peculiar and semi-tropical that I might see. Even before I had left the steamboat my imagination had already flown beyond the wilderness of cotton-bales, the sierra-shaped roofs of the sugar-sheds, the massive fronts of refineries and storehouses to wander in search of the old slave-trader's mansion, or at least of something resembling it—"built of heavy cypress, lifted up on pillars, grim, solid and spiritless." I did not even abandon my search for the house after I had learned that Tchoupitoulas "Road" was now a great business street, fringed not by villas but by warehouses; that the river had receded from it considerably since the period of the story; and that where marshlands used to swelter under the sun broad pavements of block stone had been laid, enduring as Roman causeways, although they will shudder a little under the passing of cotton-floats. At one time I tried to connect the narrative with a peculiar residence near the Bayou Road—a silent wooden mansion with vast verandahs, surrounded by shrubbery which had become fantastic by long neglect. Indeed there are several old houses in the more ancient quarters of the city which might have served as models for the description of Jean-ah Poquelin's dwelling, but none of which are situated in his original neighborhood,—old plantation-houses whose broad lands have long since been cut up and devoured by the growing city. In reconstructing the New Orleans of 1810 Mr. Cable might have selected any one of these to draw from, and I may have found his model without knowing it. Not however until the last June *Century* appeared, with its curious article upon the "Great South Gate," did I learn that in the early years of the nineteenth century such a house existed precisely in the location described by Mr. Cable. Readers of "The Great South Gate" must have

[*]Reprinted, with permission, from the manuscript (HM 11963) at the Huntington Library, San Marino, California. The essay appeared in *Century Magazine*, 27 (November, 1883), 40–47.

been impressed by the description therein given of "Doctor" Gravier's home, upon the bank of the long-vanished Poydras Canal,—a picture of desolation more than justified by the testimony of early municipal chronicles; and the true history of that eccentric "Doctor" Gravier no doubt inspired the creator of "Jean-ah Poquelin." An ancient city map informs us that the deserted indigo-fields, with their wriggling amphibious population, extended a few blocks north of the present Charity Hospital; and that the plantation-house itself must have stood near the juncture of Poydras and Villere streets,—a region now very closely built and very thickly peopled.

The sharp originality of Mr. Cable's description should have convinced the readers of *Old Creole Days* that the scenes of his stories are in no sense fanciful; and the strict perfection of his Creole architecture is readily recognized by all who have resided in New Orleans. Each one of those charming pictures of places—veritable pastels—was painted after some carefully-selected model of French or Franco-Spanish origin,—typifying fashions of building which prevailed in colonial days. Greatly as the city has changed since the eras in which Mr. Cable's stories are laid, the old Creole quarter still contains antiquities enough to enable the artist to restore almost all that has vanished. Through those narrow, multi-colored, and dilapidated streets, one may still wander at random with the certainty of encountering eccentric façades and suggestive Latin appellations at every turn; and the author of *Madame Delphine* must have made many a pilgrimage into the quaint district, to study the wrinkled faces of the houses, or perhaps to read the queer names upon the signs,—as Balzac loved to do in old-fashioned Paris. Exceptionally rich in curiosities is the *Rue Royale*, and best represents, no doubt, the general physiognomy of the colonial city. It appears to be Mr. Cable's favorite street,—as there are few of his stories which do not contain references to it; and even the scenery of incidents laid elsewhere has occasionally been borrowed from that "region of architectural decrepitude," which is yet peopled by an "ancient and foreign-seeming domestic life." For Louisiana dreamers Mr. Cable has peopled it also with many delightful phantoms; and the ghosts of Madame Délicieuse, of Delphine Carraze, of 'Sieur George, will surely continue to haunt it until of all the dear old buildings there shall not be left a stone upon a stone.

From the Canal-street corner of Royal,—ever perfumed by the baskets of the flowersellers,—to the junction of Royal with Bienville, one observes with regret numerous evidences of modernization. American life is largely and widely invading the thoroughfare,—uprearing concert-halls with insufferably pompous names, multiplying flashy saloons, and cheap restaurants, cigar-stores and oyster-rooms. Gambling indeed survives, but only through metamorphosis;—it is certainly not of that aristocratic kind wherein Colonel De Charleu, owner of "Belles Demoiselles Plantation," could have been wont to indulge. Already a line of electric lights mocks the rusty superannuation of those long-disused wrought-iron lamp-frames set into the walls of various Creole buildings. But from the corner of Conti street,—where Jules St. Ange idled one summer morning "some seventy years ago,"—*Rue Royale* begins to display a picturesqueness almost unadulterated by innovation, and opens a perspective of roof-lines astonishingly irregular, that jag and cut into the blue strip of intervening sky at every conceivable angle, with gables, eaves, dormers, triangular peaks of slate, projecting corners of balconies or verandahs,—overtopping or jutting out from houses of every imaginable tint: canary, chocolate, slate-blue, speckled grey, ultramarine, cinnamon-red, and even pale rose. All have sap-green batten shutters;—most possess balconies balustraded with elegant arabesque-work in wrought-iron,—graceful tendrils and curling leaves of metal, framing in some monogram of which the meaning is forgotten. Much lattice work also will be observed about verandahs,—or veiling the ends of galleries,—or suspended like green cage-work at the angle formed by a window-balcony with some lofty court-wall. And far down the street, the erratic superimposition of wire-hung signs—advertising the presence of many quiet, shadowy little shops that hide their faces from the sun behind slanting canvas-awnings,—makes a spidery confusion of lines and angles in the very center of the vista.

I think that only by a series of instantaneous photographs, tinted after the manner of Goupil, could the physiognomy of the street be accurately reproduced,—such is the confusion of projecting show-windows, the kaleidoscopic medley of color, the jumble of infinitesimal stores. The characteristics of almost any American street may usually be taken in at one presbyopic glance; but you might transverse this Creole thoroughfare a hundred times without being able to ordinate the puzzling details of its perspective.° Out of the bewildering multitude, of anonymous and enigmatic establishments which offer no outward indication of their interior commercial life, you might perhaps retain confused memories of two or three banks, as severely and quaintly decorous as a Creole family-portrait; several lilliputian jewelry-stores; some Italian groceries, sundry Spanish wine-houses; a Swiss tobacconist's; a lottery-office, with wooden screen concealing its low desk; some bric-à-brac establishments behind whose smoky show-panes unfashionable bronzes touch elbows with waxen figurines of Spanish-American origin, illustrating the *Costumbres Mejicanos*;—perhaps a druggist's shining signboard, gilded in two languages: "Deutsche Apotheke" "Pharmacie Française,"—making us think of Frowenfeld; two or more millinery-establishments, panelled with coquettish mirrors which duplicate the latest Paris importations; a French bookstore displaying behind its plate-glass the last novels of Maupassant or of Zola, in tantalizing yellow or blue covers;—finally, a sombre and elegant shoestore where the eye is fascinated by the exhibition of white kid shoes—one pair only;—but so dainty, so aerial, so slender, that they must have been shaped for a Creole foot.

But when the curious pilgrim reaches the corner of Royal and St. Peter streets (Rue Saint-Pierre) he finds himself confronted by an edifice whose oddity and massiveness compel special examination,—a four-story brick tenement-house with walls deep as those of a medieval abbey, and with large square windows having singular balconies, the iron-work of which is wrought into scrolls and initials. Unlike any other building in the quarter, its form is that of an irregular pentagon, the smallest side of which looks down Royal and up St. Peter street at once, and commands through its windows a simultaneous view of three street-angles. This is the house where 'Sieur George so long dwelt. It is said to have been the first four-story building erected in New Orleans; and it certainly affords a singular example of the fact that some very old buildings obstinately rebel against innovations of fashion, just as many old men do. Despite a desperate effort recently made to compel its acceptance of a new suit of paint and whitewash, the venerable structure persists in remaining almost precisely as Mr. Cable first described it. The cornices are still dropping plaster; the stucco has not ceased to peel off; the rotten staircases, "hugging the sides of the court," still seem "trying to climb up out of the rubbish"; the court itself is always "hung with many lines of wet clothes";—and the rooms are now as ever occupied by folk "who dwell there simply for lack of activity to find better and cheaper quarters elsewhere." Cheaper it would surely be easy to find,—inasmuch as 'Sieur George's single-windowed room rents—unfurnished—at ten dollars per month. There is something unique in the spectacle of this ponderous, dilapidated edifice, with its host of petty shops on the *rez-de-chaussée*,—something which recalls an engraving I once saw in some archaeological folio, picturing a swarm of Italian fruit-booths seeking shelter under the crumbling arches of a Roman theater.

Upon the east side of Rue Royale, half-a-square further up, the eye is refreshed by a delicious burst of bright green,—a garden enclosed on three sides by spiked railings, above which bananas fling out the watered-satin of their splendid leaves, and bounded at its eastern extremity by the broad, blanched, sloping-shouldered silhouette of the Cathedral. Here linger memories of Padre Antonio de Sedella (Père Antoine) first sent to Louisiana as a Commissary of the Holy Inquisition,—immediately shipped home again by sensible Governor Miro. But Padre Antonio returned to Louisiana not as an inquisitor, but as a secular priest, to win the affection of the whole Creole population by whom he was venerated as a saint even before his death. Somewhere near this little garden the Padre used to live in a curious wooden hut; and the narrow flagged alley on the southern side of the Cathedral and its garden still bears the appellation, *Passage Saint-Antoine*, in honor of [the] old priest's patron. The name is legibly inscribed above the show-windows of the Catholic shop on the corner, where porcelain angels appear to be perpetually ascending and descending a Jacob's ladder formed of long Communion-candles. The "Pères Jeromes" of our own day reside in the dismal brick-houses bordering the alley further toward Chartres street,—buildings which push out—,above the heads of passers-by, a line of jealous-looking balconies screened with lattice work in which wicket-lookouts have been contrived. On the northern side of garden and Cathedral runs another flagged alley, which affects to be a continuation of Orleans street. Like its companion-passage it opens into Chartres street; but on its way it forks into a grotesque fissure in the St. Peter-street block,—into a marvellous, medieval-looking byway, craggy with balconies and peaked with dormers. As this picturesque opening is still called Exchange Alley, we must suppose it to have once formed part of the much-more familiar passage of that name, though now widely separated therefrom by architectural reforms effected in Rue Saint-Louis and other streets intervening. The northern side-entrance of the Cathedral commands it,—a tall, dark, ecclesiastically-severe archway, in whose shadowed recess Madame Delphine might have safely entrusted her anxieties to "God's own banker";—and Catholic quadroon-women on their daily morning way to market, habitually enter it with their baskets, to murmur a prayer in patois before the shrine of *Nôtre Dame de Lourdes.* Jackson Square with its rococo flower-beds and clipped shrubbery, might be reached in a moment by either of the flagged alleys above described; but it retains none of its colonial features, and has rightly been deprived of the military titles it once bore,— *Place d'Armes*, or *Plaza de Armas.*

There stands at the corner of St. Anne and Royal streets, a one-story structure with Spanish tile-roof, a building that has become absolutely shapeless with age, and may be torn away at any moment. It is now a mere hollow carcass,—a shattered brick skeleton to which plaster and laths cling in patches only, like shrunken hide upon the bones of some creature left to die and to mummify under the sun. An obsolete directory, printed in 1845, assures us that the construction was considered immemorially old even then; but a remarkable engraving of it, which accompanies the above remark, shows it to have at that time possessed distinct Spanish features, and two neat entrances with semicircular stone-steps. In 1835 it was the *Café des Réfugiés*, frequented by fugitives from the Antilles, West-Indian strangers, filibusters, revolutionaries,—all that singular class of Latin-Americans so strongly portrayed in Mr. Cable's "Café des Exilés."

At the next block, if you turn down Dumaine street from Royal, you will notice, about half-way toward Chartres a very peculiar house, half-brick, half-timber. It creates the impression that its builder commenced it with the intention of erecting a three-story brick, but changed his mind before the first-story had been completed, and finished the edifice with second-hand lumber,— supporting the gallery with wooden posts that resemble monstrous balusters. This is the house bequeathed by "Mr. John," of the Good Children's Social Club, to the beautiful quadroon Zalli and her more beautiful reputed daughter, 'Tite Poulette. As Mr. Cable tells us, and as one glance can verify, it has now become "a den of Italians, who sell fuel by day, and by night are up to no telling what extent of deviltry." On the same side of Dumaine, but on the western side of Royal street, is another remarkable building, more imposing, larger,— "whose big, round-arched windows in the second-story were walled-up, to have smaller windows let into them again with odd little latticed peep-holes in their batten shutters." It was in this house that Zalli and 'Tite Poulette removed their worldly goods, after the failure of the bank; and it was from the most westerly of those curious windows in the second story that Kristian Koppig saw the row of cigar-boxes empty their load of earth and flowers upon the head of the manager of the Salle Condé. Right opposite you may see the good Dutchman's one-story Creole cottage. The resemblance of 'Tite Poulette's second dwelling-place to the old Spanish barracks in architectural peculiarity has been prettily commented upon by Mr. Cable; and, in fact, those barracks, which could shelter six thousand troops in O'Reilly's time, and must therefore have covered a considerable area, were situated not very far from this spot. But the only fragments of the barrack-buildings that are still positively recognizable are the arched structures at Nos. 270 and 272 Royal street occupied now, alas! by a prosaic seltzer-factory. The spacious cavalry stables now shelter vulgar mules, and factory-wagons protrude their shafts from the mouths of low broad arch-ways under which once glimmered the brazen artillery of the King of Spain.

A square west of Royal, at the corner of Bourbon and St. Phillip streets, formerly stood the famed smithy of the Brothers Lafitte; but it were now useless to seek for a vestige of that workshop, whose chimes of iron were rung by African muscle. Passing St. Phillip street, therefore, the visitor who follows the east side of Royal, might notice upon the opposite side an elegant and lofty red-brick mansion, with a deep archway piercing its rez-de-chaussée to the court-yard, which shows a glimpse of rich foliage whenever the *porte-cochère* is left ajar. This is No. 253 Royal street, the residence of "Madame Délicieuse"; and worthy of that honor it seems, with its superb tiara of green verandahs. A minute two-story cottage squats down beside it—a miniature shop having tiny show windows that project like eyes. The cottage is a modern affair; but it covers the site of Dr. Mossy's office, which, you know was a lemon-yellow Creole construction, roofed with red tiles. What used to be "the Café de Poésie on the corner" is now a hat-store. Further on, at the intersection of Royal and Hospital streets (Rue d'Hôpital, famous in Creole ballads) one cannot fail to admire a dwelling solid and elegant as a Venetian palazzo. It has already been celebrated in one foreign novel; and did I not feel confident that Mr. Cable will tell us all about it one of these days, I should be tempted to delay the reader on this corner, although Madame Delphine's residence is already within sight.

No one can readily forget Mr. Cable's description of "the small, low brick house of a story and a half, set out upon the sidewalk, as weatherbeaten and mute as an aged beggar fallen asleep." It stands near Barracks street on Royal;—the number, I think, is 294. Still are its solid wooden shutters "shut with a grip that makes one's nails and knuckles feel lacerated"; and its coat of decaying plaster, patched with all varieties of neutral tints, still suggests the raggedness of mendicancy. Even the condition of the garden-gate,—through which Monsieur Vignevielle first caught a glimpse of Olive's maiden-beauty,—might be perceived today as readily as ever by "an eye that had been in the blacksmithing business." But since the accompanying sketch was drawn, the picturesqueness of the upper part of the cottage has been greatly diminished by architectural additions made with a view to render the building habitable. Over the way may still be seen that once-pretentious three-story residence, "from whose front-door hard times have removed all vestiges of paint,"—a door shaped like old European hall-doors, and furnished with an iron knocker. It has not been repaired since Mr. Cable wrote his story, nor does it seem likely to be. Only a few paces further on yawns the dreamy magnificence of aristocratic Esplanade street, with its central broad band of grass all shadow-flecked by double lines of trees. There Royal street terminates;—Esplanade forming the southern boundary-line of the old French quarter.

If the reader could now follow me westwardly along one of the narrow ways leading to the great Rue des Ramparts, he would soon find himself in that quadroon quarter, whose denizens still "drag their chairs down to the narrow gateways of their close-fenced gardens, and stare shrinkingly at you as you pass, like a nest of yellow kittens." He would be at once charmed and astonished by the irregularity of the perspective and the eccentricity of the houses:—houses whose foreheads are fantastically encircled by wooden parapets, striped like the *foulards* of the negresses;—houses yellow-faced and sphinx-featured like certain mulatto-women,—houses which present their profiles to the fence,—so that as you approach they seem to turn away their faces with studied prudery, like young Creole-girls,—houses that appear felinely watchful in spite of closed windows and doors, gazing sleepily at the passer-by through the chinks of their green shutters, as through vertical pupils. Five minutes walk over banquettes of disjointed brickwork, through which knots of tough grass are fighting their upward way, brings one to Rampart street, where Mr. Cable found the model for his "Café des Exilés." It was situated on the west side,—No. 219,—and the *Century's* artist sketched it under a summer glow that brought out every odd detail in strong relief. But, hereafter, alas! the visitor to New Orleans must vainly look for the window of Pauline,—"well up in the angle of the broad side-gable, shaded by its rude awning of clapboards, as the eyes of an old dame are shaded by her wrinkled hand." Scarcely a week ago, from the time at which I write, the antiquated cottage that used to "squat right down upon the sidewalk, as do those Choctaw squaws who sell bay and sassafras and life-everlasting"— was ruthlessly torn away, together with its oleanders and palmettoes and pomegranates, to make room, no doubt, for some modern architectural platitude.

A minute's walk from the vacant site of the Café des Exilés will bring you to Congo Square,—the last green remnant of those famous Congo plains, where the negro-slaves once held their bamboulas. Until within a few years ago, the strange African dances were still danced and the African songs still sung by negroes and negresses who had been slaves;—every Sunday afternoon the bamboula-dancers were summoned to a woodyard on Dumaine street by a sort of drum-roll, made by rattling the ends of two great bones upon the head of an empty cask; and I remember that the male dancers fastened bits of tinkling metal or tin rattles about their ankles, like those strings of copper gris-gris worn by the negroes of the Soudan. Those whom I saw taking part in those curious and convulsive performances—subsequently suppressed by the police—were either old or beyond middle-age: the veritable Congo dance, with its extraordinary rhythmic chant, will soon have become as completely forgotten in Louisiana as the significance of those African words which formed the hieratic vocabulary of the Voudoos.

It was where Congo square now extends that Bras-Coupé was lassoed while taking part in such a dance;—it was in the same neighborhood that Captain Jean Grandissime of the Attakappas lay hiding—secure in his white man's skin "as if cased in steel"—to foil the witchcraft of Clémence;—and it was there also that a crowd of rowdy American flat-boatmen, headed by "Posson Jone'," of Bethesdy Church, stormed the circus and slew the tiger and the buffalo. Now "Cayetano's circus" was not a fiction of Mr. Cable's imagining: such a show actually visited New Orleans in 1816 or thereabouts, and remained a popular "fixture" for several seasons. The Creole-speaking negroes of that day celebrated its arrival in one of their singular ditties. Some years ago, when I was endeavoring to make a collection of patois songs and other curiosities of the oral literature of the Louisiana colored folk, Mr. Cable kindly lent me his own collection with permission to make selections for my private use; and I copied therefrom this *chanson créole*:

°C'est Michié Cayétane
Qui sorti la Havane
Avec so chouals et so macacs!
Li gagnin ein homme qui dansé dans sac;
Li gagnin qui dansé si yé la main;
Li gagnin zaut' à choual qui boi' di vin;
Li gagnin oussi ein zeine zolie mamzelle
Qui monté choual sans bride et sans selle;—
Pou di tou' ça mo pas capabe,—
Mais mo souvien ein qui valé sab'.
Yé n'en oussi tout sort bétail:
Yé pas montré pou' la négrail
Qui ya pou' douchans,—dos-brulés
Qui fé tapaze,—et pou' birlé
Ces gros madames et gros michiés
Qui ménein là tous p'tis yé
'Oir Michié Cayétane
Qui vivé la Havane
Avec so chouals et so macaca.

° " 'Tis Monsieur Gaëtano
Who comes out from Havana
With his horses and his monkeys!
He has a man who dances in a sack;
He has one who dances on his hands;
He has another who drinks wine on horseback;
He has also a young pretty lady
Who rides a horse without bridle or saddle:
To tell you all about it I am not able,—
But I remember one who swallowed a sword.
There are all sorts of animals, too;—
They did not show to nigger-folk
What they showed to the trash,—the burnt-backs [*poor whites*]
Who make so much noise,—nor what they had to amuse
All those fine ladies and gentlemen
Who take all their little children along with them
To see Monsieur Gayëtano
Who lives in Havana
With his horses and his monkeys.

And whosoever cares to consult certain musty newspaper-files, which are treasured up among the city archives, may find therein the quaint advertisements of Señor Gaëtano's circus, and the story of its violent disruption.

But Congo Square has been wholly transformed within a twelvemonth:— the high railings and gateways have been removed; the weeds that used to climb over the mouldering benches have been plucked up; new gravelled walks have been made; the grass, mown smooth, is now refreshing to look at; the trunks of the shadetrees are freshly whitewashed; and, before long, a great fountain will murmur in the midst. Two blocks westward the sombre, sinister, Spanish façade of the Parish Prison towers above a huddling flock of dingy frame dwellings, and exhales far around it the heavy, sickly, musky scent that betrays the presence of innumerable bats. At sundown they circle in immense flocks above it, and squeak like ghosts about its naked sentry-towers. I have been told that this grim building will soon be numbered among those antiquities of New Orleans forming the scenery of Mr. Cable's romances.

The scene of perhaps the most singular tale in *Old Creole Days*,—"Belles Demoiselles Plantation,"—remains to be visited; but if the reader recollects the observation made in the very first paragraph of the story, that "the old Creoles never forgive a public mention," he will doubtless pardon me for leaving the precise location of "Belles Demoiselles" a mystery, and for keeping secret its real and ancient name. I can only tell him that to reach it he must journey far from the Creole faubourg and beyond the limits of New Orleans to a certain unfamiliar point on the river's bank, whence a ferryman, swarthy and silent as Charon, will row him to the further side of the Mississippi, and aid him to land upon a crumbling levee erected to prevent the very catastrophe anticipated in Mr. Cable's tale. Parallel with the levee curves a wagon-road whose further side is bounded by a narrow and weed-masked ditch, where all kinds of marvellous wild things are growing, and where one may feel assured that serpents hide. Beyond this little ditch is a wooden fence, now overgrown and rendered superfluous by a grand natural barrier of trees and shrubs, all chained together by interlacements of wild vines and thorny creepers. This forms the boundary of the private grounds surrounding the "Belles Demoiselles" residence;—and the breeze comes to you heavily-sweet with blossom-scents, and shrill with vibrant music of cicadas and of birds.

Fancy the wreck of a vast garden created by princely expenditure,—a garden once filled with all forms of exotic trees, with all species of fantastic shrubs, with the rarest floral products of both hemispheres,—but left utterly uncared-for during a generation, so that the groves have been made weird with weeping of moss, and the costly vines have degenerated into parasites, and richly-cultured plants returned to their primitive wild shapes. The alley-walks are soft and sable with dead leaves; and all is so profoundly beshadowed by huge trees that a strange twilight prevails there even under a noonday sun. The lofty hedge is becrimsoned with savage roses, in whose degenerate petals still linger traces of former high cultivation. By a little gate set into the hedge, you can enter the opulent wilderness within, and pursue a winding path between mighty trunks, that lean at a multitude of angles, like columns of a decaying cathedral about to fall. Crackling of twigs under the foot, leaf-whispers, calls of birds and cries of tree-frogs are the only sounds;—the soft gloom deepens as you advance under the swaying moss and snaky-festoons of creepers: there is a holy dimness and calm as of a place consecrated to prayer. But for their tropical and elfish drapery one might dream those oaks were of Dodona. And even with the passing of the fancy, lo!—at a sudden turn of the narrow way, in a grand glow of light *even the Temple appears*, with splendid peripteral of fluted columns rising boldly from the soil. Four pillared façades,—east, west, north, and south,—four superb porches, with tiers of galleries suspended in their recesses;—and two sides of the antique vision ivory-tinted by the sun. Impossible to verbally describe the effect of this matchless relic of Louisiana's feudal splendors,—that seems trying to hide itself from the New Era amid the monstrosity of its neglected gardens, the savage Dorésqueness of its groves. It creates such astonishment as some learned traveller might feel, were he suddenly to come upon the unknown ruins of a Greek temple in the very heart of an equatorial forest;—it is so grand, so strangely at variance with its surroundings! True, the four ranks of columns are not of chiselled marble, and the stucco has broken away from them in places, and severe laws of architecture have not been strictly obeyed; but these things are forgotten in admiration of the building's majesty. I suspect it to be the noblest old plantation-house in Louisiana; I am sure there is none more quaintly beautiful. Would that some true artist might paint the scene even as I last beheld it!—the grand old mansion with the evening sun resting upon it in a Turneresque column of yellow glory,—and the oaks reaching out to it their vast arms through ragged sleeves of moss,—and, beyond, upon either side, the crepuscular dimness of the woods with rare golden luminosities spattering down through the serpent knot-work of lianas, and the heavy mourning of mosses, and the great drooping and clinging of multitudinous disheveled things. . . . And all this subsists only because the old Creole estate has never changed hands,—because no speculating utilitarian could buy up the plantation, to remove or remodel its proud homestead and condemn its odorous groves to the saw-mill. The river is the sole enemy to be dreaded, but a terrible one: it is ever gnawing the levee to get at the fat canefields; it is devouring the roadway; it is burrowing nearer and nearer to the groves and the gardens;—and while gazing at its ravages I could not encourage myself to doubt that, although his romantic anticipation may not be realized for years to come, Mr. Cable has veritably predicted the ghastly destiny of "Belles Demoiselles Plantation."

[Notes for a Novel, *Dr. Sevier*]

D. Warren Brickell°

Tell Cable I cant give exact date.—It was in the fall of 1856.—

Perhaps he had better use another name than Ritchie, as the wife may be alive.

A very important point I think I forgot to give was the absolute and untiring attention given the sick stranger (in her first illness) by the Quadroons and Mulatresses who kept the house, on the outside of which there hung from the gallery the sign—"Chambres à Louer."—

I dont know that his attention was ever drawn to it; but a *feature* in the history of New Orleans of the past has been the system of rooms to let carried on by these people; their quiet and genteel houses, and their real devotion to their sick tenants.—My observation as a Dr. goes back to Jan. 1/48, and I often, often think of it.—*All* the best of these people had french blood and nearly all french accent.—

Ed. Note: This memorandum is on a letterhead bearing the printed date 1881. Cable added and signed this note: "This is from Dr. D. Warren Brickell, the original of Doctor Sevier." Brickell was the Cable family doctor.

°Printed with permission from the manuscript in the George W. Cable Collection, Special Collections Division, Tulane University Library.

Mr. Cable's *Dr. Sevier*

Lafcadio Hearn[*]

The whole plan, purpose, and style are marked by a rare uniqueness;—the chapters, each a little *tableau-vivant*, reveal a fine study of certain phases of life treated for the first time by a singularly artistic pen;—the portrayal of the unfortunate vicissitudes through which the young Richlings pass suggest rather than contain a moral more effective than any number of heavy volumes upon *Self-Help*, or *Practical Education*; and the descriptions of Louisiana scenery and New Orleans localities sometimes exceed in picturesque exquisiteness the best word-coloring Mr. Cable had yet given us. Without didactic commentary upon the incidents which he paints, the author has contrived by those incidents alone to explain the secret of success in life,—the true reason why certain gifted natures, though strong in integrity and tenacious in purpose, must fall by the wayside, while less cultivated and less scrupulous aspirants for wealth reach the desired goal almost without apparent effort. Admirably conceived is the contrast between the sensitive, refined and spirited Richling,—and the subtle, taciturn, kindly but somewhat terrible Ristofalo. Indeed, the whole purpose of the work is contained in those two characters. The austere Doctor; the fantastic Narcisse; even the beautiful and true woman, who by mere force of love makes her way through the lines of steel and fire to meet her dying husband,—all, strictly speaking, perform only subordinate *roles*. It was, perhaps, in accordance with this plan that the author finally dismisses Narcisse from view with a mere hint of the future awaiting him instead of inviting the reader to follow the Creole regiment to the field and there enable him to witness the last heroic struggle. It was certainly a magnificent opportunity for the display of literary force,—an opportunity that no English novelist would have dreamed of losing; and the neglect of it by Mr. Cable can only be explained by some voluntary artistic purpose,—a purpose, however, not invariably adhered to with the same rigidity. The general impression of the book is that of a long succession of vivid and realistic life scenes, through which one comparative study is carried somewhat unsteadily but nevertheless successfully. The unsteadiness is largely due to the importance given to small detail; the frame work is often undiscernible by

[*]Reprinted from the New Orleans *Times-Democrat*, October 5, 1884. This essay appears in Lafcadio Hearn, *Essays in American Literature*, ed. Sanki Ichikawa (Tokyo: Hokuseido Press, 1929), pp. 164–70.

reason of ornamentation; the incidents overburden the purpose. But how fine the workmanship! Choose at random any description of a familiar New Orleans locality and observe the realistic correctness of treatment. . . .

Space allows of few quotations from *Dr. Sevier*; but there are a few passages which will suffice to give a just idea of the beauties the book contains. These beauties are not generally of the severer order; they are light, graceful and essentially odd. . . .

There are many passages of remarkable beauty in *Dr. Sevier*—we could wish to cite more of them;—there is no lack of originality; and the literary critics might well afford to ignore certain faults of construction or of language for the sake of much uniqueness and grace. But the critics who will judge the book most severely are not those who commit their opinions of it to print;—they form a considerable portion of that reading public—especially in New Orleans—whom Mr. Cable has necessarily antagonized by the anti-Southern tone of his work, by side-thrusts at political and social ideas which he himself once fought in defense of. We do not wish, indeed, to discuss these points with Mr. Cable; but we may certainly take opportunity to observe in a friendly way that it is more than doubtful whether the pages in which these political touches appear really add dignity or value to his novel. Impressionality is one of the qualities by which writers far greater than Mr. Cable have won universal esteem and even affection; and the best light literature of the nineteenth century is being shaped according to the pure and strong model such men have laid down.

There is no doubt that *Dr. Sevier* is a far more artistic work than *The Grandissimes*,—although it repeats some of the weaknesses of the latter. The attempts at dialect are not always successful; they are more often heavy, wearying;—for Mr. Cable cannot teach the general public to read them as readily or pleasingly as he did himself last winter. In his briefer stories the broken-English of Mr. Cable's Latin characters does not weary, because there is not too much of it. But *Dr. Sevier* contains nearly five hundred pages! Now that we can judge of the novel as a whole, we doubt whether it reveals Mr. Cable at his best;—it gives us good ground for the belief that his best work will always be confined to his short, bright, graceful stories. We still find in *Old Creole Days* something superior to his later and larger efforts,—something more artistically entire, more consummate. Nor is it discreditable in the least to Mr. Cable that his talents should have visible limits;—the same thing is true of some of the greatest story-tellers of France, who, like Mr. Cable, possess elegance, grace, originality. What Mr. Cable lacks for large work is force,—the force to buoy up the weight of five hundred pages,—the strength that subordinates details to general purpose. This Mr. Cable has not been always able to do in *Dr. Sevier*; and the vapory delicacy of his fancy, the minute finish of his drawing, do not appear to advantage in so broad and ponderous a frame. Had the exquisite pictures of this long panorama been separately mounted,—separately hung,—instead of being merged into one immense design,—we fancy they would be better appreciated, more warmly praised, and more widely studied. Nevertheless we do not hesitate to class the beauties of *Dr. Sevier* as matchless in their way, and the work generally as one of the most remarkable of recent American literary productions. Our comparisons have been drawn between two classes of Mr. Cable's own productions; and our preference for the humbler undertakings does not by any means imply insensibility to the real art of the larger ones.

Mr. Cable's History of
the Creoles

George Parsons Lathrop[*]

Contrary to the popular idea, the novelist is not always a mere purveyor of amusement: he is often a thinker. A few examples prove this. Balzac philosophized freely upon human nature in general, and analyzed the conditions of French life in particular, with trenchant insight; Fielding, quite apart from his fiction, discussed the state of the poor as a humanitarian; George Sand took the liveliest interest in political and sociological questions; George Eliot was a critic and a student of the Positivist theory, as well as a writer of stories; Irving put much of his energy into histories; Thackeray, a great lover of biography, wrote some immortal historical lectures. It need not surprise us, therefore, that Mr. Cable, who has become justly famous for his art in narrating imaginary events, should come forward as the popular historian of New Orleans.

This is virtually the character that he assumes in *The Creoles of Louisiana*. Having presented us, in *Old Creole Days*, with a bouquet of flowers of romance, he now proceeds, as it were, to explain the nature of the soil from which they sprang. The whole course of the growth of New Orleans, from its founding by Bienville, and from the early days of Ulloa, Aubry and O'Reilly, is carefully retraced in these pages. The Indian wars, the cession to Spain, the re-acquisition by Napoleon, the purchase by the United States, and the later local vicissitudes, are all related in a style of great refinement and lucidity, but with a reserve that reminds one at times of Parkman. Among the most picturesque episodes is that of the pirates of Barataria, with their chief, Jean Lafitte, who appears also in *Madame Delphine*. Nor are commercial statistics neglected: indeed, the uncommercial reader may sometimes be a little wearied by their frequency. On the other hand, Mr. Cable might, perhaps, have made more of his chapters dealing with the yellow-fever epidemics, which opened to him an opportunity for dramatic incident and pathos, the effect of which would have been stirring and ennobling. The period of the war and the progress of the colored race are judiciously passed over. One can see that, in places, Mr. Cable has written under some constraint; and his task is a delicate one in discussing the Creoles themselves, since his fictions have already excited their ire. The impartial reader will conclude that they have no ground of complaint against the present work, since,

[*]Reprinted from *Book Buyer*, 1 (December, 1884), 277–79.

although it does not hide their shortcomings, it accords them praise in full measure for their large share in the extraordinary task of building a great city in a swamp. "New Orleans," says Mr. Cable, "grew to its present importance, like the Delta sands, by the compulsory tribute of the Mississippi"; but he shows how the peculiar and little understood Creole population has aided in utilizing that tribute; what persistence, love of liberty, heroism it has shown, despite its proverbial indolence; and how it is still useful and progressive today. Incidentally, the historic mistake of supposing that Jackson fought the battle of New Orleans behind cotton-bale breastworks is corrected, and the fallacy of General Butler's claim that he reformed the sanitation of the city is exposed. Mr. Cable permits himself some slips in grammar which ought to be reproved, and he shows many felicities of expression which ought to be praised; but there is no space here to do either of these things. The illustrations by Pennell are charming. A cover with an original if *outré* design, having, in some cases, on the inside an appropriate "alligator" paper, lends outward attractiveness to what is, within, a valuable and interesting book.

The New Orleans of George Cable

W. S. Kennedy°

A recent perusal of Mr. Cable's romances has left something like a delicious perfume floating in my memory, and I came to *La Nouvelle Orléans* chiefly for the purpose of seeing something of Creole life. It is a curious truth that the immediate neighbors of a man who has achieved fame nearly always exhibit a petty spite or envy towards him. In Concord the farmers hoot at the idea of Thoreau possessing any greatness; and in New Orleans George Cable is pronounced to be a humbug, in respect of the truthfulness of his pictures of Creole life. Careful sifting of the evidence leads me to the conclusion that the charges against Cable have some slight color of right, but, in the main are unjustified. It was pretty hard for a people of pride and very slender purses—as most of the New Orleans people are—to see a man who had been getting $50 a week as clerk in a cotton establishment suddenly attain fame and wealth at a bound (Cable and Mark Twain are said here to be making $3,000 a week each by their readings). The historian of Louisiana, Judge Gayarré, is especially bitter against Cable. I was told by intimate friends of the Judge—one of whom is my host, a member of the Governor's staff—that he (Gayarré) asked Cable one day if he had ever been intimate in a Creole family. Cable replied he had not. "I thought not," said Gayarré, "for you describe things that have no existence." Dr. Melville Saunders, who for a quarter of a century has been educating the youth of the city, told me that the linguist, Alexander Dimitry, also pronounced Cable's pictures of Creole life to be fancy sketches. These are grave charges, and to them you may add one made in the Boston *Herald* some months ago by a Creole gentleman of Boston.

I wandered for several days through the French quarter, talking with the French-speaking people, and listening to them; but scarcely a hint of a resemblance could I find to the quaint French-English of Mr. Cable's Narcisses and Jules St. Anges. Feeling puzzled, I applied for information, and received the replies above detailed. The architecture, the environment of the novels is all there, and even quainter than I had imagined. But the language and the manners of the people are not those of the novels. The simple fact, as I apprehend it, is that Mr. Cable has not only idealized his material, as every creative artist

°Reprinted from *Literary World*, 16 (January 24, 1885), 29–31.

does, but has allowed his imagination to play a little too freely, so that his idealizations often fail to keep touch with the reality at all. The novelist of Creole life has seized a bit of life here and a bit of *genre* there, an idiom from this person, a lisp from that, a broken word from another, and throwing them all together has made a mosaic picture the colors of which have a glow and luster which the sober actuality of the natural facts do not present. It is something after the style of Dickens, not that of Hawthorne.

Still, as I have intimated, the essential facts of the representations are true and sharply accentuated. I have heard from different Creoles bits of speech which were familiar from my having already met with them in *The Grandissimes*, or *Old Creole Days*. You soon discover that the class feeling, the ancient national antipathy of French and Saxon, makes of Canal Street—separating the French from the American quarter—a line of demarcation as distinct as that which divides the waters of the Mississippi from those of the Gulf. The Creoles are proud and poor; they hold themselves aloof—have their own paper—*L'Abeille de la Nouvelle Orléans*—and will read no other; and have formed a society for the preservation of the French language. They hate English, rarely speaking it with willingness, or without a shrug of the shoulders. They say that there are Creoles who have lived all their lives in the city, and yet have never crossed Canal Street to the American side. And this is a credible thing. While conversely, great ignorance of the French quarter prevails among the Americans. In view of these facts it is easy to see how a dispute could arise about the *vraisemblance* of Cable's delineations.

The Creoles go about in a quiet, stealthy way, with that dangerous Latin glitter in their black eyes. Nearly all the women are extremely plain. I saw only one that might have served as the model for a 'Tite Poulette or Madame Délicieuse; her complexion was purest white, the nose thin and aquiline, and the large dreamy black eyes emitted light in flashes and gleams from under long sweeping eyelashes that almost touched her cheek when her glance was downward.

The old French houses are dilapidated and even squalid—some of them; but quaint beyond description, especially the one-story cottages. Every house in the city has roomy balconies. People live in the open air; in the French quarter I saw a shoemaker plying his trade on the sidewalk. Too poor to rent a shop, he had manfully untied his bundle and gone to work where he could; he stitched as for life; beside him a half-eaten loaf was carelessly tossed amidst his tools. At Lake Pontchartrain the tables of the hotels are set in the open air. The yards are full of greenery—roses in bloom, orange-trees laden, delicate perfumes in the air.

But I was speaking of the French balconies; they give *Rue Royal* and the abutting streets a really Oriental appearance. Through old round-arched entrances, you look into where the sunlight falls into green old courts—always this inner court. Here on St. Peter's Street you see a notice, "Chambres Garnies à Louer." You knock; the "gate," as it is called, opens; you are in a covered hall-alley, at the farther end of which a great staircase winds up; along one side of the stone floor runs a little gutter connecting with that outside. If you enter the rooms, you find them of immense size, for coolness sake; and generally scantily furnished with antique furniture. The cottages are the most picturesque. All are plastered on the outside, salmon-colored generally; tall, narrow, pedimented windows opening in the middle vertically and inward; the curved roof, sometimes tiled, sweeping far out over the sidewalk; long iron lamp-rod thrust out like a flag-pole horizontally into the narrow street; sometimes the iron fretwork of the balconies continued upward in a screen of vines; great gateways surmounted by lions—everywhere quaintness, dark interiors and dilapidation, proud, mournful memories, and—filth. I am sorry to say that the old Café des Réfugiés, corner St. Anne and Royal, is no more. A hideous American brick building is being erected on its site. Kristian Koppig's College on Dumaine Street still confronts the window of 'Tite Poulette, and, with its extremely curious honeycomb roof-balustrade—a wall of horizontally placed hollow tiles—is only less interesting than the tile-roofed house around the corner on Royal Street, the side of which is completely covered with vines through which peeps a wooden latticed window. The latter building is for sale, and as I was inspecting it, a fat, dirty, pimpled old French monster, with the egg of his breakfast on his greasy old coat, waddled out of some den over the way, and asked if I wished to see it. He asked by gesture only, for all his English consisted of grunts.

The ancient turbaned negress seems the most thoroughly at home of anybody in the French quarter. Anywhere in the city you cannot take ten steps without meeting a negro in rags and tatters. They strangely accentuate and antithesize the life. Persons of negro blood in New Orleans have only half the air of an alien and servile class. Miscegenation has broken down barriers of caste. When you see refined gentlemen and exquisite ladies, with the unmistakable marks in their faces of belonging to the ornamental class, and yet showing negro blood in their cheeks, you realize the weakening of the caste prejudice.

To one from Massachusetts it seems curious to hear negroes talking French. "You can't get a seat in here," says the conductor of the one-mule street car to an old candy-selling negress. "*Ne pas?*" she says, in a shrill voice. At the French market there is a perfect babel, an inconceivable uproar, of outlandish patois cries. One barefooted ferocious looking black had a voice that rose above all others, and he seemed fairly convulsed with excitement and fury as he descanted upon the virtues of his *souflé*, as he called his *chou-fleurs*, or cauliflower. At another stall a bare-headed old Italian veteran (all Italian fruit-sellers are nicknamed "dagoes") sung weirdly the song of his oranges, and, squatted on their haunches, a half dozen sorrowful faced Indian women presided over the sale of bags of green powdered sage and piles of fragrant wild roots. This was the Sunday morning before Christmas, and with its booths of toys, etc., the market resembled a fair more than an ordinary market. All the markets in the city do a larger business on Sunday than any other day. In the French quarter the shops are all closed; but on the American side of the city I saw shoe and clothing stores, groceries, fruit stores, shooting galleries, and cobblers' shops all open for business. One of the advertised amusements of Sunday is cock fighting.

As everybody knows, the lottery business is sanctioned by the State. After each drawing, the lucky numbers are posted up in the shop windows and elsewhere, and are eagerly scanned by those holding tickets. Your chance of getting a prize is about one in twenty.

I ought to notice two curious customs of the French quarter. When the courts are in session in the Cabild' (Cabildo), two long wavy battered pieces of sheet iron, attached each to an inch square iron bar, are sunken, as to their bars, in sockets at each end of the rough-paved street in front, and have written upon them the faded inscription "HALT!! COURTS IN SESSION."

The other custom is that of posting up funeral notices in the streets. At the head of the circular is generally a funebral cut, and below you read something like this:

"Vous êtes prié d'assister au convoi et à l'enterrement de feu so and so, natif de——décédé——. . . . Le corps est exposé rue——"

There is a homely beauty in this custom, as of exiles clinging closely together in the midst of an alien people.

Mr. Cable's house is a fit home for a poetical romancer. A story and a half cottage in drab and maroon, situated about fifty feet back from the street; the first floor reached by a broad flight of wooden steps leading up to a vine-embowered veranda extending across the whole front of the house; the rez-de-chaussée, as is the custom here in old houses, being open to the air in the rear, and enclosed by lattice in front, and used for storage purposes and as an adjunct of the kitchen; this plan also elevates the living-floors above the damp ground. The front steps are flanked by two beautiful orange-trees, which the present tenant, Joaquin Miller, tells me bear the sweetest oranges in the world. Two more just like them stand by the gate. In the rear of the house you catch a glimpse of a banana plant. With the exception of the wilted banana leaves, the whole yard is now one intense green, as are all those of the neighborhood, which is the most beautiful in the city, and occupied by the homes of the wealthiest citizens. Mr. Cable's mother and sisters live just opposite his own residence. The mother is an Indiana woman of strict Presbyterian principles. Her husband was a Southern gentleman.

P. S. Since the above was written I have caught a glimpse of the subject from an entirely new angle. A respectable gentleman of the city, Mr. J. H. P., who has been here since 1828, tells me that Cable's dialect is marvelously correct. Mr. P.'s father kept a school to which the French were accustomed to send their children, so that the son spoke "Gumbo French," as they call the broken English of Cable's books, from the time when he could talk at all. But the "Gumbo French" ceased to be commonly spoken as far back as forty years ago, he says. (My hostess, who is by birth a Creole, says there are quite a number now in the French quarter who still speak it.) Mr. P. says that Cable's characters are drawn to the life—his Innerarity, for example; also the mulatto, Fusilier, brother of Honoré Grandissime. I learn also that Cable is criticized for making

Honoré and the widow Aurora speak broken English to each other, when they both spoke French. Mr. Cable's defense is that he did this so that the slaves might not understand what was said. But this defense will not do for that broken English talk which Aurora and her daughter have when alone in bed. But these are hypercritical fault-findings, it seems to me. The real animus against Cable, I find, is that he has put the Creoles in a ridiculous light, and has drawn, they say, but one really noble Creole character, i.e., Honoré Grandissime. My Creole hostess thinks he cannot have seen the best Creole society. But this does not follow. He had a perfect right to arrange his characters as he chose. I call Madame Délicieuse a noble character, and surely there is nobility of character in Jean-ah Poquelin, 'Tite Poulette, and even poor old Agricola Fusilier. But one can never please everybody.

As to the patois songs rendered by Mr. Cable, Mr. P. says they are still sung in the French quarter. Mr. P. sang some of them for me and also gave one or two quaint street cries; the chimney sweep sings "Zamoner, Zamoner, Zamoner d'haut en bas!" And the old callas woman cries "Callas, callas, callas tous chauds!" (callas being little rice cakes fried brown in oil.) The changes rung upon the word *zamoner*, to sweep (*ramoner* is the correct word) and the weird intonations and inflections given it by the sweep are said to be very striking. By the way, the poet of the Sierras told me that Longfellow's Acadians, who live out in the Têche country, have become a puny weak-kneed race; so that for one negro to call another a "black Acadian" (pronounced A-ká-jăn) is considered to be a serious insult. I also learn from Mrs. Cable, the mother of the novelist, that the amusing character "Narcisse" of *Dr. Sevier* is drawn from the life in every essential particular except the borrowing propensity; the original having been a Creole in her son's office. Mrs. Cable further remarked that after the publication of *The Grandissimes* Mr. Cable was invited by a Creole lady of position—Madame O., living in the French quarter—to a wedding, and she assured him that she was delighted with the fidelity of his delineations of Creole life.

Freedom of Discussion

[Editor of *Century Magazine*]°

Thoughtful and unpartisan observers of the Southern situation have long been watching with interest the signs which show that the South is emerging from provincialism into a genuine spirit of nationality and of intellectual freedom. The great test of this advance is the growing liberty of opinion, as manifested in the press and on the platform, and in other quarters as well. Without this liberty of opinion there can be, of course, no genuine solution of any social or political question whatever—in the South or anywhere else.

No essay on the subject of the freedmen published for many years has attracted wider attention than Mr. Cable's "The Freedman's Case in Equity," in the January *Century*. The reception of this essay in the Southern States (though not unaccompanied by some amusing reminders of the good old-fashioned bowie-knife and fire-eating days) would seem to be a new proof that the Southern people admit of the honest and free discussion of burning questions in a manner which has not always been characteristic of that section. Not only does the South admit the distasteful opinions of thinkers from other sections, but, what is still more noticeable, it is increasingly tolerant of differences of opinion among its own writers. When one considers the intolerance recently manifested in the North and West in the matter of political independence, and the spirit of "boycotting" shown toward certain Northern leaders and periodicals, and when one sees this new attitude of Southern newspapers and leaders, one has food for reflection. Evidently a great many changes have taken place in this country during the past twenty years.

A number of more or less dissenting essays and "Open Letters" have come to us from the South since the publication of Mr. Cable's last article, but we have thought best to confine the reply, at present, to a single representative essay of some length, which is now in preparation, and which will appear in an early number of the *Century*.

Ed. Note: Henry Woodfin Grady (1850–89), editor of the *Atlanta Constitution* (1879–89), was chosen to write the essay in reply to Cable.

°Reprinted from *Century Magazine*, 29 (March, 1885), 789–90.

In Plain Black and White:
A Reply to Mr. Cable

Henry W. Grady[*]

It is strange that during the discussion of the negro question, which has been wide and pertinent, no one has stood up to speak the mind of the South. In this discussion there has been much of truth and more of error—something of perverseness, but more of misapprehension—not a little of injustice, but perhaps less of mean intention.

Amid it all, the South has been silent.

There has been, perhaps, good reason for this silence. The problem under debate is a tremendous one. Its right solution means peace, prosperity, and happiness to the South. A mistake, even in the temper in which it is approached or the theory upon which its solution is attempted, would mean detriment, that at best would be serious, and might easily be worse. Hence the South has pondered over this problem, earnestly seeking with all her might the honest and the safe way out of its entanglements, and saying little because there was but little to which she felt safe in committing herself. Indeed, there was another reason why she did not feel called upon to obtrude her opinions. The people of the North, proceeding by the right of victorious arms, had themselves undertaken to settle the negro question. From the Emancipation Proclamation to the Civil Rights Bill they hurried with little let or hindrance, holding the negro in the meanwhile under a sort of tutelage, from part in which his former masters were practically excluded. Under this state of things the South had little to do but watch and learn.

We have now passed fifteen years of experiment. Certain broad principles have been established as wise and just. The South has something to say which she can say with confidence. There is no longer impropriety in her speaking or lack of weight in her words. The people of the United States have, by their suffrages, remitted to the Southern people, temporarily at least, control of the race question. The decision of the Supreme Court on the Civil Rights Bill leaves practically to their adjustment important issues that were, until that decision was rendered, covered by straight and severe enactment. These things deepen the responsibility of the South, increase its concern, and confront it with a problem to which it must address itself promptly and frankly. Where it has

---

[*]Reprinted from *Century Magazine*, 29 (April, 1885), 909–17.

75

been silent, it now should speak. The interest of every American in the honorable and equitable settlement of this question is second only to the interest of those specially—and fortunately, we believe—charged with its adjustment. "What will you do with it?" is a question any man may now ask the South, and to which the South should make frank and full reply.

It is important that this reply shall be plain and straightforward. Above all things it must carry the genuine convictions of the people it represents. On this subject and at this time the South cannot afford to be misunderstood. Upon the clear and general apprehension of her position and of her motives and purpose everything depends. She cannot let pass unchallenged a single utterance that, spoken in her name, misstates her case or her intention. It is to protest against just such injustice that this article is written.

In a lately printed article, Mr. George W. Cable, writing in the name of the Southern people, confesses judgment on points that they still defend, and commits them to a line of thought from which they must forever dissent. In this article, as in his works, the singular tenderness and beauty of which have justly made him famous, Mr. Cable is sentimental rather than practical. But the reader, enchained by the picturesque style and misled by the engaging candor with which the author admits the shortcomings of "We of the South," and the kindling enthusiasm with which he tells how "We of the South" must make reparation, is apt to assume that it is really the soul of the South that breathes through Mr. Cable's repentant sentences. It is not my purpose to discuss Mr. Cable's relations to the people for whom he claims to speak. Born in the South, of Northern parents, he appears to have had little sympathy with his Southern environment, as in 1882 he wrote, "To be in New England would be enough for me. I was there once,—a year ago,—and it seemed as if I had never been home till then." It will be suggested that a man so out of harmony with his neighbors as to say, even after he had fought side by side with them on the battle-field, that he never felt at home until he had left them, cannot speak understandingly of their views on so vital a subject as that under discussion. But it is with his statement rather than his personality that we have to deal. Does he truly represent the South? We reply that he does not! There may be here and there in the South a dreaming theorist who subscribes to Mr. Cable's teachings. We have seen no signs of one. Among the thoughtful men of the South,—the men who felt that all brave men might quit fighting when General Lee surrendered,—who, enshrining in their hearts the heroic memories of the cause they had lost, in good faith accepted the arbitrament of the sword to which they had appealed,—who bestirred themselves cheerfully amid the ruins of their homes, and set about the work of rehabilitation,—who have patched and mended and builded anew, and fashioned out of pitiful resource a larger prosperity than they ever knew before,—who have set their homes on the old red hills, and staked their honor and prosperity and the peace and well-being of the children who shall come after them on the clear and equitable solution of every social, industrial, or political problem that concerns the South,—among these men, who control and will continue to control, I do know, there is general protest against Mr. Cable's statement of the case, and universal protest against his suggestions for the future. The mind of these men I shall attempt to speak, maintaining my right to speak for them with the pledge that, having exceptional means for knowing their views on this subject, and having spared no pains to keep fully informed thereof, I shall write down nothing in their name on which I have found even a fractional difference of opinion.

A careful reading of Mr. Cable's article discloses the following argument: The Southern people have deliberately and persistently evaded the laws forced on them for the protection of the freedman; this evasion has been the result of prejudices born of and surviving the institution of slavery, the only way to remove which is to break down every distinction between the races; and now the best thought of the South, alarmed at the withdrawal of the political machinery that forced the passage of the protective laws, which withdrawal tempts further and more intolerable evasions, is moving to forbid all further assortment of the races and insist on their intermingling in all places and in all relations. The first part of this argument is a matter of record, and, from the Southern stand-point, mainly a matter of reputation. It can bide its time. The suggestion held in its conclusion is so impossible, so mischievous, and, in certain aspects, so monstrous, that it must be met at once.

It is hard to think about the negro with exactness. His helplessness, his generations of enslavement, his unique position among the peoples of the earth, his distinctive color, his simple, lovable traits,—all these combine to hasten opinion into conviction where he is the subject of discussion. Three times has this tendency brought about epochal results in his history. First, it abolished slavery. For this all men are thankful, even those who, because of the personal injustice and violence of the means by which it was brought about, opposed its accomplishment. Second, it made him a voter. This, done more in a sense of reparation than in judgment, is as final as the other. The North demanded it; the South expected it; all acquiesced in it, and, wise or unwise, it will stand. Third, it fixed by enactment his social and civil rights. And here for the first time the revolution faltered. Up to this point the way had been plain, the light clear, and the march at quick-step. Here the line halted. The way was lost; there was hesitation, division, and uncertainty. Knowing not which way to turn, and enveloped in doubt, the revolutionists heard the retreat sounded by the Supreme Court with small reluctance, and, to use Mr. Cable's words, "bewildered by complication, vexed by many a blunder," retired from the field. See, then, the progress of this work. The first step, right by universal agreement, would stand if the law that made it were withdrawn. The second step, though irrevocable, raises doubts as to its wisdom. The third, wrong in purpose, has failed in execution. It stands denounced as null by the highest court, as inoperative by general confession, and as unwise by popular verdict. Let us take advantage of this halt in the too rapid revolution, and see exactly where we stand and what is best for us to do. The situation is critical. The next moment may formulate the work of the next twenty years. The tremendous forces of the revolution, unspent and still terrible, are but held in arrest. Launch them mistakenly, chaos may come. Wrong-headedness may be as fatal now as wrong-heartedness. Clear views, clear statement, and clear understanding are the demands of the hour. Given these, the common sense and courage of the American people will make the rest easy.

Let it be understood in the beginning, then, that the South will never adopt Mr. Cable's suggestion of the social intermingling of the races. It can never be driven into accepting it. So far from there being a growing sentiment in the South in favor of the indiscriminate mixing of the races, the intelligence of both races is moving farther from that proposition day by day. It is more impossible (if I may shade a superlative) now than it was ten years ago; it will be less possible ten years hence. Neither race wants it. The interest, as the inclination, of both races is against it. Here the issue with Mr. Cable is made up. He denounces any assortment of the races as unjust and demands that white and black shall intermingle everywhere. The South replies that the assortment of the races is wise and proper, and stands on the platform of equal accommodation for each race, but separate.

The difference is an essential one. Deplore or defend it as we may, an antagonism is bred between the races when they are forced into mixed assemblages. This sinks out of sight, if not out of existence, when each race moves in its own sphere. Mr. Cable admits this feeling, but doubts that it is instinctive. In my opinion it is instinctive—deeper than prejudice or pride, and bred in the bone and blood. It would make itself felt even in sections where popular prejudice runs counter to its manifestation. If in any town in Wisconsin or Vermont there was equal population of whites and blacks, and schools, churches, hotels, and theaters were in common, this instinct would assuredly develop; the races would separate, and each race would hasten the separation. Let me give an example that touches this supposition closely. Bishop Gilbert Haven, of the Methodist Episcopal Church, many years ago came to the South earnestly, and honestly, we may believe, devoted to breaking up the assortment of the races. He was backed by powerful influences in the North. He was welcomed by resident Northerners in the South (then in control of Southern affairs) as an able and eloquent exponent of their views. His first experiment toward mixing the races was made in the church—surely the most propitious field. Here the fraternal influence of religion emphasized his appeals for the brotherhood of the races. What was the result? After the first month his church was decimated. The Northern whites and the Southern blacks left it in squads. The dividing influences were mutual. The stout bishop contended with prayer and argument and threat against the inevitable, but finally succumbed. Two separate churches were established, and each race worshiped to itself. There had been no collision, no harsh words, no discussion even. Each race simply obeyed its instinct, that spoke above the appeal of the bishop and dominated the divine influences that pulsed from pew to pew. Time and again did the bishop force the experiment. Time and again he failed. At last he was driven to the confession that but one thing could effect what he had tried so hard to bring about, and that was miscegenation. A few years of experiment would force Mr. Cable to the same conclusion.

The same experiment was tried on a larger scale by the Methodist Episcopal Church (North) when it established its churches in the South after the war. It essayed to bring the races together, and in its conferences and its churches there was no color line. Prejudice certainly did not operate to make a division here. On the contrary, the whites and blacks of this church were knit together by prejudice, pride, sentiment, political and even social policy. Underneath all this was a race instinct, obeying which, silently, they drifted swiftly apart. While white Methodists of the church North and of the church South, distant from each other in all but the kinship of race and worship, were struggling to effect once more a union of the churches that had been torn apart by a quarrel over slavery, so that in every white conference and every white church on all this continent white Methodists could stand in restored brotherhood, the Methodist Church (North) agreed, without serious protest, to a separation of its Southern branch into two conferences of whites and of blacks, and into separate congregations where the proportion of either race was considerable. Was it without reason—it certainly was not through prejudice—that this church, while seeking anew fusion with its late enemies, consented to separate from its new friends?

It was the race instinct that spoke there. It spoke not with prejudice, but against it. It spoke there as it speaks always and everywhere—as it has spoken for two thousand years. And it spoke to the reason of each race. Millaud, in voting in the French Convention for the beheading of Louis XVI., said: "If death did not exist, it would be necessary to-day to invent it." So of this instinct. It is the pledge of the integrity of each race, and of peace between the races. Without it, there might be a breaking down of all lines of division and a thorough intermingling of whites and blacks. This once accomplished, the lower and the weaker elements of the races would begin to fuse and the process of amalgamation would have begun. This would mean the disorganization of society. An internecine war would be precipitated. The whites, at any cost and at any hazard, would maintain the clear integrity and dominance of the Anglo-Saxon blood. They understand perfectly that the debasement of their own race would not profit the humble and sincere race with which their lot is cast, and that the hybrid would not gain what either race lost. Even if the vigor and the volume of the Anglo-Saxon blood would enable it to absorb the African current, and after many generations recover its own strength and purity, not all the powers of earth could control the unspeakable horrors that would wait upon the slow process of clarification. Easier far it would be to take the population of central New York, intermingle with an equal percentage of Indians, and force amalgamation between the two. Let us review the argument. If Mr. Cable is correct in assuming that there is no instinct that keeps the two races separate in the South, then there is no reason for doubting that if intermingled they would fuse. Mere prejudice would not long survive perfect equality and social intermingling; and the prejudice once gone, intermarrying would begin. Then, if there is a race instinct in either race that resents intimate association with the other, it would be unwise to force such association when there are easy and just alternatives. If there is no such instinct, the mixing of the races would mean amalgamation, to which the whites will never submit, and to which neither race should submit. So that in either case, whether the race feeling is instinct or prejudice, we come to but one conclusion: The white and black races in the South must walk apart. Concurrent their courses may go—ought to go—will go—but separate. If instinct did not make this plain in a flash, reason would spell it out letter by letter.

Now, let us see. We hold that there is an instinct, ineradicable and positive, that will keep the races apart, that would keep the races apart if the problem were transferred to Illinois or to Maine, and that will resist every effort of appeal, argument, or force to bring them together. We add in perfect frankness, however, that if no such instinct existed, or if the South had reasonable doubt of its existence, it would, by every means in its power, so strengthen the race prejudice that it would do the work and hold the stubbornness and strength of instinct. The question that confronts us at this point is: Admitted this instinct, that gathers each race to itself. Then, do you believe it possible to carry forward on the same soil and under the same laws two races equally free, practically equal in numbers, and yet entirely distinct and separate? This is a momentous question. It involves a problem that, all things considered, is without a precedent or parallel. Can the South carry this problem in honor and in peace to an equitable solution? We reply that for ten years the South has been doing this very thing, and with at least apparent success. No impartial and observant man can say that in the present aspect of things there is cause for alarm, or even for doubt. In the experience of the past few years there is assuredly reason for encouragement. There may be those who discern danger in the distant future. We do not. Beyond the apprehensions which must for a long time attend a matter so serious, we see nothing but cause for congratulation. In the common sense and the sincerity of the negro, no less than in the intelligence and earnestness of the whites, we find the problem simplifying. So far from the future bringing trouble, we feel confident that another decade or so, confirming the experience of the past ten years, will furnish the solution to be accepted of all men.

Let us examine briefly what the South has been doing, and study the attitude of the races towards each other. Let us do this, not so much to vindicate the past as to clear the way for the future. Let us see what the situation teaches. There must be in the experience of fifteen years something definite and suggestive. We begin with the schools and school management, as the basis of the rest.

Every Southern State has a common-school system, and in every State separate schools are provided for the races. Almost every city of more than five thousand inhabitants has a public-school system, and in every city the schools for whites and blacks are separate. There is no exception to this rule that I can find. In many cases the law creating this system requires that separate schools shall be provided for the races. This plan works admirably. There is no friction in the administration of the schools, and no suspicion as to the ultimate tendency of the system. The road to school is clear, and both races walk therein with confidence. The whites, assured that the school will not be made the hot-bed of false and pernicious ideas, or the scene of unwise associations, support the system cordially, and insist on perfect equality in grade and efficiency. The blacks, asking no more than this, fill the schools with alert and eager children. So far from feeling debased by the separate-school system, they insist that the separation shall be carried further, and the few white teachers yet presiding over negro schools supplanted by negro teachers. The appropriations for public schools are increased year after year, and free education grows constantly in strength and popularity. Cities that were afraid to commit themselves to free schools while mixed schools were a possibility commenced building school-houses as soon as separate schools were assured. In 1870 the late Benjamin H. Hill found his matchless eloquence unable to carry the suggestion of negro education into popular tolerance. Ten years later nearly one million black children attended free schools, supported by general taxation. Though the whites pay nineteen-twentieths of the tax, they insist that the blacks shall share its advantages equally. The schools for each race are opened on that same day and closed on the same day. Neither is run a single day at the expense of the other. The negroes are satisfied with the situation. I am aware that some of the Northern teachers of negro high-schools and universities will controvert this. Touching their opinion, I have only to say that it can hardly be considered fair or conservative. Under the forcing influence of social ostracism, they have reasoned impatiently and have been helped to conclusions by quick sympathies or resentments. Driven back upon themselves and hedged in by suspicion or hostility, their service has become a sort of martyrdom, which has swiftly stimulated opinion into conviction and conviction into fanaticism. I read in a late issue of *Zion's Herald* a letter from one of these teachers, who declined, on the conductor's request, to leave the car in which she was riding, and which was set apart exclusively for negroes. The conductor, therefore, presumed she was a quadroon, and stated his presumption in answer to inquiry of a young negro man who was with her. She says of this:

> "Truly, a glad thrill went through my heart—a thrill of pride. This great auto-crat had pronounced me as not only in sympathy, but also one in blood, with the truest, tenderest, and noblest race that dwells on earth."

If this quotation, which is now before me over the writer's name, suggests that she and those of her colleagues who agree with her have narrowed within their narrowing environment, and acquired artificial enthusiasm under their unnatural conditions, so that they must be unsafe as advisers and unfair as witnesses, the sole purpose for which it is introduced will have been served. This suggestion does not reach all Northern teachers of negro schools. Some have taken broader counsels, awakened wider sympathies, and, as a natural result, hold more moderate views. The influence of the extremer faction is steadily diminishing. Set apart, as small and curious communities are set here and there in populous States, stubborn and stiff for a while, but overwhelmed at last and lost in the mingling currents, these dissenting spots will be ere long blotted out and forgotten. The educational problem, which is their special care, has already been settled, and the settlement accepted with a heartiness that precludes the possibility of its disturbance. From the stand-point of either race the experiment of distinct but equal schools for the white and black children of the South .aas demonstrated its wisdom, its policy, and its justice, if any experiment ever made plain its wisdom in the hands of finite man.

I quote on this subject Gustavus J. Orr, one of the wisest and best of men, and lately elected, by spontaneous movement, president of the National Educational Association. He says: "The race question in the schools is already settled. We give the negroes equal advantages, but separate schools. This plan meets the reason and satisfies the instinct of both races. Under it we have spent over five million dollars in Georgia, and the system grows in strength constantly." I asked if the negroes wanted mixed schools. His reply was prompt: "They do not. I have questioned them carefully on this point, and they make but one reply: They want their children in their own schools and under their own teachers." I asked what would be the effect of mixed schools. "I could not maintain the Georgia system one year. Both races would protest against it. My record as a public-school man is known. I have devoted my life to the work of education. But I am so sure of the evils that would come from mixed schools that, even if they were possible, I would see the whole educational system swept away before I would see them established. There is an instinct that gathers each race about itself. It is as strong in the blacks as in the whites, though it has not asserted itself so strongly. It is making itself manifest, since the blacks are organizing a social system of their own. It has long controlled them in their churches, and it is now doing so in their schools."

In churches, as in schools, the separation is perfect. The negroes, in all denominations in which their membership is an appreciable percentage of the whole, have their own churches, congregations, pastors, conferences, and bishops, their own missionaries. There is not the slightest antagonism between them and the white churches of the same denomination. On the contrary, there is sympathetic interest and the utmost friendliness. The separation is recognized as not only instinctive but wise. There is no disposition to disturb it, and least of all on the part of the negro. The church is with him the center of social life, and there he wants to find his own people and no others. Let me quote just here a few sentences from a speech delivered by a genuine black negro at the General Conference of the Methodist Episcopal Church (South), in Atlanta, Georgia, in 1880. He is himself a pastor of the African Methodist Church, and came as a fraternal delegate. This extract from a speech largely extempore is a fair specimen of negro eloquence, as it is a fair evidence of the feeling of that people toward their white neighbors.

In their social insitutions, as in their churches and schools, the negroes have obeyed their instinct and kept apart from the whites. They have their own social and benevolent societies, their own military companies, their own orders of Masons and Odd-fellows. They rally about these organizations with the greatest enthusiasm and support them with the greatest liberality. If it were proposed to merge them with white organizations of the same character, with equal rights guaranteed in all, the negroes would interpose the stoutest objection. Their tastes, associations, and inclinations—their instincts—lead them to gather their race about social centers of its own. I am tempted into trying to explain here what I have never yet seen a stranger to the South able to understand. The feeling that, by mutual actions separates whites and blacks when they are thrown together in social intercourse is not a repellent influence in the harsh sense of that word. It is centripetal rather than centrifugal. It is attractive about separate centers rather than expulsive from a common center. There is no antagonism, for example, between white and black military companies. On occasions they parade in the same street, and have none of the feeling that exists between Orangemen and Catholics. Of course the good sense of each race and the mutual recognition of the possible dangers of the situation have much to do with maintaining the good-will between the distinct races. The fact that in his own church or society the negro has more freedom, more chance for leadership and for individual development, than he could have in association with the whites, has more to do with it. But beyond all this is the fact that, in the segregation of the races, blacks as well as whites obey a natural instinct, which, always granting that they get equal justice and equal advantages, they obey without the slightest ill-nature or without any sense of disgrace. They meet the white people in all the avenues of business. They work side by side with the white brick-layer or carpenter in pefect accord and friendliness. When the trowel or the hammer is laid aside, the laborers part, each going his own way. Any attempt to carry the comradeship of the day into private life would be sternly resisted by both parties in interest.

We have seen that in churches, schools, and social organizations the whites and blacks are moving along separately but harmoniously, and that the "assortment of the races," which has been described as shameful and unjust, is in most part made by the instinct of each race, and commands the hearty assent of both. Let us now consider the question of public carriers. On this point the South has been sharply criticised, and not always without reason. It is manifestly wrong to make a negro pay as much for a railroad ticket as a white man pays, and then force him to accept inferior accommodations. It is equally wrong to force a decent negro into an indecent car, when there is room for him or for her elsewhere. Public sentiment in the South has long recognized this, and has persistently demanded that the railroad managers should provide cars for the negroes equal in every respect to those set apart for the whites, and that these cars should be kept clean and orderly. In Georgia a State law requires all public roads or carriers to provide equal accommodation for each race, and failure to do so is made a penal offense. In Tennessee a negro woman lately gained damages by proving that she had been forced to take inferior accommodation on a train. The railroads have, with few exceptions, come up to the requirements of the law. Where they fail, they quickly feel the weight of public opinion, and shock the sense of public justice. This very discussion, I am bound to say, will lessen such failures in the future. On four roads, in my knowledge, even better has been done than the law requires. The car set apart for the negroes is made exclusive. No whites are permitted to occupy it. A white man who strays into this car is politely told that it is reserved for the negroes. He has the information repeated two or three times, smiles, and retreats. This rule works admirably and will win general favor. There are a few roads that make no separate provision for the races, but announce that any passenger can ride on any car. Here the "assortment" of the races is done away with, and here it is that most of the outrages of which we hear occur. On these roads the negro has no place set apart for him. As a rule, he is shy about asserting himself, and he usually finds himself in the meanest corners of the train. If he forces himself into the ladies' car, he is apt to provoke a collision. It is on just one of these trains where the assortment of the passengers is left to chance that a respectable negro woman is apt to be forced to ride in a car crowded with negro convicts. Such a thing would be impossible where the issue is fairly met, and a car, clean, orderly, and exclusive, is provided for each race. The case could not be met by grading the tickets and the accommodations. Such a plan would bring together in the second or third class car just the element of both races between whom prejudice runs highest, and from whom the least of tact or restraint might be expected. On the railroads, as elsewhere, the solution of the race problem is, equal advantages for the same money,—equal in comfort, safety, and exclusiveness,—but separate.

There remains but one thing further to consider—the negro in the jury-box. It is assumed generally that the negro has no representation in the courts. This is a false assumption. In the United States courts he usually makes more than half the jury. As to the State courts, I can speak particularly as to Georgia. I assume that she does not materially differ from the other States. In Georgia the law requires that commissioners shall prepare the jury-list for each county by selection from the upright, intelligent, and experienced citizens of the county. This provision was put into the Consitution by the negro convention of reconstruction days. Under its terms no reasonable man would have expected to see the list made up of equal percentage of the races. Indeed, the fewest number of negroes were qualified under the law. Consequently, but few appeared on the lists. The number, as was to be expected, is steadily increasing. In Fulton County there are seventy-four negroes whose names are on the lists, and the commissioners, I am informed, have about doubled this number for the present year. These negroes make good jurymen, and are rarely struck by attorneys, no matter what the client or cause may be. About the worst that can be charged against the jury system in Georgia is that the commissioners have made jurors of negroes only when they had qualified themselves to intelligently discharge a juror's duties. In few quarters of the South, however, is the negro unable to get full and exact justice in the courts, whether the jury be white or black. Immediately after the war, when there was general alarm and irritation, there may have been undue severity in sentences and extreme rigor of prosecution. But the charge that the people of the South have, in their deliberate and later moments, prostituted justice to the oppression of this dependent people, is as false as it is infamous. There is abundant belief that the very helplessness of the negro in court has touched the heart and conscience of many a jury, when the facts should have held them impervious. In the city in which this is written a negro, at midnight, on an unfrequented street, murdered a popular young fellow, over whose grave a monument was placed by popular subscription. The only witnesses of the killing were the friends of the murdered boy. Had the murderer been a white man, it is believed he would have been convicted. He was acquitted by the white jury, and has since been convicted of a murderous assault on a person of his own color. Similarly, a young white man, belonging to one of the leading families of the State, was hung for the murder of a negro. Insanity was pleaded in his defense, and so plausibly that it is believed he would have escaped had his victim been a white man.

I quote on this point Mr. Benjamin H. Hill, who has been prosecuting attorney of the Atlanta, Ga., circuit for twelve years. He says: "In cities and towns the negro gets equal and exact justice before the courts. It is possible that, in remote counties, where the question is one of a fight between a white man and a negro, there may be a lingering prejudice that causes occasional injustice. The judge, however, may be relied on to correct this. As to negro jurors, I have never known a negro to allow his lawyer to accept a negro juror. For the State I have accepted a black juror fifty times, to have him rejected by the opposing lawyer by order of his negro client. This has occurred so invariably that I have accepted it as a rule. Irrespective of that, the negro gets justice in the courts, and the last remaining prejudice against him in the jury-box has passed away. I convicted a white man for voluntary manslaughter under peculiar circumstances. A negro met him on the street and cursed him. The white man ordered him off and started home. The negro followed him to his house and cursed him until he entered the door. When he came out, the negro was still waiting. He renewed the abuse, followed him to his store, and there struck him with his fist. In the struggle that followed, the negro was shot and killed. The jury promptly convicted the slayer."

So much for the relation between the races in the South, in churches, schools, social organizations, on the railroad, and in theaters. Everything is placed on the basis of equal accommodations, but separate. In the courts the blacks are admitted to the jury-box as they lift themselves into the limit of qualification. Mistakes have been made and injustice has been worked here and there. This was to have been expected, and it has been less than might have been expected. But there can be no mistake about the progress the South is making in the equitable adjustment of the relations between the races. Ten years ago nothing was settled. There were frequent collisions and constant apprehensions. The whites were suspicious and the blacks were restless. So simple a thing as a negro taking an hour's ride on the cars, or going to see a play, was fraught with possible danger. The larger affairs—school, church, and court—were held in abeyance. Now all this is changed. The era of doubt and mistrust is succeeded by the era of confidence and good-will. The races meet in the exchange of labor in perfect amity and understanding. Together they carry on the concerns of the day, knowing little or nothing of the fierce hostility that divides labor and capital in other sections. When they turn to social life they separate. Each race obeys its instinct and congregates about its own centers. At the theater they sit in opposite sections of the same gallery. On the trains they ride each in his own car. Each worships in his own church, and educates his children in his schools. Each has his place and fills it, and is satisfied. Each gets the same accommodation for the same money. There is no collision. There is no irritation or suspicion. Nowhere on earth is there kindlier feeling, closer sympathy, or less friction between two classes of society than between the whites and blacks of the South to-day. This is due to the fact that in the adjustment of their relations they have been practical and sensible. They have wisely recognized what was essential, and have not sought to change what was unchangeable. They have yielded neither to the fanatic nor the demagogue, refusing to be misled by the one or misused by the other. While the world has been clamoring over the differences they have been quietly taking counsel with each other, in the field, the shop, the street and cabin, and settling things for themselves. That the result has not astonished the world in the speediness and the facility with which it has been reached, and the beneficence that has come with it, is due to the fact that the result has not been freely proclaimed. It has been a deplorable condition of our politics that the North has been misinformed as to the true condition of things in the South. Political greed and passion conjured pestilential mists to becloud what the lifting smoke of battle left clear. It has exaggerated where there was a grain of fact, and invented where there was none. It has sought to establish the most casual occurrences as the settled habit of the section, and has sprung endless jeremiads from one single disorder, as Jenkins filled the courts of Christendom with lamentations over his dissevered ear. These misrepresentations will pass away with the occasion that provoked them, and when the truth is known it will come with the force of a revelation to vindicate those who have bespoken for the South a fair trial, and to confound those who have borne false witness against her.

One thing further need be said, in perfect frankness. The South must be allowed to settle the social relations of the races according to her own views of what is right and best. There has never been a moment when she could have submitted to have the social status of her citizens fixed by an outside power. She accepted the emancipation and the enfranchisement of her slaves as the legitimate results of war that had been fought to a conclusion. These once accomplished, nothing more was possible. "Thus far and no farther," she said to her neighbors, in no spirit of defiance, but with quiet determination. In her weakest moments, when her helpless people were hedged about by the unthinking bayonets of her conquerors, she gathered them for resistance at this point. Here she defended everything that a people should hold dear. There was little proclamation of her purpose. Barely did the whispered word that bespoke her resolution catch the listening ears of her sons; but, for all this, the victorious armies of the North, had they been rallied again from their homes, could not have enforced and maintained among this disarmed people the policy indicated in the Civil Rights bill. Had she found herself unable to defend her social integrity against the arms that were invincible on the fields where she staked the sovereignty of her States, her people would have abandoned their homes and betaken themselves into exile. Now, as then, the South is determined that, come what may, she must control the social relations of the two races whose lots are cast within her limits. It is right that she should have this control. The problem is hers, whether or not of her seeking, and her very existence depends on its proper solution. Her responsibility is greater, her knowledge of the case more thorough than that of others can be. The question touches her at every point; it presses on her from every side; it commands her constant attention. Every consideration of policy, of honor, of pride, of common sense impels her to the exactest justice and the fullest equity. She lacks the ignorance or misapprehension that might lead others into mistakes; all others lack the appalling alternative that all else failing, would force her to use her knowledge wisely. For these reasons she has reserved to herself the right to settle the still unsettled element of the race problem, and this right she can never yield.

As a matter of course, this implies the clear and unmistakable domination of the white race in the South. The assertion of that is simply the assertion of the right of character, intelligence, and property to rule. It is simply saying that the responsible and steadfast element in the community shall control, rather than the irresponsible and the migratory. It is the reassertion of the moral power that overthrew the scandalous reconstruction governments, even though, to the shame of the republic be it said, they were supported by the bayonets of the General Government. Even the race issue is lost at this point. If the blacks of the South wore white skins, and were leagued together in the same ignorance and irresponsibility under any other distinctive mark than their color, they would progress not one step farther toward the control of affairs. Or if they were transported as they are to Ohio, and there placed in numerical majority of two to one, they would find the white minority there asserting and maintaining control, with less patience, perhaps, than many a Southern State has shown. Everywhere, with such temporary exceptions as afford demonstration of the rule, intelligence, character, and property will dominate in spite of numerical differences. These qualities are lodged with the white race in the South, and will assuredly remain there for many generations at least; so that the white race will continue to dominate the colored, even if the percentages of race increase deduced from the comparison of a lame census with a perfect one, and the omission of other considerations, should hold good and the present race majority be reversed.

Let no one imagine, from what is here said, that the South is careless of the opinion or regardless of the counsel of the outside world. On the contrary, while maintaining firmly a position she believes to be essential, she appreciates heartily the value of general sympathy and confidence. With an earnestness that is little less than pathetic she bespeaks the patience and the impartial judgment of all concerned. Surely her situation should command this, rather than indifference or antagonism. In poverty and defeat,—with her cities destroyed, her fields desolated, her labor disorganized, her homes in ruins, her families scattered, and the ranks of her sons decimated,—in the face of universal prejudice, fanned by the storm of war into hostility and hatred,—under the shadow of this sorrow and this disadvantage, she turned bravely to confront a problem that would have taxed to the utmost every resource of a rich and powerful and victorious people. Every inch of her progress has been beset with sore difficulties; and if the way is now clearing, it only reveals more clearly the tremendous import of the work to which her hands are given. It must be understood that she desires to silence no criticism, evade no issue, and lessen no responsibility. She recognizes that the negro is here to stay. She knows that her honor, her dear name, and her fame, no less than her prosperity, will be measured by the fullness of the jusice she gives and guarantees to this kindly and dependent race. She knows that every mistake made and every error fallen into, no matter how innocently, endanger her peace and her reputation. In this full knowledge she accepts the issue without fear or evasion. She says, not boldly, but conscious of the honesty and the wisdom of her convictions: "Leave this problem to my working out. I will solve it in calmness and deliberation, without passion or prejudice, and with full regard for the unspeakable equities it holds. Judge me rigidly, but judge me by my works." And with the South the matter may be left—must be left. There it can be left with the fullest confidence that the honor of the republic will be maintained, the rights of humanity guarded, and the problem worked out in such exact justice as the finite mind can measure or finite agencies administer.

Mr. Cable and the Creoles

Edward E. Hale°

Hundreds of thousands of Northern people have taken the chances of the last winter to verify Mr. Cable's account of the Creoles of Louisiana. He has had the help of the Great Exhibition in making people of another race and of other training understand how "a Latin civilization, sinewy, valiant, cultured, rich and proud, holds out against extinction." The more sensible of these people carried with them as their best guide-book the elegant volume which the Scribners issued last fall, *The Creoles of Louisiana*—and all the most enthusiastic of the sensible ones peered into the garden gates of New Orleans with his charming novels in their hands, and felt quite sure that they had discovered the homes of Madame Nancanou and of Palmyre Philosophe.

There is something a little pathetic and very amusing in the faint protest which a few of the old Creoles make against Mr. Cable—as if he had dishonored a race to which, in fact, he has paid most loyal and noble tributes. But we may see the same sensitiveness anywhere. The perfect Knickerbocker of New York never saw the fun of Irving's *History of New York, from the Beginning of the World to the End of the Dutch Dynasty*. And at this moment, whoever is fortunate enough to sit at an old-fashioned Boston dinner-table, will hear it explained by his next neighbor at some length, that Mr. Howells, in his exquisite portraiture from Boston life, does not understand the limits of the Back Bay, nor know the true Bostonian when he sees him. But the world of American readers, on the whole, will remember Irving and Howells and Cable together, and will remember them very gratefully. Mr. Cable has revealed a new world to most American readers, and he has done it so truly, and with such thorough sympathy, that he might have been sure of the gratitude and applause of the Creole race. It seems as if his books, with such aid for the moment as the Exhibition has given, might at last teach the great multitude of frozen people who hibernate in New York, New England, Wisconsin, Minnesota and other countries which are warmed by the North Star, what a wonderful and beautiful and fascinating region they have close under their lee, for semi-tropical travel, and—which is so much better—semi-tropical rest. The happy end of the Rebellion made it possible for a Northern man to go into a Southern State without losing his self-respect. A vigorous effort to colonize Florida from the North helped on a certain

°Reprinted from *Critic*, 7 (September 12, 1885), 121–22.

languid flow, every spring, to St. Augustine, Jacksonville and Magnolia, of a few thousand people with delicate lungs and their sisters—with occasionally a brother or a father who could be spared so long from the grinding. But, let us confess it in the still secrecy of this reading, the resources of Florida for the adventurer who wishes four-months' relief from goloshes and splash are somewhat limited. One cannot make sketches in St. Augustine for two months in every year, and shoot alligators for two more. It is then a benefaction to America at large—certainly to all that part of America which prefers living in plenty, gladness, perfume and sunshine, to dying in labor, wretchedness, cold and thaw,—a benefaction, when Mr. Cable opens the portals of Louisiana, shows us its charms, and tempts us perhaps to follow a lead so attractive, and carry the great adventure farther, even to "San Antone," to El Paso, and to the Halls of Montezuma. Up to his time there were twenty Northerners every winter in Pau, in Mentone, in Nice, and on the rest of the Mediterranean coast, for one who escaped a wintry spring by going to our own Gulf of Mexico. In future years, as with Mr. Joseph Jefferson, we eat the sunny side of an orange and hear legends of Lafitte, or as with Mr. Robertson we compare a Fire Rose against the old Solfaterra, we shall all thank Mr. Cable who showed to us a way so excellent.

It is fair to say that all the readers of the *Critic* have read Mr. Cable's stories. The exceptions are so few and so insignificant that they need not be counted. Now they all want to know how much is historically true and how much is imaginary in this; "also especially"—as our dear transplanted German friends say so nicely,—they want to see exactly the frame in which such charming pictures are to be hung. All their questions are answered by Mr. Cable in his book on the Creoles. He was a historical student before he was a novelist, as every one knows who in the old days had the good fortune to consult him, on any matter which bore on the French occupation of the great valley of the great River. And what a marvellous story all this is which he has to tell of that occupation. The old slow-coach line of Phi Beta Kappa orators and other heavyweights used to tell us fifty years ago that there was going to be an Augustan Age of American poets and novelists who were going to write about—, about—"our magnificent prairies, our immeasurable rivers, and our pathless forests." Nay, some of us can remember a bookseller's advertisement of those days which said, day after day, "A supply of the 'Yamoyden' kept constantly on hand,"—as you might say of skullcap, or any other native sedative. But, to tell the truth, this unbounded prairie literature had in it but few of those broken lights which the carnal eye longs for. They were like the gigantic landscape representations which the artists of that pre-historic time used to bring down from the White Mountains in October. All the same, when a man of genius appears, it proves that every fascinating scene for romance, and every critical moment are ours. Take this beautiful book of Mr. Cable's, and read his sketch of the history of the first planting of Louisiana. Why, really, it was only the turn of a straw that d'Artagnan and Aramis and Porthos in their old age did not look in on the "coast," and shoot alligators, and crack pecan nuts, or feast on pompano, with their friends D'Iberville and the youngster Bienville. Who shall say that you could not still find in Paris the hostelry where those dear old heroes fought their battles over to the delight of their Canadian friends, a hundred and fifty years before Dumas spun on the threads of the old story? Why, here was an establishment maintained by those gorgeous, fatuous, indolent and elegant courts of Louis XVI. and XVII., and of the Regency between. None of them knew what they maintained them for. If they had inquired and looked up among their own papers, they would have found that there was a certain wax-tree there, and that the King expected some day or other to have some candles from it. Was there cotton or sugar? Not an ounce. Silk? Not a fibre. Wheat? Not a grain. What was there? A steady outgo of crown expenses, for a hundred years, to maintain a colony where a handful of gentlemen held the mouth of a great river. At the end of the hundred years the King gives away this costly colony to his cousin, the particular idiot who at that moment fills the throne of Spain. At the end of a hundred years more, the valley which that river waters supplies food, not to say clothing, to the people of half the world. Beginning with the days of Louis XVI. and coming down to the Civil War nearly two hundred years after, think what romance is woven in with this Creole history. Bienville's matchless leadership, the mysteries of interior adventure, the Natchez massacre. All of a sudden we are ceded to Spain; then we are at war with England; this Yankee, Oliver Pollock, begins sending powder to Pittsburgh. Meanwhile we have insurrections at home and bloody suppressions of the same. Then the English get a foothold in Florida. They are very disagreeable neighbors. Down the river come these dirty-shirt people from Tennessee and Kentucky—"half horse and half alligator." Here is Philip Nolan one day, bothering the Governor about a pass; and he shows John James Audubon a gull he shot yesterday. All of a sudden we find ourselves Americans; and here is the rascal Wilkinson, with his rascal friend Burr, crossing the Place d'Armes. A little later and here is Andrew Jackson; and yonder, alas! are Packenham and Gibbs and Keane. A short hour, and before nine o'clock in the morning, an English army is driven away from New Orleans, and two thousand brave men are dead or wounded; and this sixteen days after the two nations were at peace, had they only known it. All through this wilderness of romance survives this sturdy scion of the French race which celebrates the carnival with unheard-of display, which rejoices on the fourth of July; and ten days later, with far greater enthusiasm, commemorates that great Fourteenth that saw the fall of the Bastile.

Mr. Cable has carefully followed out the lines of this fascinating history in his book on the Creoles. Exquisite engravings, and the perfect descriptions wrought in by this pen of his, so light and so firm, make real the actors in the varied scene. If his Creole friends are not satisfied this time, both with the historian and the history, they must indeed be hard to please.

[Review of *The Silent South*]

Anonymous°

Clearly, the old provincialism which used to be the bane of "Southern literature" before the War, is fading away. Southern readers are no longer content to wrap themselves up in the contemplation of "them intellektle giants, Simms an' Maury" (to quote from Lowell's *Biglow Papers*), and declare this or that local poet or novelist one of the world's geniuses, kept from his dues by malignant cabals of Boston critics. Neither, on the other hand, are the foremost Southern authors afraid to utter anything but indiscriminate praise of the politics, society, and institutions in which they live. That "nationalism in literature" of which Mr. Cable has so admirably spoken, as opposed to sectionalism, is beginning to make the South content to have its authors measured by standards of general criticism; while those authors themselves are realizing that literature can be thoroughly indigenous and yet broad and free. Meanwhile Northern and Western readers should not forget that colonialism, in their own sections, is not quite dead yet, nor is the mutual admiration society and the indignant sensitiveness of provincialism wholly extinct.

This hopeful element in Mr. Cable's new volume—containing his well known *Century* papers on "The Silent South," "The Freedman's Case in Equity" and "The Convict Lease System," impresses the literary student quite as strongly as does the discussion of the political and social questions involved. Mr. Cable boldly, strongly and convincingly tells the South that it is on honor in its treatment of the Freedmen, now that bayonets from Washington are withdrawn; that the case will not "down," but must be settled; that civil rights are one thing, social equality quite another; that the former must ultimately be given and secured, though, of course, social communism, in the thousand details of life, will come no sooner in the South than in the North; and that the irregularity in the treatment of the negro—who has far better treatment in South Carolina than in Georgia or Tennessee—must be done away. Finally, he makes a vigorous attack on the convict lease system and the white jury system, whereby negroes are punished more severely and more constantly than whites, even when we take into account their average social standing and consequent proclivity to petty crime. Not all readers, North or South, will agree with all Mr. Cable's statements; but they certainly must admit that here is a book to be

°Reprinted from *Critic*, 6 (January 9, 1886), 14–15.

considered, and either accepted in the main or refuted in the main. Mr. Cable writes with vigor, courtesy and moderation—sometimes with eloquence. In this book, however, there is an occasional muddiness of style and lack of clearness, which make the reader reread a sentence or a paragraph. This fault is one not found in the author's other books, and which could easily have been remedied by more careful revision of the manuscript before printing.

[Review of *Strange True Stories of Louisiana*]

Anonymous°

These records of early French and Creole life have been rescued from oblivion by Mr. George W. Cable at the expense of infinite pains and research. In more than one case the documents necessary to verify the tale were discovered, one by one, in days of rummaging in the garret of one of the old court buildings. Several of the stories, noted enough in their day, had perished from the memory of men, and survived only in the dusty and half-illegible records of a law suit. One of these is the history of "Salome Muller," the child of a German "redemptioner," sold into slavery, and for many years treated and regarded as a slave; another, that of Attalie Brouillard, which, as Mr. Cable says, is a tradition based on "lawyers' talk."

Better accredited and much prettier is the story of the "Adventures of Françoise and Susanne," daughters of Pierre Bossier, planter of the parish of St. James, who, in the year 1795, took with their father a voyage up the Mississippi to the wild and hardly explored Attakapas country, where, twenty years before, the exiled Acadians had settled. They traveled in a flat-boat with a motley company. The owner of the boat, Mario Carlo, had his wife and four children with him; they were mulattoes. Of his two partners one was Irish, with an Amazonian wife who smoked a pipe and was as good a shot with a rifle as her husband; the other, Joseph Charpentier, was a French carpenter, who had saved from the guillotine, during the Reign of Terror, his foster-sister, an exquisite little French countess, by the expedient of a form of marriage. He got her safely across to England and there, according to his promise, offered her freedom; but the little creature, left alone in the world by the death of every near relative, had learned to love her low-born husband, and elected to share his fortunes in the new world. This fairy shape among the rude surroundings of the flat-boat, protected and indulged with a reverent fondness by her adoring spouse, makes a charming picture. The party have many adventures, and in the end preëmpt and occupy valuable tracts of land along the Bayou Teche, where their descendants are to be found to this day. The history of the voyage was told many years later to her grandchildren by the little Françoise, and finally written down by one of them. It is full of the spirit of youthfulness; its aged narrator evidently went back to the standpoint of her girlhood, looking at things and men with untroubled youthful gaze, and renewing in memory the sparkle and zest of that by-gone time. This fact gives its special charm to the story.

°Reprinted from *Literary World*, 20 (December 21, 1889), 473–74.

George W. Cable and
John March, Southerner

Paul van Dyke°

It is unusual nowadays for a novelist whose last book sold well to wait three years before he sends out another. But the patient work in *John March, Southerner* cannot have been tedious to Mr. Cable. The little study opening from the sitting-room is part of a home filled with life and affection, and the friend of the house soon finds that the story is looked upon and spoken of as simply and as naturally as if it were another child. Thirty yards behind the house are the woods, and the master can point you to a specimen, often struggling for life in the deepest part of some sapling thicket, of each of the sixty or seventy kinds of hardwood bush or tree that grow on his acres. It is a good rest to visit the protégés who have had a fairer chance for survival given them by his hatchet, and end up with a little stroll along the Mill River, which seems to have forgotten the score of wheels it has already turned and to be loafing along through the woods on the way to the work still to be done below. And so it happens that, when you have dropped in a few evenings to hear the single page of manuscript just written as finely and clearly as if engraved from a copper-plate, you see that here is a maker of stories who thinks his art is sacred, and to whom no time seems long because he loves his work and is happy in it.

That Mr. Cable should abandon the field of which he was the discoverer with its obvious romance, seems at first a little startling. And one who had nothing to judge by but the few hasty essays which he has printed recently, might easily have suspected in the announced change of theme a sign of loss of power. But it needs only a glance at "The Taxidermist" published last spring, or at the first chapters of *John March*, to see a technical skill greater than that of his best previous work. The courage which surrenders this advantage is that of a craftsman conscious of a certain mastery in his art.

And this boldness in taking a big subject is something our literature needs. Even the best of our story tellers have been too prone to gather social antiquities and curiosities. Cooper painted the Indian as we like to think of him. Hawthorne caught the atmosphere of pensive romance that haunts the decaying gables of New England towns. Bret Harte distilled agreeable sentiment from a character who vanishes as soon as a community is old enough to have a police force. Cable himself, like the old workers in Dresden porcelain, has made delicate and charming figures from a small society of the past. But in this book

°Reprinted from *Book Buyer*, 12 (April, 1894), 118–20.

he attempts a picture of a great historic crisis, and shows life as it is lived by millions of our fellow-countrymen.

For it is an American story—with an Americanism very sturdy because entirely unconscious of self. Our modern novelists have been much in the habit of taking the measurement of our life in terms of English society. Mr. James, loyal as he is to his own country, has pointed out some hundreds of particulars in which we have better morals and worse manners than Europeans. And even Mr. Howells, who has given us several great American novels, is, or rather *was*, prone to bring out the characteristics of his New England heroine by introducing her to some one who had lived in London. But no character of *John March* has a Cunard label on his hand-baggage. And the best of it is that no one of them has any idea that in being an American and living all his life in Dixie, he is doing anything extraordinary. Here is not a trace of what Lowell came to hate so heartily in his *fin de siècle* countrymen—"being vulgar precisely because we are afraid of being so." To every man in this story we can apply the phrase of one of his letters:

"Thank God, if he hasn't the manners of Vere de Vere, he has at least that first quality of a gentleman, that he stands squarely on his own feet and is as unconscious as a prairie."

And there is distinction also in the method of *John March*. The writer applies to the novel of reflection the objective treatment which has in the last decade given such vogue to the novel of action. Like *David Copperfield*, *John March* tells the story of a life, the growth of a soul. All its situations are *spiritual* crises, but it contains nothing but action, conversations, and description of actors or background. There are no pages of moral reflections, nor is the reader told confidentially by the author what has been happening in the inner life of the actors. We get to know the story of John March and his friends as nearly as possible in the same way in which we might get to know it if we lived in Suez, just around the corner from Weed & Usher's drug store.

Not that Mr. Cable is a *doctrinaire* who makes fetters out of rules. But rather, like the older school of etchers, he chooses to limit the means he employs. And, keeping the self-imposed law of his art in the spirit, he does not hesitate to break it in the letter. He even uses a long soliloquy when necessary, though he does not imitate the great master of romance and introduce it by a page of apology, pointing out that, though "there are no such soliloquies in nature, . . . they must be received as a conventional means of communication between the poet and the audience."[1]

But in spite of these exceptions the rigor of his self-restraint is evident by a comparison. *The Three Musketeers* is a story of action entirely without ideas. It refers to no spiritual qualities except courage and personal fidelity, to be seen in the higher animals as well as in man. The tale of four brilliant young pagans has no relation whatever to religion, patriotism, family affection or the love of woman, which form the very atmosphere of *John March*. Its time is only eighteen months, and it is twice as long as *John March*. Yet the first quarter of *John March*, already published, contains no larger number of reflections made by the author to his reader or descriptions of what is passing in a character's mind, than the same amount of this masterpiece of the novel of action. The four southern gentlemen who surround the hero's boyhood are distinctly drawn, and their portraits are the result of very careful analysis of character. But they are not accompanied by a descriptive catalogue. The saints in *John March* wear no halo of the author's approval, and the sinners are just as agreeable companions as those who walk in slippery places often continue to be for many years. We like all these men—three of them are gallant soldiers, and the fourth is a simple-hearted gentleman, a sort of southern Colonel Newcome. The dry rot of moral character gives, in the book as in life, only scattered suggestions for distrust, which we cannot estimate except in the light of the catastrophe.

Nothing is so uncertain as literary prophecy. But whether *John March* be felt by the people or not, it certainly must be recognized by all who have any ability to judge art as a skillful, consistent and courageous attempt to do something seldom attempted and very difficult.

Notes

1. [Sir Walter Scott] *Fortunes of Nigel*, vol. 2.

[Review of *John March, Southerner*]

Anonymous*

In *John March, Southerner*, Mr. George W. Cable has made the most careful and thoroughgoing study of the reconstruction period in the South which has yet been offered the world in the form of fiction. Behind this novel there is evident to any one who reads it closely a great amount of serious thinking and of close observation, for many things are wrought into it which do not appear upon a casual reading. With the instinct of the novelist, Mr. Cable has seized upon dramatic points, has brought into relief striking characters, and has shown in action the influence of different ideals, standards, faiths, and aims upon a large group of people. The plot is, in a way, complicated, and the number of persons engaged in its working out is very considerable—large enough to afford studies of a good many types. Behind these persons one feels continually the conflict of old and new ideas, the stress and turbulence of a transition period; and one sees the new world gradually rising in a very disorderly fashion, as it always does, out of the wreck of the old. It is the birth of a new society and the advent of a new period which are celebrated in this story. There is a great deal of keen observation, a great deal of strong characterization, and there are many of those delicate, artistic touches which are never absent from Mr. Cable's work, and the presence of which, with other qualities, puts him in the foremost rank of American men of letters. This story is full of ability; but one is obliged to judge a writer of Mr. Cable's standing by his own standards, and by those standards *John March, Southerner* is not so satisfactory a work of art as some of its predecessors. It is not so firmly knit together; it has not the same narrative flow; it does not command the same attention. It is full of ability, but its execution is uneven; it is full of delicate and acute characterization, but its characters are not always perfectly realized; there is a great deal of dramatic action in it, and yet as a whole the story lacks coherence of dramatic movement. It has not quite the touch which marked Mr. Cable's earlier work, and which appears with equal distinctness in several stories which he has written since this longer novel was elaborated. "The Taxidermist," for instance, one of the most recent of Mr. Cable's stories, shows him at his very best, and points the way to the fine, true, strong work which lies before him in the future.

*Reprinted from *Outlook*, 51 (March 2, 1895), 356.

[Review of *John March, Southerner*]

Anonymous*

In view of the number and variety of figures in *The Golden House*, it seems clear that Mr. Warner is possessed by the prevalent belief among novelists in the seriousness of their profession, and set himself to include in one volume a comprehensive presentation of life in New York. It takes a large imagination and great constructive skill to give unity, force, value to this comprehensive fiction, and so far no American except Mr. Howells, in many volumes, has come within sight of success. Doubtless, Mr. Cable was animated by the same ambition in the composition of *John March, Southerner*; at all events, it is soothing to find so worthy an excuse for such a maddening performance. Seventy-eight chapters are ostensibly devoted to John from childhood to maturity, but what he was or is or shall be remains an enigma. John's father, a judge, presumably an old-time Southern gentleman, talking an atrocious dialect, dies in the twenty-third chapter, bequeathing to his son an irrelevant, futile, verse-writing mother, and a great deal of unimproved land. The remaining chapters are presumably intended to develop the methods adopted by John for repressing his mother and colonizing his land, several of them being abandoned to these topics. The incidental information is various and unrelated. John has a tedious love affair, meandering through much talk to a second passion. He gets religion, and also gets rid of it at the penitent bench. He insults the British flag, but does not make an international episode. He is casually engaged in a shooting affray with a mountaineer; the mountaineer is shot, and one wishes it had been John. All the time the inhabitants of Suez, in the State of Dixie (generals, colonels, white women, negroes), keep on talking about the war and each other, apparently trying to display astonishing invention in corrupting the English language. Such fiction as this might have been an invaluable agent for reform in the old days when the novel-reading habit was regarded as pernicious. No boy would hide it under his pillow, hoping to snatch a fearful joy at dawn. No woman would, for love of it, neglect her baby and darning.

*Reprinted from *Nation*, 60 (March 14, 1895), 206.

[Review of *John March, Southerner*]

Anonymous*

John March is a novel of undoubted power, of lavish and often masterly workmanship, which engages our full sympathies a dozen times in its course, though it does not keep them unbroken all the way through. For this last fact we take our share of the blame. The fashion of the day in fiction permits the greatest psychological complexity, but is all against complexity of plot and incident, unless, as in detective stories, the complexity be of a very regular mechanical pattern. Mr. Cable's plot turning on land difficulties in the Southern States of America after the war, would doubtless be more easily followed by those to whom such difficulties have been matters of long familiarity. To us they are a distinct hindrance in the understanding of the story; we admit there is something of indolence in our objection; but we also protest that the author has done little to smooth our way. Besides this there is no other fault to be found, but it is an important matter. For we tried reading on without having done all the unravelling, and we had to turn back again; so closely are the difficulties woven in with the story. As a novel of character we know no American novel of late years to compare with it. John March the ardent young Southerner, his mother the poetess, Fannie the vivacious young beauty, the double-natured Garnet, Barbara, Jeff-Jack, the clever black rascal Cornelius—this is not to name one half of the men and women that live and move and have their actual being in these pages. We do not need to give extravagant praise and call them great creations; but there is not a personage introduced that has not been framed out of the novelist's best knowledge of human nature. Those in want of easy reading may not finish *John March*; but those who finish it will have read it with delight, and with an astonished gratitude to the man who can lavish so much thought and work on one single story.

*Reprinted from *Bookman*, 7 (May, 1895), 56.

[Review of *John March, Southerner*]

Anonymous°

It is a pleasure to see Mr. Cable's name on the title-page of a novel, even though we perceive, with a slight pang of disappointment, that the environment of the tale is no longer that which was made so entrancing in *Old Creole Days* and *The Grandissimes*. We very soon find, however, that Mr. Cable treats greater Dixie with the same genial wit and candid sympathy which he lavished upon old Louisiana. If we miss something of the optimism and hilarity which pervaded many of his earlier pages, this may simply mean that we are all grown older, or it may be due to the geographical position of Suez. "In the last year of our civil war," begins Mr. Cable, and proceeds to one of the freshest and most delightful bits of word-painting in any recent book,—"in the last year of our civil war, Suez was a basking town, with rocky streets and break-neck sidewalks; its dwellings dozing most months of the twelve among roses and honeysuckles, behind anciently whitewashed, much broken fences, and all the place wrapped in that wide sweetness of apple and acacia scents that comes from whole mobs of dog-fennel. The Pulaski City turnpike entered at the northwest corner, and passed through to the court-house green, with its hollow square of stores and law-offices; two sides of it blackened ruins of fire and war. Under the town's southeasternmost angle, between yellow banks and overhanging sycamores, the bright green waters of Turkey Creek, rambling round from the north and east, skipped down a gradual stairway of limestone ledges, and glided, alive with sunlight, into that true 'Swanee River,' not of the maps, but which flows forever 'far, far away' through the numbers of imperishable song. That river's head of navigation was, and still is, at Suez."

The fortunes of John March and of Suez are closely identified. The changes wrought in both by the Land Company and the Construction Company, the brief prosperity and the subsequent ruin,—for a full account of these things and all that they implied the curious reader must go to the book itself. Mr. Cable's plots are apt to be over-complicated. This one is far too much so to admit of any brief abstract. The square in front of the old court-house is perpetually thronged with conspirators, mulattoes, mountaineers, Northern "promoters," and Southern irreconcilables. The air is thick with oaths and powder, and,

°Reprinted from *Atlantic Monthly*, 75 (June, 1895), 821–22.

under cover of the same, one intrigue succeeds another with bewildering rapidity. Yet the central figures stand out boldly from this chaotic background. John March, the hero, has two lady-loves,—Fannie Halliday and Barbara Garnet. Barbara's father is the white villain of the tale, and Cornelius Leggett is his mulatto confederate. No reckless actor in the strange drama of reconstruction in the South has ever been presented in a more masterly manner than this half-breed, with his abrupt alternations of cringing servility and insolent bravado. Both as a politician and as a lover, whether he is looking about for bribes in the House or courting the impish maid Daphne-Jane, whom he playfully entitles his "Delijah,"—in every capacity of life, in short, Leggett is constitutionally and shamelessly immoral; while Mr. Garnet, notwithstanding his white skin and thin varnish of civilized manners, is his fitting associate. Neither of the two is really a clever villain. Garnet could never have compassed John's ruin without the fatuous and gratuitous assistance of his victim; and a very little practical shrewdness would have sufficed to show him that it was by no means his cue to destroy March, but rather to build up his fortunes and marry him to Barbara. Cable is never at his best, however, in depicting people of supposed brains. How admirably, for instance, in this present book, does he introduce his professedly clever man Ravenel, and how shadowy and incoherent has the character become before we part from him! We are utterly at a loss to understand what it is the man wants, and a shrewd suspicion visits us that Mr. Cable knows no better than we. And yet what infinite possibilities he seems to possess when he is first presented to us, "at scant nineteen, a war-veteran, tattered and battered, but with courage unabated, and heart 'still ready to play out the play' "! We continue to believe in him through all his early career as editor in Suez. We feel the fascination he exercises over Fannie Halliday, and can quite understand her putting aside John March with his calf love for this more developed suitor. The first false note is struck when we are invited to behold Ravenel volubly drunk upon his wedding-day. We cannot credit it. Ravenel, we know, hated *words*. He must needs have learned by experience, long before that date, just how many glasses he could imbibe without becoming loquacious, and it would have taken a far more exciting event than his own wedding to induce him to overpass that limit. It must be owned that they all drank freely at Suez; while as for the sudden deaths upon streets and stairways, one wonders that the place was not depopulated. John March gets his own first experience of these epidemic frays in company with his father, and wins his spurs gallantly at Judge March's side. Cable has never drawn a more lovable character than this of the chivalrous, dreamy, devoted old Southerner; never painted a sweeter picture than the one where the father and son are introduced, mounted upon the same horse, the boy "in his eighth year, . . . fast asleep, with his hands clutched in the folds of the judge's coat, and his short legs and browned feet spread wide behind the saddle;" never compassed a keener pathos, not even in the Belles Demoiselles Plantation, than in the scene of the judge's death. This one character is well worth the book, and there are others here whose acquaintance we are glad to have made. There is many a clear side-light thrown upon the stiff problems, by no means all solved as yet, which beset the destiny of the New South, and there are frequent flashes of Mr. Cable's own quaint wit. We wish, of course, that he could better defend the good English which is his by right against the inroads of such literary *canaille* as this: "Breakfus' at next stop, seh! No, seh! It's yo' only chaynce till dinneh, seh! Seh? No, seh, not tell one o'clock dis afte'noon, seh!" And when we read how this man "whisperously asked," and that woman "sighed an unresentful envy," we think we know too well from which "one of our conquerors" he has borrowed his inspiration.

[Preface to *Madame Delphine*]

George W. Cable°

The writing of this story grew out of the receipt of an anonymous letter which I found on my study desk in New Orleans one day when I returned from my first visit to the North.

Once, in childhood, I had spent part of three years in Indiana, but that I do not count. This time I came back flushed with the elations of a Southern writer's first month in New York City, where my publishers had just put forth my first book, the group of short stories to which they—not I—had given the happy title of *Old Creole Days*. In this group there is a tale, one of my earliest, called "'Tite Poulette." It tells of a girl of that pet name, amazingly fair, yet reputed to be the daughter of "Madame John," a palpable quadroon. In the days when European immigration was a feature in New Orleans, a young Dutchman loved her, championed her, got a murderous beating and stabbing for her, was nursed by her down to the grave's edge and back again—the rest is easy guessing. Yet I may take room enough to add that in the midst of his anguish between race-loyalty and his love of a pure sweet maiden, Madame John, after the good old romantic fashion, rushed in with the confession that 'Tite Poulette was not her child, but the offspring of Spanish yellow fever patients whom she had nursed until they died, leaving their infant in her care.

How many New Orleans stories earlier writers, in less literary-fortunate times, had already made to end in this same way, I have never had time to count; but on my return to my native city, there, on the desk, lay, as I say, this anonymous letter. I read it twice, the young mistress of my home standing by my chair.

"You'll not pay any attention to that, will you?" she said.

I replied that I thought I should.

"You can't answer an anonymous letter," she suggested.

I read it through again. It said its writer had just read "'Tite Poulette." It thanked me for the story in touching terms. "But," it said, "the ending is not the truest truth." I haven't the letter at hand to give it word for word, but I do not need it to remember precisely its tone and import. "If you have a whole heart for the cruel case of us poor quadroons," it continued, "change the story, even yet, and tell the inmost truth of it. Madame John lied! The girl was her own

---

°Reprinted from *Madame Delphine* (New York: Charles Scribner's Sons, 1896).

daughter; but like many and many a real quadroon mother, as you surely know, Madame John perjured her own soul to win for her child a legal and honorable alliance with the love-mate and life-mate of her choice."

"How can you answer it?" asked my companion again. "Where can you send the answer?"

"I shall answer it by another story," I replied, and the next day I began this one, of *Madame Delphine*. It is better than "'Tite Poulette"; of that I am sure; and, whatever its shortcomings are, some of which I am well aware of, I have a notion I shall always be glad I wrote it.

George W. Cable

W. M. Baskervill°

In the far South is a region unique in its scenery, its climate, and its civilization. It is the southern portion of Louisiana and is known as the land of the creoles. The soft, luxurious climate is said to be enervating, but, though its languid airs have induced a certain softness of utterance in the speech of the inhabitants, they have lost little of the old Gallic alertness, intrepidity, and strength of mind and of body. For this civilization was born of purely French enterprise, modified somewhat by Spanish association and control, but steadily impervious to English influences. The pushing, all-embracing American has brought this region into the family of states, but he himself was stopped upon the threshold of its inner life and admitted to the charmed circle only upon the acceptance of the manners and the ideas of the creole.

The creoles, like their French ancestors, are seen to best advantage in the city. By nature and habit they are adapted to society and in their city of New Orleans they have built up a lesser Paris. As her latest and most delightful historian remarks, the creole capital should be personified as the most feminine of women, and her whole character was brought entire from France—her good qualities and defects, her tempers and furies, her gaiety and pleasure-loving disposition, her singular delicacy and refinement, her strength and nobility in sorrow and misfortune. Charming she is, and also individual and interesting, "an enigma to prudes and a paradox to puritans."

In this capital of the creoles, George W. Cable was born, October 12, 1844. On his father's side he came of an old colonial Virginian family, which left England in the earliest years of the eighteenth century, and is now largely represented in Virginia. Owing perhaps to the early death of Mr. Cable's father, or for some other cause, he has given few tokens of his Virginian ancestry. The old New England stock represented in his mother constitutes, it would seem, the warp and woof of his nature, though it has been not a little influenced by the characteristics of his Gallic neighbors. His father and mother met in Indiana and were married in 1834, and after the financial crash in 1837 they moved to New Orleans. The father prospered for a time in business, then came misfortune, and after a second disastrous failure, in 1859, he died, leaving his family in such straitened circumstances that the fourteen-year-old boy was obliged to leave school and begin life as a clerk to help in the support of the household.

°Reprinted from *Chautauquan*, 25 (May, 1897), 179–84.

At this occupation he continued till 1863, when he went "through the lines" and entered the Confederate Army in General Win Adams' brigade of Mississippians. The hardships of camp and army life quickly transformed the raw recruit into a sober, thoughtful young man; and he is described as having been a good soldier, scrupulously observant of discipline, always at his post, and always courageous and daring. From early childhood he was studious, and he carried his studious habits with him into camp. At such times as he could command, he employed his leisure moments in the study of the Bible, in keeping up his knowledge of Latin, and in working out problems of higher mathematics.

The war left Mr. Cable, as most of his comrades, absolutely penniless. Returning to New Orleans, he became errand-boy, clerked for six months in Kosciusko, Miss., studied engineering, joined a surveying expedition, and in the Teche country and along the banks of the Atchafalaya River he took in enough malaria to keep busy for the next two years nursing himself back into health. Returning again to the bookkeeper's desk, he was in one and another position of trust in mercantile affairs, with the exception of a little less than a year's experience as reporter for the *Picayune*, till he abandoned commercial pursuits altogether to devote himself to letters.

His first experience in writing was as a contributor to a special column of the *Picayune*, over the signature of "Drop Shot." The contributions were critical and humorous papers, with an occasional poem. Then he was attached to the staff of the paper, with the understanding, however, that he was not to be called upon to report theatrical matters. Later it was considered necessary to place him in charge of this column, and upon his refusal to do the work he was informed that his services could be dispensed with. Vowing never to have anything to do with a newspaper again, he went back to bookkeeping. Very soon, however, the fascinating episodes of early New Orleans life again tempted him to use his pen and he now began to put this material into short stories. Three of these had been written, at odd moments in the midst of clerical duties, when the old *Scribner's Monthly*, now the *Century Magazine*, sent a commission to New Orleans to write and illustrate the "Great South Papers." At Mr. Cable's request a member of this commission, Mr. Edward King, sent one of the stories to the magazine, and, though it was returned, a second venture "was not only successful, but called forth a sympathetic and inspiring letter from Richard Watson Gilder, the young associate editor to Dr. Holland." "'Sieur George," it was called, and the very first words were significant—"In the heart of New Orleans."

"Belles Demoiselles Plantation," "'Tite Poulette," "Jean-ah Poquelin," "Madame Délicieuse," and "Café des Exilés" now appeared at intervals, covering about two years, and then, with the inimitable "Posson Jone'," published in *Appletons' Journal*, were issued in a single volume under the title of *Old Creole Days*. These stories made a twofold revelation—a new field of romance, rich in the contrasts and colors of an old, unique, and varied civilization, steeped in sentiment and passion and enveloped in the poetic, many-tinted haze of a semitropical clime, and also the master hand of a literary artist, who, to the moral energy and sinewy fiber of English character, added the grace, delicacy, airy lightness, and excitability of the Latin race. They also showed that the author was a born story-teller.

In this first volume there was no suggestion of the amateur, nothing crude, unfinished. The pictures of life are as exquisitely clear as they are delicately tender or tragically sorrowful. Arch humor and playful fancy throw a bright ray into scenes of pure pathos, or give a joyous note to the tender tones of happy loves, which would otherwise grow monotonous; but in the tragic story of "Jean-ah Poquelin" the slow martyrdom is painted in gloomy shadows, and the pathos, imagery, and dramatic force of this sketch first suggested comparison with Hawthorne. These stories are all good, but "Posson Jone' " is the master-piece of the collection.

In "Jules St. Ange," a perfect creation in miniature, Mr. Cable has so perfectly caught the very spirit of the French race that it would seem down-right rude and coarse to apply matter-of-fact English words and standards of morals and conduct to the gay, pleasure-loving, kind-hearted, volatile little creole. With rare skill, too, does the author cast the idealizing light of genius upon the awkward backwoods preacher, the street, the drinking-place, the vulgar confidence game, the gambling saloon, the bull ring and motley crew of spectators, the calaboose, the departing boat, the returning prodigal, which lifts them forever out of the realm of the sordid and commonplace into that of pure art and abiding beauty. This elegant little heathen is as much a monument to the author's heart as it is to his dramatic skill.

At the accountant's desk two more years were now spent without further literary activity. But even during the period of convalescence from malarial fever the young man had eagerly applied himself to the study of natural history and laid the foundation for those beautiful pictures of swamp, bayou, prairie, and still life which are such marked features of his writings, in exact scientific knowledge as well as in close observation. So at this time and later Mr. Cable extended his studies and researches into the speech, songs, manners, customs, personal traits, and characteristics of the creoles, covering their entire history from the earliest settlements in Louisiana to the present time.

Thus equipped he was ready to give immediate attention to the request of the *Century Magazine* for a twelve months' serial. The result was *The Gran-dissimes*. Before him lay the story of "Bras Coupé," which had been offered for publication as a short story and rejected, and this now became the central idea of a genuine romance of Louisiana at the beginning of this century. Over the differences of race, the bitterness of caste prejudice, restiveness under imposed rule, jealousy of the alien ruler, and suspicion of the newcomer, which largely constituted the situation at that time, was cast the warm coloring of a poetic imagination.

But a note struck only here and there in the short stories now becomes the theme of all Mr. Cable's writings. It did not occur to him, it would seem, that an artist out of his domain is not infrequently the least clearsighted of mortals. If the poet is to be our only truth-teller, he must let politics alone. But to this Mr. Cable has answered: "For all he was the furthest removed from a mere party contestant, or spoilsman, neither his righteous pugnacity nor his human sympathy would allow him to 'let politics alone' "; for he doubtless had himself in mind when he wrote these words in regard to Dr. Sevier. Indeed he belongs to the class of thorough-going men governed by thorough-going logic—lovers of abstract truth and perfect ideals, and it was his lot to be born among a people who by the necessities of their situation were controlled by a practical expediency. They were compelled to adopt an illogical but practical compromise between two extremes which were logical but not practical. This conflict between theory and actuality, of abstract truth with practical expediency has so affected the sensitive nature of an extremely artistic temperament as to make this writer give a prejudiced, incorrect, unjust picture of southern life, character, and situation. This domination of one idea has vitiated the most exquisite literary and artistic gifts that any American writer of fiction, with possibly one exception, has been endowed with since Hawthorne, though in respect to intellectuality, to imagination, to profound insight into life, to a full, rich, large, and true humanity, one would be overbold to institute comparison between him and America's greatest writer.

Both the time and Mr. Cable's methods—now that of the ardent conversationalist espousing the extremest measures of partisan politics and again that of the consummate artist holding up a people to the scorn and detestation of the world—were unsuited either to a philanthropic and benevolent, or to a true artistic handling of this theme. The southerners were suffering from the desolations of a devastating war and the humiliating experiences of "reconstruction." Under these adverse and almost blinding conditions many of them felt the call of duty to deal righteously with the most difficult problem any people has ever been called upon to work out, and at last time and the practical common sense of the American people have made it possible to give to this question the solution of a slow, patient, and orderly growth. We are now concerned only with tracing the effect produced upon the writer by this protracted struggle between the artist and the man with a mission, begun in *The Grandissimes* and completed in *John March, Southerner.*

In *The Grandissimes* Mr. Cable has forsaken the beaten track of character study, with its brilliant, indefinite conversation and subtle moral and intellectual problems, and returned to the old romance. Yet he is modern and has taken with him into the older field an artist's nice eye for color and the picturesque, an artist's fine sense of workmanship, and an artist's aim of producing effect in a natural way and by dramatic skill. The story itself is interesting. The Grandissimes and the De Grapions emerge from the haze of a romantic past into the actual present with the reader's keenest interest aroused in their fortunes, their feud, the ancient and honorable character of their ancestry, and their pride and family feeling. The hero and heroine, Honoré Grandissime and Aurora De Grapion, who unite at last the fortunes of the two families, are the author's best portraits of higher creole life. Aurora in naturalness and finish is as much a creation of genius as Jules St. Ange, Raoul, Narcisse—a kind of characterization in which Mr. Cable excels. In the delineation of the gentleman, Honoré and Dr. Sevier for examples, this author succeeds about as well as most writers of fiction—that is, very poorly. A few realistic touches, at best a type, are as a rule the most we may expect.

The theme of *The Grandissimes* is the effect produced upon a tropical society by an institution which deprives a human being of his liberty, produces a feeling of caste, and the maintenance of which involves a separation in thought and feeling from the rest of the civilized world. In the portion of the South in which Mr. Cable was reared slavery had fewer mitigating circumstances than in any other; and he seems to have approached the study of the question from the point of view of the French Revolution and with the philosophy of Rousseau. The latter is the basis of the Bras Coupé story. Over the entire romance, over action and incident and scene and character, hangs the pall of slavery, with just enough light and color introduced to deepen the shadows. The effect upon the individual and upon society is brought out admirably, now by skilful word-painting and again by a still more skilful dramatic action. But too frequently the author throws his puppets aside and appears in person upon the scene. The man with a mission throttles the artist. At such times he makes sententious comments or utters commonplaces now universally accepted, and still more frequently he indulges in sharp thrusts and biting sarcasms—all, from the point of view of art, not only blemishes, but "palpable intrusions." The abundance of these remarks in Mr. Cable's writings may perhaps account for the creoles' peculiar affection for him. "Like all other luxuries, the perpetration of an epigram has to be paid for."

Mr. Brander Matthews has drawn a nice distinction between humor and the sense of humor, observing that the ownership of one does not insure possession of the other. "Probably," he adds, "if the sense of humor had been more acutely developed in Dickens he might have refrained from out-Heroding Herod in his massacre of the innocents." But melodrama seems to be a part of the nature of some authors. A sense of humor equal to the author's rich gift of humor would have been necessary to save our nerves from the tragico-sentimental story of Bras Coupé, the wanton murder of Clemence, the revolting death of the pot-hunter in the beautiful idyl of *Bonaventure*. In at least two of these instances the author's nice artistic sensibility has been dulled by partisan feeling. Partisanship of any kind implies a more or less one-sided view, for a complete man never takes one-sided views.

In *Madame Delphine* we see the most perfect specimen of the author's literary art and constructive ability. The story is so quickly told and handled so skilfully as almost to leave us unaware of the utter improbability of the plot. While its compass does not admit of the same exhibition of strength as in *The Grandissimes*, it also prevents the digressions and extravagances which mar that story. If the author had been content to leave it a fairy tale for quadroons, we might have accorded it the unalloyed enjoyment that we give to those delightful creations of the fancy. But the ethical element is made so prominent that the story demands nearer scrutiny.

In 1879 Mr. Cable formally entered upon a literary life. Since that time his productions may be divided into four kinds: politico-sociological, editorial, historical, and creative. The writings of the first kind, dealing mainly with the political and social status of the negro in the South, have been collected into two volumes, entitled *The Silent South* (containing also his well-known papers "The Freedman's Case in Equity" and "The Convict Lease System in the Southern States") and *The Negro Question*. His editorial work may more properly be classed here, as it was apparently designed to promote rather his political than his literary reputation. The most important effort of this kind is *Strange True Stories of Louisiana*.

The same style, finish, and spirit found in his literary productions Mr. Cable has carried into his historical writings. His facts have been gathered with abundant research and painstaking labor; but in *The Creoles of Louisiana* particularly they are so highly colored and suffused with prejudice that the value of this vivid, charmingly written volume as history has been greatly lessened. The titles are "New Orleans Before the Capture," "The Dance in the Place Congo" (two short sketches), "New Orleans" in the Census of 1880 and again in the Encyclopedia Britannica, and *The Creoles of Louisiana*.

But Mr. Cable is always best in creative work. *Dr. Sevier*, in which some of the author's finest and most poetic thought is contained, and *Bonaventure*, that pure white flower standing alone in the turbid pool of partisan controversy, are specially noteworthy. Public readings and political writings now kept Mr. Cable from bringing out another work of fiction till he essayed a long novel in *John March, Southerner*—one of the most dismal failures ever made by a man of genius. There are few true notes in the entire volume. "The Taxidermist" and one or two other rare gems of more recent date serve to show that the divine fire yet burns. Would that it could be religiously consecrated to pure art!

A Note on Mr. Cable's
The Grandissimes

James M. Barrie[*]

To sit in a laundry and read *The Grandissimes*—that is the quickest way of reaching the strange city of New Orleans. Once upon a time, however, I took the other route, drawn to the adventure by love of Mr. Cable's stories, and before I knew my way about the St. Charles Hotel (not, as Mr. Cable would explain, the St. Charles of *Dr. Sevier*, but its successor), while the mosquitos and I were still looking at each other, before beginning, several delightful Creole ladies had called to warn me. Against what? Against believing Mr. Cable. They came singly, none knew of the visits of the others, but they had heard what brought me there; like ghosts they stole in and told their tale, and then like ghosts they stole away. The tale was that Mr. Cable misrepresented them: Creoles are not and never were "like that," especially the ladies. I sighed, or would have sighed had I not been so pleased. I said I supposed it must be so: no ladies in the flesh could be quite so delicious as the Creole ladies of Mr. Cable's imagination, which seemed to perplex them. They seemed to be easily perplexed, and one, I half think, wanted to be a man for an hour or two just to see how those ladies would impress her then. But by the time she regained the French quarter she was probably sure that she had convinced me. And she had, they all did, one after the other—that the sweet Creoles who haunt these beautiful pages were not always ghosts, but always ghost-like. They come into the book like timid children fascinated by the hand held out to them, yet ever ready to fly, and even when they seem most real, they are still out of touch; you feel that if you were to go one step nearer they would vanish away. Such is the impression they leave in all Mr. Cable's books, and his painting of them would be as faulty as the masterpiece exhibited by Honoré Grandissime's cousin in Mr. Frowenfeld's window if their descendants were not a little scared by it, they who had for so long peeped from behind veils and over balconies to be at last introduced to that very mixed society, the reading public. What would Aurora of this book have said to it? She is the glory of the book; no one, not even Mr. Cable (who rather disgracefully shirks the question) can tell why Joseph Frowenfeld "went over" from her to Clotilde (I am sure Joseph did not know) after feeling that to be with her was like "walking across the vault of heaven

[*]Reprinted from *Bookman*, 7 (July, 1898), 401–03.

with the evening star on his arm" (which is exactly what talking to a Creole lady in the St. Charles Hotel is like); yet had Aurora been of a later age and heard what Mr. Cable was about she would certainly, without consulting that droll little saint Clotilde have slipped out of bed some night to invoke the naughty spirits, when the novelist awoke he would have been horrified to find in one corner of his pillow an acorn, in another a joint of cornstalk, in a third a bunch of feathers. And though he had gone mad with terror she would have held that it served him right. And she would have had more acorns and feathers for the pillows of suspicious visitors to the St. Charles Hotel.

You may still see what was the home of Aurora after she came into her fortune, the house where the little comedy was played (in the last chapter of this book) which I venture to call one of the prettiest love scenes in any language. Of course it is in the French (or Creole) quarter, for though many of the Americans of New Orleans doubtless go to Paris even before they die, the city has still its bit of France, far more truly French than the Paris boulevards of to-day. New Orleans was twice in French hands and once in Spanish before it became part of the United States, and the Creoles are the descendants of the French and Spaniards left behind. Canal street, which may be said to cut the city in two, is their English Channel; on the one side the English tongue and ways of living, though a fourth of the inhabitants are "coloured" (but not all coloured black); on the other lies France (and a little of Spain), the France of a time when railways were not; the names of the streets, the names over the shops, the life, the language, these are nearly all French, often somewhat decayed and as often intermarried perplexingly with interlopers, as the Creoles themselves are said never to intermarry. Those of the French side seem to be reluctant to cross Canal Street even on business, and they go still less frequently for pleasure; it is only when they die that all the people of New Orleans meet (except those who must be content with what is grimly called a "water funeral"), in the strange cemeteries which the swampy soil compels them to build above ground. Each family has its mausoleum of marble or granite, many of them palatial, so that the cities of the dead at New Orleans are infinitely more handsome than the city of the living, and as you walk under the magnolia trees along streets of tombs that look like beautiful dwelling-houses, you may see by the door of one of these houses a woman sitting on a chair knitting, and it is almost as if she had stepped out to enjoy the sun again. Or is it Aurora slipping away for an hour from Clotilde, whom she loved but sometimes found in the way?

There are a quarter of a million people in New Orleans now; there were ten thousand in the days when Joseph Frowenfeld mistook a lady and her daughter for sisters, and walked the vault of heaven with his future mother-in-law on his arm. Even now it is perhaps the most picturesque city in America, but it was still more brightly coloured then, every nationality represented in its arcades and at its lattices and dormer windows, its government just passing into the hands of the English, and every family "a hive of patriots who did not know where to swarm." Every family of white people, that is to say, for the blacks are supposed to be out of it all; whatever happens in Louisiana, their condition must remain the same. Gradually we realize that the rivalry between French and English is a trumpery matter in New Orleans compared to the question of blacks and whites, and even the blacks can well afford to wait when their case is put beside that of those who are neither black nor white. Mr. Cable is the impassioned advocate of the rights of the black man, who has surely never had such an artist for champion as here, in the story of Bras-Coupé, yet I like him best when his one arm protects some poor wounded quadroon, and he is fighting for her with the other. The Honoré Grandissime, who is, I suppose, the hero of the book, is a Creole of whom his race have some right to be proud, but the other Honoré is the most memorable figure; he, a white man to all appearance, who told the whole tragedy of his life in the simple words, "I am not white, monsieur."

Mr. G. W. Cable in London: An Interview

Anonymous*

The *British Weekly*, with characteristic promptitude, has interviewed Mr. G. W. Cable, who is at present staying with Mr. J. M. Barrie in Kensington. Mr. Cable is known to English readers as the writer of that masterpiece, *Old Creole Days*, published when he was thirty-five, and other stories of creole and negro life. This is Mr. Cable's first visit to London:

"Had you ever crossed the Atlantic before?" asked the interviewer.

"No," said Mr. Cable; "this is my first stay of any length in a foreign country. I ought not, however, to say foreign in speaking of England, for I find this country very homelike and seem to be constantly meeting my own people. London is very charming—such a delightful confirmation of a lifetime of reading and pictorial illustration. The pictures seem to have come out of the books, although magnified to life-size."

"You propose, I think, to give some readings in England?"

"Yes," said Mr. Cable, "at the suggestion of English friends, I have come over at last, after many years of delay, during which I put off the idea. In America I have been in the habit of giving readings to public audiences. The old entertainment of elocutionary reading by professional elocutionists has long since quite gone out of fashion, but there is still a very strong interest in hearing and seeing authors render their own pages by word of mouth. That kind of entertainment is common all over the States from Maine to Mexico, where the population is not too sparse to maintain it."

"What passages from your books do you find most popular in America?"

"It is rather difficult to give an accurate reply to that question. My sustained novels seem to be all about equally favoured, but among my shorter stories 'Posson Jone'' is perhaps the one which audiences most like to hear. Along with 'Posson Jone'' I may mention 'The Story of Madame Delphine,' and the middle story in the trilogy of *Bonaventure*, entitled 'Grande Pointe.' These are beyond doubt the most popular single passages. Then I choose pieces from two or three of my novels, always confining myself to one book or story, and reading passages selected for their literary and dramatic quality, but at the same time making the story plain to the hearers."

*Reprinted from (London) *Academy Supplement*, 53 (May 7, 1898), 497–98.

"Do you ever read a whole story at once?"

"Sometimes, as in the case of 'Grande Pointe' and 'Posson Jone'.' The latter is really almost a play."

"Do your audiences in America consist chiefly of the richer and more cultured classes?"

"There is a system of lyceums all over the country," said Mr. Cable. "These provide a series of entertainments lasting over the season, to which admission is by course-ticket. People of every social rank attend these entertainments, and the audiences are as varied as those of a theatre."

"And how about the creole songs, Mr. Cable?"

"Well, many years ago, when I discovered that these Folk-songs of the slaves of former Louisiana creoles had a great charm of their own, and were preserved by tradition only, I was induced to gather them and reduce them to notation. I found that others were so strongly interested in the songs that, without pretending to any musical authority or original charm of voice, I was tempted to sing one or two of them before public audiences. The first time I did so was in Boston, and since then I have rarely been allowed to leave them out of my entertainment when the length of my literary programme left room for them."

"What of your present literary work, Mr. Cable? Shall you be making any progress with that in London?"

"Certainly," said Mr. Cable, "in fact, one thing that has brought me over besides my lifelong desire to see the mother country of our own great nation and the home of our language and literature, is the hope that by taking my days very quietly and in much retirement, I may carry on at a moderate pace my present literary work even here. So I have brought my knitting with me. It is a novel based upon my experience as a cavalry soldier in the American Civil War."

"Have you fixed on the name?"

"I never succeed in naming a story till I have finished it. I name it to myself a dozen times, but these names are mere scaffolding, and the real task and agony of getting the right name is one of the finishing touches. I have another story, by the way, in the hands of *Scribner's Magazine* which is now awaiting publication. It is called 'The Entomologist,' and the scene is laid in New Orleans during the great epidemic of 1878."

Mr. Cable lived in New Orleans through that terrible time, and had many strange experiences in nursing the sick.

[Cable's Readings in London]

Anonymous[*]

Mr. G. W. Cable's first reading, in Mrs. Barrie's drawing-room, last Tuesday afternoon, delighted his audience. To be accurate, it was not a reading at all, but a dramatic recitation, in the late Mr. Brandram's manner; but Mr. Cable allows himself a greater latitude in emotion and gesture. It was his own work he recited (scenes from *Dr. Sevier*); he felt it strongly, and he communicated the thrill to his audience. For properties Mr. Cable allowed himself a book and a handkerchief, and he used them only for the Widow Riley—the book as a fan, the handkerchief for her Irish tears. The text itself was in the author's head. Neat, sincere, and gay is his literary style; neat his manner; and neat, intimate, and mobile is his method of delivery. He passes easily from the lightest of light comedy to the imminent tragedy of battle. But best of all his characters he loves to put on the flexible, caressing voices that go with the short-stepping nimble movements of his own Creoles. Mr. Cable's rendering of the quaint, cunning utterances of the matchless Narcisse was comedy at its best, and "Mary's Night Ride" was admirable narrative tragedy. In fact, the hour and a half's traffic with *Dr. Sevier* called up so many delightful reminiscences that at least one of the audience went away hot-foot to the Kensington bookshops. But none of them had *Dr. Sevier* in stock, or, indeed, any of Mr. Cable's books; which must be remedied. Perhaps some publisher will give us Mr. Cable's works on the Edinburgh Stevenson model.

In appearance Mr. Cable is slim and slight, with a high, broad forehead. He wears a bristling gray moustache, and might be mistaken for a military man were it not for the sensitive play of expression of his features. Not the least interesting incident of the afternoon was his rendering of a story told by a Creole woman to a child, and his crooning of a Creole song.

All who care for fine literature and fine acting should make a note of the two other readings Mr. Cable will give in London—at Bay Tree Lodge, Frognal, to-day (Saturday), and at 88, Portland-place, next Wednesday.

[*]Reprinted from (London) *Academy*, 53 (May 21, 1898), 551.

Mr. Cable in England

Anonymous*

"Whatever may be the state of the political relations between Great Britain and the United States," said the London *Times* on May 18, "there is fortunately no need to advocate an *entente cordiale* between the men-of-letters of the two countries. English writers have long been able to count upon something more than cordiality when they have visited America, and reciprocal courtesies in this country await any author from the United States whose work is favorably known on this side of the Atlantic. It is not long since Mr. Anthony Hope returned from a tour during which he had given readings from his stories in many cities of the United States, and he was only following in the footsteps of several other English writers of note. Now we are able on our part to extend a welcome to an American novelist, widely known and admired for his clever studies of southern life, who has been persuaded during his visit to London to give a few of those readings from his books that have delighted his own countrymen. Mr. George W. Cable has created many original and amusing characters in his *Old Creole Days* and other books, and his dramatic talent enables him to bring them before an audience with vivid effect.

"At his first reading, given yesterday at Mr. J. M. Barrie's house in South Kensington, Mr. Cable read from *Doctor Sevier*, his tale of life in New Orleans about the date of the Civil War; and in the passages of humor and pathos that he chose, he soon won the hearts of his audience. Very skilfully he took the parts of the various figures of the tale—the creole Narcisse, with his childlike chatter and vanity and his intense 'Byronism'; the Irish-American Widow Riley; the matter-of-fact Italian, with his soothing, purring ways, who wins the widow's heart; but even more remarkable was the suggestion of 'atmosphere' which Mr. Cable managed to convey. He seemed to bring into a London drawing-room the languorous, scent-laden air of a southern state, to make his hearers see the brilliant coloring and the rich profusion of a summer in the south, to leave a clear impression in every passage of the scene as well as of the characters who figured in it. Reciting entirely from memory, Mr. Cable was able to get the utmost dramatic value out of his selections, and the power with which he worked up the thrilling story of a night ride through the Confederate army's

*Reprinted from *Critic*, NS 29 (June 11, 1898), 387.

lines, came as a surprise to those who had looked only for the humorous effects of the earlier pieces.

"A little speech by Mr. Birrell, M. P., introduced the reader to his audience, and the few words of Sir John Leng, M. P., at the close, served to express the pleasure which Mr. Cable had given. The next reading will be at 88 Portland place, on the 26th inst., when Sir Henry Irving will preside."

The Stories of George W. Cable

Cornelia Atwood Pratt[°]

The attempt to explain why charm is charming is always a thankless task. There are other literary qualities which may be reduced to their constituents, and these last weighed and ticketed, but the charm of a tale, like that of a personality, is always irreducible, defying the critic and delighting the world at large, apparently elusive and yet, so far as fiction is concerned, the one indestructible element. A little charm carries far and lasts forever.

It is the possession of this element of charm that gave Mr. Cable's early work its immediate success and insured its lasting popularity. The long-famous collection of stories published under the title of *Old Creole Days* has, it is true, many more tangible excellences. The tales dealt with wholly fresh material, and opened, to Northern readers, a new world in a land which they had always vaguely apprehended to be the region of romance. This material was deftly handled. The stories were told in a manner sufficiently direct and vigorous to give the effect of intensity, and yet sufficiently deliberate and measured to convey the alluring golden atmosphere of a land where it is always afternoon. They were unencumbered with any lengthy, tiresome explanations of the social conditions which made the very essence of their dramatic intensity, and yet managed to make those conditions perfectly clear. They were full of the picture-conveying phrases which throw such strong illumination upon the background of a situation. For one instance out of a hundred, recall Père Jerome's dingy and carpetless parlor where "one could smell distinctly the vow of poverty," or the latter-day aspect of Madame Delphine's house, whose batten shutters are closed "with a grip that makes one's knuckles and nails feel lacerated." They appealed exquisitely to the finer feelings—we are all frankly glad when literature does that, perhaps because it is personally reassuring to find the finer feelings responding promptly to the appeal—and their handling of things emotional is always that delicate, sane, sweet touch which puts the emotions safe upon the high levels we would have them always keep. Even when they were painful stories, their pain was always on the side of righteousness or moral beauty. But chiefly they were playful, tender, human. Over their pages dripped softly the luxurious Creole-English which affects the eye and ear as honey does the palate. Whether charm subsists in the sum of all these qualities or is a

[°]Reprinted from *Critic*, 24 (March, 1899), 250–53.

product arising from their chemical combination, or is something behind and beyond them all, does not greatly matter if only the world is so cordially agreed concerning its presence as has been the case in *Old Creole Days*. It is almost twenty years since these stories became a part of our literature, but the fact is one difficult to realize, since the book has the gift of the perennial youth and freshness always seeming to belong, if not exactly to the current hour, at least to a near and beloved yesterday.

Of a lovableness almost equal to *Old Creole Days* are Mr. Cable's stories of Acadian Louisiana, *Bonaventure* and the rest. It is only in facing the author's longer novels that the critic escapes from the tyranny of charm, and becomes able to use again the implements of his trade which the magnetic qualities of the other work we have been considering render useless for the time.

Perhaps the best test of the absolute finality of a man's call to labor in any field of art is found in his persistent devotion to the ends of art through middle age and after, and in the power his work shows of resisting the encroachment of the other mental interests which are naturally and righteously far more absorbing to the normal man than are the ends of art. The question is not only, to paraphrase Mr. James, "Can he keep his talent fresh when other elements turn stale?" but even more is it, "Can he keep his talent disentangled from his religion, his sense of affairs, his political perceptions, his historical sense, and all the invading horde of lively and legitimate interests which go to make up the intellectual life of a man beyond thirty?" The implication of the question is not, of course, that all these things cannot serve art, but rather that art must not serve them.

If one were to arraign any of Mr. Cable's work for any cause—and in its mildest form the labor is not a gracious one—it would be his novels, on the ground that they are overweighted with other than the human interest which is the compulsory one in fiction. Other things are good only so long as they make or explain personality; they begin to be bad when personality is made subservient to them. The law is as simple and as rigid as the law of ornament in design. Even in *The Grandissimes* the problem is more absorbing than the people. The book has the setting which so delights us in the shorter stories, and possesses many of their most alluring qualities, but the reader feels that the writer has studied so deeply the political and social aspects of life at that time and place, that he is possessed by the result of his study rather than by the personality of his creations. So, Louisiana in the early part of this century is more heroine than the ladies Nancanou and more hero than the brothers Grandissime or the studious Frowenfeld, to whom is assigned, indeed, what may be called a thinking part, since he does little save to act as mouthpiece for the reflections of his creator upon events and their causes, and to permit himself to be happily married in the end. There is, however, so much atmosphere in the book, and that of so suave a quality, that one may read it happily for the story's sake and be undisturbed by the elements which were dearer to the author than the story. In *Dr. Sevier* the atmosphere is less rich and the problem more insistent. The thread of the story is slender, and no personality in the tale is strong enough to carry on the interest from painful phase to more painful phase of its evolution. It is a study of the development of a man's comprehension of life and society through the most harrowing experiences of poverty and vicarious as well as personal suffering, and the reader, who has a right to be warm-hearted, reproaches the author for cruelty because his problem is dearer to him than the fortunes of John Richling, who might have been allowed to live and use his hard-won wisdom without any detriment to our respect for the processes by which he learned it. Just here one stops to reflect that carelessness of the individual is Nature's way as well as Mr. Cable's, and this would be an irresistible argument for the method were it not that the only ultimate use of fiction is to strengthen our belief in the power of personality and hide the mercilessness of Nature a little from our eyes:

> " A veil to draw 'twixt God his law,
> And man's infirmity;
> A shadow kind to dumb and blind
> The shambles where we die."

In *John March*, again, some of the questions of reconstruction dwarf to a certain extent our appreciation of the people who are solving the questions. The mental attitude which one thus seems to discern in these three books is essentially manly, intellectually vigorous, and natural, but it is not the attitude of one who is fundamentally an artist. Also, his attitude, while it does not make the books any less good to read in a large way, does distinctly lessen their legitimacy and excellence as fiction. They have interest as history and ethics rather than as life and art. They hold us by chapters and pages rather than as wholes, because in them the writer's creative ability has been sacrificed to his power of reflection.

It seems safe to assume that this sacrifice must have occurred by conscious or unconscious choice, since Mr. Cable's novelettes and short stories give abundant evidence of his ability to tell a story that is a story, existing for its own sake and moving directly, if with the grace of leisure, to its appointed end. This being the case, we can only regret that the choice has been so made, for reflective work in literature is as plentiful as creative work is rare, and to spend upon the one a talent capable of the other seems an unpardonable rudeness to the gods who give of their best sparingly.

Mr. G. W. Cable's Aurora and Clotilde Nancanou

W. D. Howells[*]

The heroines of Mr. Cable's admirable novel, *The Grandissimes*, could be proved, at least to the satisfaction of their present elderly adorer, easily first among the imaginary ladies with whose sweetness novelists have enriched and enlarged our acquaintance . . . .

I

I am not going to urge the right of Mr. Cable to lead the Southern writers who have done such notable work in fiction since the Civil War. There may very well be two opinions as to that, and it is quite sufficient for my purpose here that the reader should agree with me concerning the positive excellence of *The Grandissimes*. That seems to me one of the few American fictions which one can think of without feeling the need of forbearance; or without wishing, in the interest of common honesty, strongly to qualify one's praises of it. Ample, yet shapely, picturesque in time and place, but essentially faithful to the facts of both, romantic in character but realistic in characterization, it abounds in varieties and contrasts of life mellowed but not blurred in the past to which they are attributed. Without accusing the author of slighting any of the rich possibilities of such an historic moment as that of the cession of Louisiana to the United States by France, and the union of the old province with the new nation against the prejudices of nearly all the native population, one may note that the political situation is subordinated to the social and personal interests, and the dark presence of slavery itself is perceptible not in any studied attitude, but in the casual effects of character among the Creole masters and the Creole slaves.

It is well known that the author's presentation of this character dissatisfied (to use a word of negative import for the expression of a positive resentment) the descendants of the Creole masters at least, who fancied their race caricatured in the picture. But the fact only testified to the outside spectator of the extreme difficulty, the impossibility, indeed, of satisfying any people with any portraiture by an alien hand. To such a spectator Mr. Cable's studies of Creole character in his New Orleans of the early nineteenth century seem affection-

[*]Reprinted from *Heroines of Fiction* (New York: Harper & Brothers, 1901), pp. 234–44.

123

ately, almost fondly, appreciative, and they convince of their justice by that internal evidence which it is as hard to corroborate as to overthrow. No dearer or delightfuller figures have been presented by the observer of an alien race and religion than Mr. Cable has offered in Aurora and Clotilde Nancanou, and in none does the artist seem to have penetrated more sympathetically the civilization, so unlike his own, which animated them with a witchery so diverse yet so equal. Without blaming his Creole critics, one wonders what would have satisfied them if they are not content with the vivid and lawless caprice of Aurora, the demure, conscientious, protesting fascination of Clotilde.

In this mother and daughter the parental and filial relations are inverted with courageous fidelity to life, where we as often see a judicious daughter holding an impulsive mother in check as the reverse, Clotilde is always shocked and troubled by her mother's wilful rashness, and Aurora, who is not so very much her senior, is always breaking bounds with a girlish impetuosity, which is only aggravated by the attempt to restrain it. These lovely ladies, who are in their way ladies to their finger-tips, and are as gentle in breeding as they are simple in circumstance, shine to each other's advantage in the situations which contrast them; and it is in such situations that they are mostly seen. One such situation fixed itself in my mind at a first reading, and has remained there unfaded during the twenty years that have since elapsed, though I will not deny that I have several times refreshed my original sense of it. The reader who knows the book will not have forgotten the passage descriptive of Sieur Frowenfeld's call upon the ladies in their little house, when Clotilde and he try to ignore their unspoken love for each other in a sober discussion of the Creole's peculiarities, and Aurora, from whom their passion is of course less hidden than from themselves, dashes irrelevantly into the conversation from time to time, and turns the train of Frowenfeld's ideas topsy-turvy. It is all done with a delicacy, a gracious tenderness, enhanced by the author's sensitive rendering of the Creole ladies' accents in the English which they employ with the English-speaking young German pharmacist; but one despairs in quoting it, knowing that the quaint beauty of the characterization can be only suggested in such a fragment . . . .

II

It may very justly be urged that this is not drama; and very often in the illustrative passages I have given in this series of studies I have felt that they did not represent the heroines in those lime-lighted moments in which a heroine is supposed most to live. One has to choose between such moments and some quieter episode in which character softly unfolds itself, and its fascination penetrates like a perfume to the reader's sympathy while his more tumultuous sensations are left unstirred. Then, one has one's conscience as to the quality of the whole work in which the character is rooted, and of which it is the consummate flower. One must somehow do justice to that; and in reading Mr. Cable's novel one is afraid that nothing short of entreating the reader to go to it and do it justice himself will suffice. Not to make this baggarly default, however, one may remind him of the opalescent shimmer in which the story is wrapped, and from which keenly sparkle its facts and traits of comedy and tragedy. For a certain blend of romance and reality, which does no wrong to either component property, I do not know its like in American fiction, and I feel that this is saying far too little; I might say in all fiction; and not accuse myself of extravagance. Short of this I may safely declare it the author's masterpiece, on which he has lavished his happiest if not his most conscious art; and Aurora Nancanou is its supreme grace. What she is otherwise will not be readily put into words, even her own words. She is always the wild, wilful heart of girlhood, which the experiences of wifehood, motherhood, and widowhood have left unchanged. She is a woman with a grown-up daughter, but essentially she is her daughter's junior, and, adorable as Clotilde is in her way, she pales and dulls into commonplace when Aurora is by.

That last chapter, which is so apt to be an anti-climax in a novel, is so good in *The Grandissimes*, and is so subtly interpretative of Aurora's personality— the sort of personality which coquettes with itself to the very end—that I should like to give it entire, though I know that I should have still a haunting fear that without everything that had gone before the portrait of this bewitching creature would want its full effect. Honoré Grandissime, who has loved her through all the involutions of her caprice, has offered himself and been refused, and a scene follows which, among love scenes, has to my knowledge scarcely been surpassed in its delicious naturalness . . . .

[Letter to Charles Scribner]

George W. Cable[*]

Northampton, Mass., Dec. 20, 1901

Dear Mr. Scribner:

The notion that I have written a story "to catch the market" strikes me more drolly than I suppose it can possibly strike anyone else. The fact is, the real beginning of *The Cavalier* dates almost ten years back. It was then that I began to plan a group of character stories, but stories of character portrayal through the medium of romantic and dramatic incidents. They were to be short stories, beginning with a very brief one, and each succeeding one to be longer than the one before.

However, very early in 1893, the year of the Chicago Exposition, I had gone no further than to plan one story which threatened to be long and which did not promise sufficient portrayal of strong characters to suit me. Its scenes were laid in New Orleans and in the regions which have furnished the scenes of *The Cavalier*. I pigeonholed it and wrote for a "Columbian number" of Scribner's magazine "The Taxidermist." It was the first of my character group. Once more I should have turned to the earlier planned story, but a still older project was my "Gregory's Island" or "The Solitary"—fourteen years old, it was—and I wrote it because I knew I could make it brief. Thus followed a story suggested by my taxidermist as a foil to him, "The Entomologist."

And then once more I turned to my pigeonholed sketch, and began to borrow from it certain features whose use in *The Cavalier* makes it certain that the early sketch will never become a printed tale. So I planned and began really to write *The Cavalier*—in 1897—in the spring of the year. But I was greatly interrupted that year. In 1898 I made much progress. I at first proposed to make the story about equal in length to the other three combined, which presently appeared in one volume as "Strong Hearts." This fourth story was to be the completing tale of the group; and in fact that is what it is. The four stories are told by "Richard Thorndyke Smith" out of his own experiences, he says, though of course how true that is I don't know. I finished the first draft of *The Cavalier* in 1899, laid it by for many months, revised it in 1900 and ended the task at the end of the year.

[*]Printed, with permission, from manuscript in Scribner Archives, New York.

If I had published *The Grandissimes* last October, instead of twenty five years ago, it would have seemed as if I certainly had written it to catch the market. Oh, no, I'm too slow a story-teller to do that sort of thing successfully, or even try to do it. From first to last *The Cavalier* was in the egg about nine years before I succeeded in hatching it, and I sitting on it (rather fitfully) all that time.

Ever

Yours truly
G. W. Cable

[Review of *The Cavalier*]

Anonymous[*]

It may seem a little tame to turn from such a feast as this [Rudyard Kipling's *Kim*] to the autumn exhibit of home products in fiction, but we need no more to reanimate us than the announcement of a new book by Mr. Cable, bearing the suggestive title of *The Cavalier*. The regular machine-made novel of our time, whether dealing with contemporary or (supposed) ancestral manners, is ofter very admirable in its way,—learnedly designed, accurately studied, and sometimes beautifully finished. But the stories of Mr. Cable are of a different order,—not made, but born. They are living organisms, which take on the image of their creator as they grow. We have had but one supreme master of imaginative romance among us, as yet; but I know of no one fitter to stand— *quocumque intervallo*—in the place next Hawthorne's than the author of "Posson Jone' " and *The Grandissimes*. The latter is indeed one of the very few American stories which can be read more than once or twice, and seem fuller and finer at each reperusal. The obscurities of the narrative become clear, the crowding characters fall into natural and noble groups; the various Creole dialects, which give the page, at first sight, so discouraging an aspect, become things of pure delight when we realize with what marvelous ingenuity the oddest vocables have been employed to express a singularly dulcet and caressing variety of human speech; finally, the incomparable climax of the main love story—"Mock me no more, Aurore Nancanou!"—lingers upon the ear as one of the most deliciously combined and entirely satisfactory of concluding chords.

That the new novel is quite equal to *The Grandissimes* one cannot pretend; but it has more of the witchery of that favorite story than anything which Mr. Cable has written for a long time. There is a fire, a dash, and a general exaltation of feeling about these memoirs of the Southern Confederacy in its brief hour of highest hope which continually suggest youth in the annalist, and incline one to fancy that the book may have been written some time ago, and wisely, if not compulsorily, withheld from publication while the passions born of civil strife were still running high. Yet the tale is not flagrantly partisan. The types upon either hand are rather highly idealized,—the superb Yankee captain hardly less than the patrician stripling, Master Richard Thorndyke Smith, who is the titular hero of the book, and the all-daring, all-beguiling Confederate

[*]Reprinted from *Atlantic Monthly*, 83 (December, 1901), 847–48.

spy, who is its chief heroine. An acid critic might describe *The Cavalier* as a "jingo" book, in that it extols, without distinction of caste or cause, the fine old military virtues,—pluck, resource, gayety in hardship and pain, simple and unquestioning self-surrender. No doubt the writer's inveterate faults are here in plenty. His plot is excessively intricate, his narrative hurried and elliptical; he has a tendency to weaken by oversentimentalizing the sadder scenes of his drama. Nevertheless, *The Cavalier* is good reading for a dull, materialistic day. It quickens the slack pulses like an episode out of Froissart, or the nerve-twanging notes of one "singing of death, and of honor that cannot die." It makes its gallant appeal, moreover, to a reconciled and united nation, with a common tradition of chivalrous deeds; and whenever the tale may have been written, it appears fitly now, when the heart of the whole country is melted by a common sorrow; when, too, so much has been reclaimed by the vanquished, and restored by the victors, of what was thought, for a time, to have been lost and won in the great fight of forty years ago.

[Review of *The Cavalier*]

E. H. Cortissoz[*]

In pleasant contrast to the cheap sensationalism of Mr. Hall Caine come the genial romance and refined sentiment of *The Cavalier*. Mr. Cable illustrates the other extreme of what the author of *The Eternal City* has attempted to do. He deals with a theme of political upheaval and bloody war, but he has not undertaken to write an hysterical epic. He draws as one who loves them his Confederate soldiers and their sweethearts, but he has not overdone the gallantry and beauty of face and character which most "Southland" novelists are disposed to paint—as though valor and virtue had been invented and patented south of Mason and Dixon's line. He has told easily and winningly his tale of modest bravery and unselfish love, and his reader's sympathy and interest are held from first to last. It is plain that personal experiences have furnished something to these scenes of Civil War, and therein the story has gained largely in vigor and dramatic unction.

[*]Reprinted from *Book Buyer*, 23 (December, 1901), 404.

[Notes for a Novel:
Bylow Hill]

S. Weir Mitchell°

A young New England clergyman of the Episcopal Church, and rather high church tendencies and of the highest education and accomplishments, and of good ancestry, met a typical Southern woman at a Summer watering place and fell desperately in love with her. She was tender, gentle, self indulgent, pretty and longed for sympathy.

They were married, and he went to his first parish in a New England village. The house was situated in a well kept garden running down to an old mill dam, which had long since ceased to be useful. The clergyman was liked in the neighborhood, and particularly was he thought well of by one of his church wardens, a handsome young man, a lawyer, and belonging to well known people in the village.

The lawyer became intimate with the clergyman and his wife, and grew attached to them. A child was born about a year after the marriage.

One day, after three years acquaintance, the clergyman became possessed with the idea that too close an intimacy existed between the lawyer and his wife. There was no foundation of truth in this. But coming from a neurotic family his tendency to morbidness became more and more apparent and he watched closely to ascertain some distinct cause for his suspicions. Finally he told the Warden that he must no longer visit his wife and became more and more suspicious until he developed an insanity with fixed delusions on the subject, and exhibited all the cunning and care to conceal his feelings which is exercised by this class of people.

Accidently he saw his wife and the lawyer in conversation (they having met by pure chance) and he was filled with rage.

At this time he dreamed often of his suspicions, dreamed of murder, and his wife became frightened at his unusual actions. At last under the effects of a dream he seized his wife by the throat, then he awakened. In awful alarm she got under the bed and he was left under the dreamed impression that he had killed her. Much excited, he went from [the] room in search of her, the wife meanwhile having fled for security to another part of the house. He was more &

°Printed, with permission, from the manuscript in The George W. Cable Collection, Special Collections Division, Tulane University Library.

more filled with the idea that he had killed her and carried the body down to the old mill pond & there weighted it with stones, etc.

Meanwhile his wife had fled from the house in her thin night clothes seeking shelter in her mother's house which adjoined her own. Her mother sheltered her and listened to the horrible story which she told of suspicious fear & of having been choked.

The next morning the husband called to state that his wife had disappeared, and the mother claimed to know nothing of her whereabouts. The mother wished to look afer the child, but the clergyman refused to give it up.

Wife in terror left the town unseen & went to—the south—until maternal instinct overcame fear. Excuses for absence easy on part of husband & mother.

Meanwhile he became sadder and sadder, and one evening on returning to his home he found his wife standing by the side of the child's cradle. Being convinced that she was dead, he thought what he saw her ghost, and went so violently insane that he was obliged to be restrained in an asylum, where he remained for two years. During this time his wife, her child and her mother were killed in a railroad accident,† and when he was discharged from the asylum as cured he was alone in the world.

Ten or fifteen years after this he consulted me as to whether I thought it right for him to marry again. After his recovery he was told the truth of the matter.

I hope you can read this my Dear—Fictioner—You will need some coaching on insanity, & if in any way I can further help you I am at your disposal— Some alienist could assist you—I presume the tale would scare the boldest novelist.

SWM

Ed. Note: In a letter of November 18, 1896, Mitchell wrote Cable that he was pleased to fulfill his promise and added: "The story is a simple one, and the person who related it to me was exceedingly desirous that it should be put in print. All the parties concerned are long since dead and I feel no hesitation in putting the material in your hands for use. It is not a subject much to my taste; perhaps I see too much of the morbid side of life." Cable appended a note saying that this was Dr. Weir Mitchell's story, on which he founded his.

† Really in quite other ways.

Review of *Bylow Hill*

Mr. Cable's romances have heretofore pertained exclusively to the South. Those with which fame first was won had Louisiana for their theme. His most recent success before *Bylow Hill* appeared—indeed with the reading public the greatest of all his successes—was a story of the Civil War, *The Cavalier.*

It is now many years since Mr. Cable took up his home in Northampton. He was long unheard from in that retreat. The public knew, however, that he was deeply interested in sociological questions. He was printing a magazine in which, with fine humanity, he was seeking to uplift those who stood in dire need of light and cheer. A feeling grew up that he might not go on repeating his early successes in writing fiction. Newer writers had reached the front and wide was the acclaim of them. Mr. Howells continued to charm a new generation. Mr. Stockton kept his followers in thrall, as had been his wont since *Rudder Grange.* But where was Mr. Cable?

Out of this wondering silence came *The Cavalier.* He leaped to a popularity never before known—not even when *The Grandissimes* and *Old Creole Days* were on the applauding tongues of all who read current books.

And now, within six months after that success, comes *Bylow Hill,* in which his genius, following late upon his own footsteps, comes North. Men who know him have doubtless always felt secure in the faith that New England would in time become at his hands the scene of a new romance. He was merely waiting for the opportune time when he should be able to grasp the life and spirit of the people among whom he had made a new home.

Bylow Hill is a story with jealousy for its moving impulse—and a clergyman is the person possessed with that passion; possessed to the point of madness. His wife blameless, the other man in reality his devoted friend, Arthur Winslow, worshipped by his congregation, alike for his power in the pulpit and his personality in social life, wrecks the happiness of his wife and goes to his own death, because of this hallucination. In the opening scenes of the story we have New England pictures as charming as they are restful, with scarcely a note of the tragedy ahead until the book has been half read through.

Isabel Morris, to whom Arthur Winslow is married, had come to Bylow Hill from the South—a woman of deep, strong and yet open nature, a type

° Reprinted from *Book Buyer*, 24 (July, 1902), 469–70.

moreover to which the New England type, with its burden of conscience, its introspection, its narrowness, presents a contrast. Out of Winslow's failure to understand a larger nature than his own, a nature larger indeed than he had been wont to see in the home of his own people, sprang his jealousy. Miss Morris had rejected another suitor. She loved him not, but after she was married to Winslow the two remained friends. Winslow could not discriminate between this and a deeper attachment. Mr. Cable obviously has sought to show wherein in these matters New England and the South are wide asunder. It was a theme well worth his while. He might indeed have wrought it out on an ample canvass and to broader purposes. As it stands, the story is slight—something between the short story and the novelette. There is power in it and there are passages of good artistic work. It does not stir the blood, save in anger at Winslow's crass stupidity, amounting almost to a crime. Nor does it start a tear. But it is a tale well told.

How I Write My Novels

George W. Cable[*]

How do I write my novels? No two of them are results of the same method. Even as to their mechanical production, I no longer put my pages into handwriting, but typewriting. When writing away from home I make them in pencil, reducing them to typewriting on my return to my study—a lodge of two rooms, one above the other, in the midst of my small grove garden, known to my family as the "power house."

But, of course it is trivial to dwell on the hand and tool work of a literary craftsman. Yet, let me add that because my wits refuse to work on any but a clean page, and because I have to revise so much and so often, I put my pages on large sheets and limit each to a hundred and fifty words, using the broad margins for revisions. This is about the only thing in the mechanical part of my work that I sufficiently approve of to recommend it to others. It has its emphatic drawbacks, but it has a number of values.

As to the mind work, my method for the novel I am just now completing (*Kincaid's Battery*) seems to me so much the best I have ever followed that I prefer to speak exclusively of it. I began with the idea of presenting a phase of life unfamiliar both to general experience and to literature, yet to the portrayal of which I could bring an exceptional familiarity, whether acquired by experience or by a vivid imaginative study, of some period of history—or by the two combined. I chose New Orleans for the centre of my scene because I am of New Orleans, by birth and more than half a lifetime's residence. I chose our civil war for time and circumstances, as hanging fullest of ripe fruit in the gardens of my imagination and actual experience. I put my hero and others into the artillery service because while still writing *The Cavalier*, a cavalry story, I noticed that the artillery arm seems to have least attention from tellers of military stories, yet offers a superb phase of soldiers' life. I set myself to make a story which should be a strong combination of character portrayal with plot; with, I mean, a conflict of passions, wills, schemes and adventurous and tragic fates; and to harmonize these entirely with historic events of the time.

Next I made a scenario, as though projecting a play, yet was careful that it should be the framework of a novel and not a play; and this anatomy I studied and revised for months before writing a page of narrative. Thus, incidentally, I

[*] Reprinted from the New York *Herald*, October 25, 1908.

135

found myself so well acquainted with each character in the tale before beginning to write it that if any one of them ever "balked" (as you say) I do not know it.

I believe I am blameless in this story of trying to prove anything or preach anything. It is supremely a love story, a tale of love and constancy. Certainly it is a war story, but not for history's sake or war's sake, much less for the praise of war; the story of a war within a war, a war of beautiful characters (with plenty of faults to make them human and real) against characters ugly and evil, yet not without charm. I hope it may preach as character and conduct always will and must whenever they are, as the critics say, convincing.

I write six days of each week, "at home or abroad, on the land, on the sea," from nine to one, and confine all the other tasks and joys of life, including research, relaxation, proofreading and correspondence, to the other hours.

And I hope no one will ever take me for an example.

[Review of *Gideon's Band*]

Anonymous[*]

It is interesting to note that we have this season pictures of the old-time Mississippi passenger boat from two well-known American novelists. The background, and, for that matter, the foreground, of Miss Murfree's "Story of Duciehurst" is the Mississippi River and its banks; while Mr. Cable's *Gideon's Band* is played on one of the palatial boats of our fathers. The time is eight years before the Civil War. The *dramatis personae* are members of the families who are rivals for the control of the passenger traffic of the Mississippi River. On the same steamer are the father and son to whom the boat belongs, and the wife, daughter, and three sons of their rival. A feud, one of long standing, has been in abeyance. It suddenly comes to life on the decks of the steamer, for there is plenty of combustible material in the temperaments of the various actors. While this drama is rapidly formulating itself, so to speak, a greater tragedy involves the steamer itself; for cholera breaks out among the immigrants on the crowded lower decks. The crisis is met by the different groups of passengers according to their temperaments. The young people, eager to forget for a time their danger, organize an amateur entertainment; but all the while there is an almost panicky sense of danger in the air. A revivalist preacher takes the opportunity of driving home a sense of their impotence to his excited auditors. The story is told largely in conversation. It is distinctly melodramatic. There are passages in which it is not easy to trace the line of development, and the story becomes blurred; in the scenes in which incidents are described Mr. Cable shows his power of vivid realization.

[*] Reprinted from *Outlook*, 108 (December 9, 1914), 844.

[Cable in New Fields of Romance]

Fred Lewis Pattee*

Harte in *Gabriel Conroy* glimpsed the new fields of romance; George Washington Cable (1844————), the earliest of the new Southern school, was the first fully to enter them. His gateway was old New Orleans, most romantic of Southern cities, unknown to Northern readers until his pen revealed it. It seemed hardly possible that the new world possessed such a Bagdad of wonder: old Spanish aristocracy, French chivalry of a forgotten *ancien régime*, creoles, Acadians from the Grand Pré dispersion, adventurers from all the picturesque ports of the earth, slavery with its barbaric atmosphere and its shuddery background of dread, and behind it all and around it all like a mighty moat shutting it close in upon itself and rendering all else in the world a mere hearsay and dream, the swamps and lagoons of the great river.

Cable was a native of the old city. During a happy boyhood he played and rambled over the whole of it and learned to know it as only a boy can know the surroundings of his home. His boyhood ended when he was fourteen with the death of his father and the responsibility that devolved upon him to help support his mother and her little family left with scanty means. There was to be no more schooling. He marked boxes in the custom house until the war broke out, and then at seventeen he enlisted in the Confederate army and served to the end. Returning to New Orleans, he found employment in a newspaper office, where he proved a failure; he studied surveying until he was forced by malarial fever caught in the swamps to abandon it; then, after a slow recovery, he entered the employ of a firm of cotton factors and for years served them as an accountant. It was an unpromising beginning. At thirty-five he was still recording transfers of cotton, and weights and prices and commissions.

But his heart, like Charles Lamb's, was in volumes far different from those upon his office desk. He had always been a studious youth. He had read much: Dickens, Thackeray, Poe, Irving, Scott; and, like a true native of the old city to whom French was a mother tongue, Hugo, Mérimée, About. He loved also to pore over antiquarian records: *Relations* of the priest explorers, and old French documents and writings. His first impulse to write came to him as he sat amid

---

* Reprinted from *A History of American Literature Since 1870* (New York: Century, 1915), pp. 246–53.

these dusty records. "It would give me pleasure," he once wrote in a letter, "to tell you how I came to drop into the writing of romances, but I cannot; I just dropt. Money, fame, didactic or controversial impulse I scarcely felt a throb of. I just wanted to do it because it seemed a pity for the stuff to go so to waste."

Cable's first story, "'Sieur George," appeared in *Scribner's Monthly* in October, 1873. Edward King, touring the Southern States in 1872 for his series of papers entitled *The Great South*, had found the young accountant pottering away at his local history and his studies of local conditions and had secured some of his work for Dr. Holland. During the next three years five other articles were published in the magazine and one, "Posson Jone'," in *Appletons'*, but they caused no sensation. It was not until 1879, when the seven stories were issued in book form as *Old Creole Days*, that recognition came. The long delay was good for Cable: it compelled him, in Hawthorne fashion, to brood over his early work in his rare intervals of leisure, to contemplate each piece a long time, and to finish it and enrich it. He put forth no immaturities; he began to publish at the point where his art was perfect.

The reception accorded to *Old Creole Days* was like that accorded to Harte's "Luck of Roaring Camp." It took its place at once as a classic, and the verdict has never been questioned. There is about the book, and the two books which quickly followed it, an exotic quality, an *aura* of strangeness, that is like nothing else in our literature. They seem not American at all; surely such a background and such an atmosphere as that never could have existed "within the bounds of our stalwart republic." They are romance, one feels; pure creations of fancy, prolongations of the Longfellowism of the mid century—and yet, as one reads on and on, the conviction grows that they are not romance; they are really true. Surely "Posson Jone'" and *Madame Delphine* are not creations of fancy. The elided and softly lisping dialect, broken-down French rather than debased English, is not an invention of the author's: it carries conviction the more one studies it; it is not brought in to show: it adds at every point to the reality of the work. And the carefully worked-in backgrounds—let Lafcadio Hearn speak, who settled in the city a few months after "Jean-ah Poquelin" came out in *Scribner's Monthly:*

> The strict perfection of his Creole architecture is readily recognized by all who have resided in New Orleans. Each one of those charming pictures of places— veritable pastels—was painted after some carefully selected model of French or Franco-Spanish origin—typifying fashions of building which prevailed in the colonial days. . . . The author of *Madame Delphine* must have made many a pilgrimage into the quaint district, to study the wrinkled faces of the houses, or perhaps to read the queer names upon the signs—as Balzac loved to do in old-fashioned Paris.[1]

It is realism, and yet how far removed from Zola and Flaubert—Flaubert with his "sentiment is the devil"! It is realism tempered with romance; it is the new romance of the transition. There is seemingly no art about it, no striving for effect, and there is no exhibition of quaint and unusual things just because they *are* quaint and unusual. Rather are we transported into a charmed atmosphere, "the tepid, orange-scented air of the South," with the soft Creole *patois* about us and romance become real. The very style is Creole—Creole as Cable knew the Creoles of the quadroon type. There is a childish simplicity about it, and there is a lightness, an epigrammatic finesse, an elision of all that can be suggested, that is Gallic and not Saxon at all.

One can feel this exotic quality most fully in the portraits of women: 'Tite Poulette, Madame Delphine, Aurora Nancanou, Clotilde, and the others, portraits etched in with infinitesimal lightness of touch, suggested rather than described, felt rather than seen. These are not Northern women, these daintily feminine survivals of a decadent nobility, these shrinking, coquettish, clinging, distant, tearful, proud, explosive, half barbarous, altogether bewitching creatures. A suggestion here, a glimpse there, an exclamation, a flash of the eyes, and they are alive and real as few feminine creations in the fiction of any period. One may forget the story, but one may not forget Madame Delphine. If one would understand the secret of Cable's art, that Gallic lightness of touch, that subtle elision, that perfect balance between the suggested and the expressed, let him read the last chapter of *The Grandissimes*. It is a Cable epitome.

"Posson Jone'," "Jean-ah Poquelin," and *Madame Delphine*, which, despite its length and its separate publication, is a short story belonging to the *Old Creole Days* group, are among the most perfect of American short stories and mark the highest reach of Cable's art.

The Grandissimes, his first long romance, appeared in 1880. Never was work of art painted on broader canvas or with elements more varied and picturesque. Though centering in a little nook among the bayous, it contains all Louisiana. Everywhere perspectives down a long past: glimpses of the explorers, family histories, old forgotten wrongs, vendettas, survivals from a feudal past, wild traditions, superstitions. Grandissime and Fusilier, young men of the D'Iberville exploring party, get lost in the swamps. "When they had lain down to die and had only succeeded in falling to sleep, the Diana of the Tchoupitoulas, ranging the magnolia groves with bow and quiver, came upon them in all the poetry of their hope-forsaken strength and beauty, and fell sick of love." The love of this Indian queen begins the romance. Both eager to possess her, they can settle the matter only with dice. Fusilier wins and becomes the founder of a proud line, semibarbarous in its haughtiness and beauty, the Capulets to De Grapion's Montagues. The culmination comes a century later when the old feudal régime in Louisiana was closed by Napoleon and the remnants of the warring families were united according to the approved Montague-Capulet formula.

But the theme of the book is wider than this quarrel of families, wider than the conflict of two irreconcilable civilizations and the passing of the outworn. In a vague way it centers in the episode of Bras Coupé, the African king who refused to be a slave and held firm until his haughty soul was crushed out with inconceivable brutality. The cumulative and soul-withering power of an ancient wrong, the curse of a dying man which works its awful way until the pure love of innocent lovers removes it—it is *The House of the Seven Gables* transferred to the barbarous swamps of the Atchafalaya.

The strangeness of the book grows upon one as one reads. It is a book of lurid pictures—the torture and death of Bras Coupé, the murder of the *négresse* Clemence, which in sheer horror and brutal, unsparing realism surpasses anything in *Uncle Tom's Cabin*, anything indeed in the Russian realists. It is a book too with a monotone of fear: the nameless dread that comes of holding down a race by force, or as Joel C. Harris has phrased it, "that vague and mysterious danger that seemed to be forever lurking on the outskirts of slavery, ready to sound a shrill and ghostly signal in the impenetrable swamps and steal forth under the midnight stars to murder and rapine and pillage"; the superstitious thrill when at dead of night throbs up from a neighboring slave yard "the monotonous chant and machine-like time-beat of the African dance"; the horror of finding morning after morning on one's pillow voodoo warnings and ghastly death charms placed seemingly by supernatural hands. No one has ever surpassed Cable in making felt this uncanny side of the negro. His characterization of the voodoo quadroon woman Palmyre with her high Latin, Jaloff-African ancestry, her "barbaric and magnetic beauty that startled the beholder like the unexpected drawing out of a jeweled sword," her physical perfection—lithe of body as a tigress and as cruel, witching and alluring, yet a thing of horror, "a creature that one would want to find chained"—it fingers at one's heart and makes one fear.

And with all this strangeness, this flash after flash of vivid characterization, a style to match. "Victor Hugo," one exclaims often as one reads. Let us quote, say from chapter five. The stars are Cable's:

> There Georges De Grapion settled, with the laudable determination to make a fresh start against the mortifyingly numerous Grandissimes.
>
> "My father's policy was every way bad," he said to his spouse; "it is useless, and probably wrong, this trying to thin them out by duels; we will try another plan. Thank you," he added, as she handed his coat back to him, with the shoulder-straps cut off. In pursuance of the new plan, Madame De Grapion—the precious little heroine!—before the myrtles offered another crop of berries, bore him a boy not much smaller (saith tradition) than herself.
>
> Only one thing qualified the father's elation. On that very day Numa Grandissime (Brahmin-Mandarin de Grandissime), a mere child, received from Governor De Vaudreuil a cadetship.
>
> "Never mind, Messieurs Grandissime, go on with your tricks; we shall see! Ha! we shall see!"
>
> "We shall see what?" asked a remote relative of that family. "Will Monsieur be so good as to explain himself?"
>
> Bang! Bang!
> Alas, Madame De Grapion!
> It may be recorded that no affair of honor in Louisiana ever left a braver little widow.

It is French, too, in its sudden turns, its fragmentary paragraphs, its sly humor, its swift summings-up with an epigram:

> "Now, sir," thought he to himself, "we'll return to our senses."
> "Now I'll put on my feathers again," says the plucked bird.

But as one reads on one realizes more and more that this style comes from no mere imitation of a master: it is Creole; it is the style that is the counterpart of the Creole temperament. It is verisimilitude; it is interpretation.

Thus far the strength of the book; there are weaknesses as great. Cable failed, as Harte failed, as most of the masters of the short story have failed, in constructive power. The magnificent thesis of the romance is not worked out; it is barely suggested rather than made to dominate the piece. Moreover, the interest does not accumulate and culminate at the end. It is a rich mass of materials rather than a finished romance. The emphasis is laid upon characters, episodes, conditions, atmosphere, to the neglect of construction. From it Cable might have woven a series of perfect short stories: some parts indeed, like the tale of Bras Coupé, *are* complete short stories as they stand. The book is a gallery rather than a single work of art.

Dr. Sevier, 1885, marks the beginning of Cable's later style, the beginning of the decline in his art. The year before he had taken up his permanent residence in Massachusetts and now as a literary celebrity, with Boston not far, he became self-conscious and timid. His art had matured in isolation; there had been an elemental quality about it that had come from his very narrowness and lack of formal education. In the classic New England atmosphere the Gallic element, the naïve simplicity, the elfin charm that had made his early writings like no others, faded out of his art. It was as if Burns after the Kilmarnock edition had studied poetry at Oxford and then had settled in literary London. *Doctor Sevier* is not a romance at all; it is a realistic novel of the Howells type, a study of the Civil War period as it had passed under Cable's own eyes, with no plot and no culminating love interest. It is a running chronicle of ten years in the lives of John and Mary Richling, tedious at times, impeded with problem discussion and philosophizing. Its strength lies in its characterization: the Italian Ristofalo and his Irish wife are set off to the life; but why should the creator of Madame Delphine and Posson Jone' and Palmyre turn to Irish and Italian characterization? The story, too, has the same defects as *The Grandissimes:* it lacks proportion and balance. With a large canvas Cable becomes always awkward and ineffective. With *Bonaventure,* graphic as parts of it unquestionably are, one positively loses patience. Its plan is chaotic. At the end, where should come the climax of the plot, are inserted three long chapters telling with minute and terrifying realism the incidents of a flood in the canebrakes. It is magnificent, yet it is "lumber." It is introduced apparently to furnish background for the death of the "Cajun," but the "Cajun" is only an incidental figure in the book. To deserve such "limelight" he should have been the central character who had been hunted with increasing interest up to the end and his crime and his punishment should have been the central theme.

With *Madame Delphine* (1881) had closed the first and the great period in Cable's literary career. The second period was a period of miscellany: journalized articles on the history and the characteristics of the Creoles, on New Orleans and its life, on Louisiana, its history and traditions, on phases of social reform. Necessary as this work may have been, one feels inclined to deplore it.

When one has discovered new provinces in the realm of gold one does not well, it would seem, to lay aside his magic flute and prepare guide books to the region.

The New England atmosphere brought to life a native area in Cable. His mother had been of New England ancestry. Moral wrestlings, questions of reform, problems of conscience, were a part of his birthright. One feels it even in his earliest work: he had seen, we feel, the problem of *The Grandissimes* before he had found the story. After his removal to Northampton, Massachusetts, it may be said that reform work became his real profession. Not that we criticize his choice, for life ever is greater than mere art; we record it simply because it explains. He formed home culture clubs for the education and the esthetic culture of wage-earners, and conducted a magazine in the interest of the work; he interested himself actively in the cause of the negro; so actively, indeed, that after his *Silent South* and *The Negro Question* and the problem novel *John March, Southerner,* the South practically disowned him.

His third period begins, perhaps, with his novel *Strong Hearts* in 1899. The pen that so long had been dipped in controversy and journalism and philanthropic propaganda again essayed fiction, but it was too late. The old witchery was gone. His later novels, all his fiction indeed after *Madame Delphine,* with the exception perhaps of parts of *Bonaventure,* read as if written by a disciple of the earlier Cable. The verve, the sly humor, the Gallic finesse, the Creole strangeness and charm, have disappeared. There is a tightening in the throat as one reads the last page of *Madame Delphine,* there is a flutter of the heart as one reads the love story of Honoré and Aurora, but nothing grips one as he reads *The Cavalier.* A pretty little story, undoubtedly, but is it possible that the author of it once wrote "Posson Jone' " and "Jean-ah Poquelin"? And *Gideon's Band,* a romance with an attempt to win back the old witchery of style—it was all in vain. Why say more?

Cable as a short story writer, a maker of miniatures with marvelous skill of touch, was most successful perhaps with dainty femininities of the old régime. Once, twice, thrice the light of romance glowed upon his page. Then he became a reformer, a journalist, a man with a problem. But he who gave to American literature *Madame Delphine* and *Old Creole Days* need not fear the verdict of coming days. Already have these works become classics.

Notes

1. Lafcadio Hearn, "The Scenes of Cable's Romances," *Century Magazine,* 27 (November, 1883), 40.

[Review of *The Flower of the Chapdelaines*]

H. W. Boynton[*]

. . . We who are old codgers or of codgerly proximity, who recall as new books *The Grandissimes* and *Dr. Sevier* must hail as a delightful gift the grateful familiar delicacy and humour of *The Flower of the Chapdelaines*. With sure touch and inimitable grace, Mr. Cable has done a very difficult thing. For though this is a romance in the old setting, the old aristocratic Creole quarter in New Orleans, it is also a romance of this time, almost of this hour. Faded now are the glories of the *vieux carré*, scattered its ancient names, hemmed in its shabby mansions by tides of alien approach, Italians, Yankees, and worse. Yet a little corner remains, a little coterie in Royal Street, who, in humbler terms, maintain the old traditions and the old charm. Here still live, not as mere relics, that childlike ingenuousness, that fine feeling for beauty and dignity and the obligations of good blood and breeding, that exquisite sensitiveness to high quality in people and things, which enchanted us in *The Grandissimes* of blessed memory. And here, above all, in Aline Chapdelaine—with her tender beauty, her pride, her destiny of a single and great love—is the right descendant of those bewitching ladies of the older tales. Within the main story, with its slight yet sufficient action, is a fabric of briefer tales, linked together by a certain community of theme; and, by their origin, linking together fair Aline Chapdelaine and her southern but not Louisianian lover.

[*] Reprinted from *Bookman*, 47 (May, 1918), 347.

From an Older Time

Randolph Bourne°

Those of us who began our reading careers after 1900 are inclined, perhaps unjustly, to neglect the school of excellent writers who delighted the youth of our fathers and mothers. The eighties and nineties saw a very deliberate and serious attempt to found a "national" American literature, and that attempt deserves far more respect and investigation from those of us who pretend to be still wanting that very thing than we usually give it. The approach to this enterprise was sectional but not separatist, sectional in the sense that if each great region—New England, Virginia, the Tennessee mountains, Louisiana, California, the Western plains—were fittingly embodied in fiction, their distinctive types of personality and ways of speech artistically presented, the federated picture would produce us a veritable American contemporary literature, comparable in depth of life and beauty of pattern to the French and Russian material that we were beginning to admire. With this motive more or less at the bottom of their hearts, writers like Miss Jewett, Miss Wilkins, G. W. Cable, Bret Harte, Hamlin Garland, Thomas Nelson Page, and James Lane Allen worked conscientiously to catch and fix the distinctiveness of the life that each one knew. And over this school presided with unquestioned authority Mr. Howells, that incredible genius who had come from humble Ohio to capture the Brahmin citadel itself, and—when the kings had been gathered to their fathers—to reign in royal Cambridge himself. Mr. Howells himself was never consciously sectional; he conveyed the simple homeliness of that naive middle-class age which got itself recognized everywhere as broadly and pervasively "American." But it was in his mellow art and under his pontifical blessing that the school felt itself sustained and encouraged.

Of all these writers, Mr. Cable is the only one who continues to produce novels of the same quality and with the same motive. Those of his school who are not dead, have earned an honorable retirement in other fields. *Lovers of Louisiana* (Scribner; $1.50) comes to us from this fine veteran of seventy-five, with his unmistakable characteristics, after a literary career of much more than forty years. And, as if to show his perennial vigor, he has not gone lazily back to his Creole life of the past, but writes his romance about a very modern New Orleans of the last three or four years. This gives him the opportunity to show

° Reprinted from *Dial*, 65 (November 2, 1918), 363–65.

the Creole life in all its unfading charm, in the beautiful flower of a Rosalie Durel, in the courtliness and finesse of her banker father, and even in the wickedness of her wonderfully named cousin Zéphire. And it enables him to confront and then to mingle with this inexhaustible Creole theme the other molding element of modern New Orleans, the rather stiffly admirable Philip Castleton, with his sociological modernity and his critical love for the South. It is rather an astonishing thing for so veteran a novelist to do—to keep so much of the old flavor of romance and yet pour so much intellectuality into his work. The interest of the feat almost disarms our criticism of the artistic creation.

Mr. Cable has always blended his romance and sociology. From many of his contemporaries we could excusably have acquired our current legend that his generation was serenely oblivious of "social problems." But we could never have got it from him. From the very first he seems to have seen the South as an impartially criticizable society as well as the beloved Dixie of romance. And it was the South's very energetic dislike to be looked at in any such light that sent him long ago to make his home in Massachusetts. If it was his upbringing in ante-bellum New Orleans that gave him his tender love of her picturesque life, it must have been his Northern, and perhaps his partly German heritage, that gave him a fatally critical sense of the poisons that continued to beset the South's convalescence of reconstruction. To my Northern mind he seems the fairest of critics, with a justice that is sincerely tempered by love. His defense of the freedman, those pamphlets he wrote in the eighties about the "silent South" and the post-slavery problems, are restrained in tone and earnest with a high-minded persuasiveness. Only a South that would stand for nothing but a servile adulation of its ways could resist such a prophet. He spoke as a lover of Dixie, but it was just that plea Dixie would not listen to—that only through political fairness to the Negro would the South be released from the clutch of its "Negro problem."

In this latest novel Philip Castleton is Mr. Cable's attitude personified. Those Southerners who do not complain about Mr. Cable's strictures on the South put their complaints against him on the ground that he is too much the sociologist at all times and too little the artist. I do not know whether he wrote *John March, Southerner* (1894) to prove his impartiality. But it happens that this story, with its pugnacious and chivalrous young hero of reconstruction and its rascally Negro politicians, is one of his best novels. Mr. Cable was artist enough to draw vivid portraits which were the reverse of special pleading for the sociological idealisms he had been expressing. Into that book he got pretty nearly the entire life of a turbulent and proud Southern community in its welter of personal and political feuds and aspirations to develop its suddenly dis-covered resources. No mere apologia could have been so convincing.

But in *Lovers of Louisiana* the reader who missed the artist in Mr. Cable would have a better case. Philip rarely becomes more than an abstraction. If he is not exactly priggish, he is little more than a voice calling upon his great city to lead the South to modernity. He comes back from Princeton to take his place in the public life of the city. He gives a course at Tulane in political history. He delivers before a Negro society an address which is taken by his proud Creole rival for the hand of Rosalie as an apology for being a white man. He heads the Grand Jury, and menaces the mysteries of Creole clairvoyants and quadroon girls. In his high-minded courtship of Rosalie he invades the precincts of the finest Creole families closed till then to ideas, and not only saves her father from bankruptcy but wins him to a larger tolerance. Philip is always less a lover, less even a reformer, than he is a walking idea of what Mr. Cable would like the effective modern Louisianan young man to be. Even when he secures his Rosalie Durel—her whom he has once identified with his city, and his city with her—our romantic interest is less stirred by their union than by that of the two touching old figures behind them, the grandmère and the Judge, who find their belated happiness after forty years.

The romance that is embodied in Rosalie and her family scarcely compensates for the abstractions of Philip and the Castletons. Of course she is utterly charming, and charming in a more vigorous and intelligent way than Mr. Cable's other Creole heroines, such as the Nancanous. Her creator spares us much of the enormity of dialect, and is thus able to save both her and her really admirably drawn father from that belittling and patronage which seems the inevitable effect of dialect on the modern taste. In this book Mr. Cable's phonetic atrocities are so much milder than usual and his conversations so much briefer as to bring his story completely within the range of what, I take it, is our demand today. Nothing cuts off his school from us quite so much as that lavish cultivation of dialect. Our eye simply balks at untangling the paragraphs of a character like Narcisse in *Dr. Sevier*, so that that youth, who is so obviously intended to be a most amusing and winning figure, falls as flat as a Petrouchka who has lost his sawdust. Mr. Cable seems well aware of this change of taste. *Lovers of Louisiana* is brief and pointed in its style. It has few of those leisurely wastes of conversation which that school copied Mr. Howells in pouring out upon us. Mr. Howells himself was saved by the fact that even in his most prairie-like stretches there is always a faint amusingness, in its transcript, of the literal banality of life. The other writers are seldom so fortunate. When they use dialect they produce books which will, I think, become progressively unreadable.

Mr. Cable's romance is still old-fashioned, however modern his literary manner may have become. His generation also followed Mr. Howells in what H. L. Mencken calls a "kittenishness" in all references to love. *Lovers of Louisiana* sounds stilted; deprived of the flow of conversation, the romance is a little bare and angular. For a short book, it has a bewildering ingenuity of plot. So short a story will scarcely carry so much interweaving of themes without fatiguing the reader, and fatiguing him justifiably. At times the meaning almost sinks out of sight under the weight of the financial intrigue, and of the influence of the young people's romance upon the shy reunion of their elders. Here are not only a Creole grandmother and an "English" grandfather who should have married years before, but were kept apart by social prejudice. There is also a broken love-match between Rosalie's father and Philip's mother, which was prevented by the same beloved Aunt Castleton who now works against Philip's suit. Add to this a financial complication in which the Castletons rather quixotically attempt to make up to the Durels the losses suffered by the embezzlements of the wicked cousin Zéphire, rival suitor for Rosalie's hand, and get the aid of an ex-slave of the Durels as well as a Scotch banker who intrigues ceaselessly to bring Rosalie and Philip together. Weave into this the realization that this indebtedness stands between Rosalie and Philip, and you produce a network that at times baffles your intelligence. To the author these intricacies of property and family pride have a significance that a younger novelist would be inclined to yawn over. For the mere situation of these two families (not hostile, still unmingling, though each represents its kind of aristocratic best in the fascinating life of New Orleans) would have been motif enough. He would not have felt so much the need of elaboration. There would have been more to understand of the people themselves and less of the too neat intermingling of their objective fortunes.

Lovers of Louisiana therefore helps us to understand, I think, the limitations of that "national" school of fiction. For our interest today is vaguely in "life" itself rather than in the distinctive trappings of life, picturesque as they may be. We like to understand characters from their cradles to their graves. We pry around the intimacies of their souls in a way that seems almost ribald in the light of these scrupulous older novelties. It is not even "American" life we are after. We are on a restless search for "human life," almost as the thing in itself. We feel a craving to look beyond and through the particular type or the odd individual to some calm, immemorial current of personal truth. Any deliberately sectional portrayal comes to seem dangerously near an exploitation. The novelist is exploiting his material, digging out his marketable ore instead of making his human landscape reveal some significant veracity. This is the difference between books like *John March, Southerner* and *The Grandissimes*. In the latter one feels the exploiting touch. But fundamentally, to Mr. Cable's honor, it must be said that he does not deserve that stigma. He has felt deeply enough about his land to be its sound and bravely passionate counselor. And he has been artist enough not to let either this idealism nor his own very strict personal moralism impede his portrayal of all the sweetness and gayety of that life which his youth loved.

Citizen of the Union

Edmund Wilson[*]

The publication of *George W. Cable: His Life and Letters* by his daughter, Lucy Leffingwell Cable Bikle, reminds us how completely this once-popular novelist has now passed into eclipse. Few people read Cable today; and the critics never discuss him. Yet in the eighties and the nineties he was enormously read both at home and abroad; and he deserved the high standing he was given. The decline of Cable's reputation is, I believe, mainly due to the general lack of interest, on the part of the critics of the new generation, in the American literature of the period just behind them. We are rediscovering Irving Babbitt and Paul Elmer More, but we have not yet discovered John Jay Chapman; we leave Stephen Crane in half-shadow, and George Cable in complete eclipse.

The prevalent notion of Cable today seems to be that he was a romantic novelist, of a species now obsolete, who made a good thing of exploiting the sentiment and charm, the quaintness and picturesqueness, of a New Orleans long gone to decay. This idea seems, indeed, to some extent, to have been shared by the public who read Cable, that public for whom taste and intellect were represented by Richard Watson Gilder, the editor of the *Century Magazine*. When George Cable was presented with an honorary degree of Master of Arts by Yale, it was "with the desire of recognizing publicly the eminent success which you have achieved in embalming in literature a unique phase of American social life which is rapidly passing away." Yet Cable himself had no idea that he was engaged in embalming anything: he supposed himself to be dealing with the realities of contemporary life—and, in the work of his best years, this was true.

The New Orleans of George Cable's time—and even the New Orleans of today—is a laboratory where certain American situations present themselves, if not in a form necessarily more acute than elsewhere, at least in more vivid colors. Louisiana, originally French, was transferred in 1762 to Spain, with the result of arousing extreme hostility between the French and the Spanish inhabitants. At the beginning of the nineteenth century, it was transferred back from Spain to France, and then sold by Napoleon to the United States, with the result

[*] Reprinted from *The Shores of Light: A Literary Chronicle of the Twenties and Thirties* (New York: Farrar, Straus and Young, 1952), pp. 415–20. This review was first published, in a slightly different form, in the *New Republic*, 57 (Feb. 13, 1929), 352–53.

of provoking a new kind of hostility, this time between the original Latin Americans, Spanish and French, on the one hand, and the Anglo-Saxon Americans who had come in to take possession, on the other. At the same time, the mingling of the whites with the large Negro element of the population had resulted in a class of mulattoes who constituted a special problem. Thus, one found in New Orleans simultaneously in a concentrated field and in intensified form, the conflict of European nationalities, as between the Spanish and the French; the conflict of the Latins and the Anglo-Saxons; and the conflict of two totally different races, as between the Negroes and the whites. Add to this the sectional conflict at the time of the Civil War, of the American South with the North, a conflict felt so much more painfully and for so much longer a time after the war by the South than by the North. The whole American problem of diversity and unity was here, and no writer ever studied it more thoroughly or thought about it more intelligently than George Washington Cable did.

For Cable was essentially a sociologist. He was not in the least a fancier of lavender and old lace. He was a good deal closer to Upton Sinclair than he was to Myrtle Reed. He had a real sense of beauty, but there was too much of the Puritan in him—his mother had been a New Englander, and it was only comparatively late in life that Cable was able to make up his mind that the theater was not immoral—to allow him much to cultivate his sensibility. Though his books have their own sort of atmosphere, which seems to have enchanted his readers, it is certainly not the atmosphere of Cable's novels which appears most successful today. Compare one of Cable's Louisiana descriptions with a description of the same region by Lafcadio Hearn. The lush background that Hearn is so good at investing with color and glamor has a way of turning flat in Cable. Beneath the floridity of the Southerner and his courteous and affable manner, we catch a glimpse of William Wetmore Story and his statue of Cleopatra. And so, though Cable had a most remarkable, an almost unexcelled ear for human speech, though he reported it with the most scrupulous accuracy, he did little to make it attractive. Just as he listened with attention to the songs of birds and transcribed them into musical notation, so he studied the different varieties of the French, Spanish and Negro Creole dialects and the language of the Acadians, both English and French, with a scholarly exactitude that must be as valuable to the phonetician as it is forbidding to the ordinary reader. This rendering, with pitiless apostrophes, of these special pronunciations was complained of even in the period of Cable's greatest popularity, and it constitutes a formidable obstacle to appreciating him today.

Cable's own conception of his craft comes out plainly in certain of the letters included in this biography. Of *The Grandissimes*, he writes that the editors of *Scribner's*, in which it first appeared, did not know "that the work I should by and by send them was going to have any political character. But that was well-nigh inevitable. It was impossible that a novel written by me then should escape being a study in the fierce struggle going on around me, regarded in the light of that past history—those beginnings—which had so differentiated Louisiana civilization from the American scheme of public society. I meant to make *The Grandissimes* as truly a political work as it has ever been called. . . . My friends and kindred looked on with disapproval and dismay, and said all they could to restrain me. 'Why wantonly offend thousands of your own people?' But I did not intend to offend. I wrote as near to truth and justice as I knew how, upon questions that I saw must be settled by calm debate and cannot be settled by force or silence."

The Grandissimes was the first full-length instalment of Cable's anatomy of Southern society. He prepared at about the same time for the United States Census of 1880 a report on the "social statistics" of New Orleans which was specially commended by the authorities; and it was this blending of what may perhaps be taken as a New England respect for facts with a humanism quite alien to New England which left Louisiana, in Cable's writings, perhaps the most satisfactorily studied of nineteenth-century American communities. For Cable, who had never been in France, had read and spoken French all his life and who, brought up as a Presbyterian, had come to manhood in a Catholic community, could penetrate Louisiana in every layer and all directions.

In *The Grandissimes* Cable incorporated a story that he had never been able to sell to the "family" magazines of the period and that had consequently not been included in the popular *Old Creole Days*. The reason for rejecting this manuscript that had been given by George Parsons Lathrop, writing for William Dean Howells, then editor of the *Atlantic Monthly*, was "the unmitigatedly distressful effect of the story." This was the *Story of Bras-Coupé*, the adventures of an African king sold into slavery in the United States. When Bras-Coupé is brought to Louisiana and taken into the fields, and he first comes to understand that it is intended for him to work with common Negroes, he hits the foreman over the head with his hoe, picks up one of the other slaves and bites him in the leg and throws him away, and raises havoc till the overseer shoots him down. A woman slave, who speaks his language, is brought to interpret to him, and he instantly falls in love with her and allows himself to be ruled through her. He demands to marry her; and, on the night of his wedding, gets drunk and forgets his status; he knocks down his master, who has already resented being treated by him as king to king. He is brutally hunted to death. As a study of what man can make of man, of the deformation of human relations by unnatural social institutions, the story of Bras-Coupé is as powerful in its smaller scope as *Uncle Tom's Cabin* itself. With the story of Mme. Lalauré in *Strange True Stories of Louisiana* and some other detached episodes, it almost puts Cable in the class of the great Russian chroniclers of serfdom.

For it is not the love stories in Cable's fiction that really interest Cable: it is the social and political situations. It is human life throttled in the web of society that arouses all his emotion, at the same time that he can trace with nicety every one of the tangled strands and explain the necessities that have strung it. One of the features of this biography is a hitherto unpublished account by Cable of the development of his political ideas. He had fought in the Confederate Army, but had afterwards come to unorthodox conclusions in regard to the Negro question and the relations of the North and the South. About the time that he began to give public expression to his opinions on these subjects, he moved his family from New Orleans to New England. The real occasion for this change of residence was the ill-health of Cable's wife; but, in spite of the fact that he made it a rule never to publish an opinion in the North which he had not first put forward in person from a public platform in the South, returning there expressly for the purpose, there can be no doubt that Cable's native city was no longer very comfortable for him. He was one of the clearest-minded Americans of his time, and in the South, after the Civil War, so detached and realistic an intelligence was uncommon and unwelcome. It was not common or welcome anywhere. Cable understood both South and North; the American and the European; the white man and the Negro; and he would not become the partisan of any of them. What he believed in were democratic principles of the kind that he understood the American Republic to have been founded to put into practice; and he devoted all his study and art to the attempt to impress their importance on a public that were occupied for the most part—during our period of industrial development after the Civil War—with aims that ran counter to these. The moral of Cable's stories is always that distinctions between human beings on social or national or racial grounds must be regarded as merely provisory; that there can never be a true equilibrium, that there can only be conflict and agony, where such discriminations are used as pretexts for unequal privilege.

George W. Cable: History and Politics

Philip Butcher*

George W. Cable, apostate Southerner, is commonly considered in American literary history as a writer worthy of attention solely for his novel, *The Grandissimes*, and his classic short stories, *Old Creole Days*, which exploit the fabulous New Orleans and the old Creole Louisiana which were his chief provinces in fiction. The practice has been to dismiss Cable as an early, though able, writer in the local color tradition, a literary school which was the precursor of regionalism and realism but which was itself romantic.[1] Sociologists and astute modern critics have been less prone to confine this prophet to so restricted a pigeonhole. Gradually Cable's virtues as an early realist of the Howells type are being recognized and it is apparent that those virtues are most evident in his extensive portrayal of the Negro. Sterling A. Brown points out that Cable "is one of the finest creators of Negro character in the nineteenth century."[2] A careful reading of all Cable's fiction—not merely the best known pieces—bears out this contention.[3]

But Cable wrote a great deal of non-fiction which cannot be overlooked in evaluating his work and assessing his attitude and influence. In respect to the Negro, his fiction and non-fiction supplement one another. He wrote two books specifically on the Negro problem and published several articles on the subject in a period of reaction when his liberal views were particularly unpopular. His history, *The Creoles of Louisiana*, though largely concerned with the Creole, is also a revealing treatment of the Negro in ante-bellum Louisiana. Cable's non-fiction is a vigorous expression of political doctrines which are evident but less obvious in his fiction.

The Creoles of Louisiana, published in 1884, is an elaboration of the census study Cable wrote with George E. Waring, Jr., and is one of his most important works. Though it relies in part on the work of Charles Gayarré, Creole historian, it involves much original research and is still one of the important references for any modern scholarship in its field.[4] Cable gives full credit to the role of the Negro soldiers in the early wars and to the field hands and artisans who helped build and support the very society which oppressed them.

*Reprinted from *Phylon: The Atlanta University Review of Race and Culture*, 9 (June, 1948), 137–45, by permission of *Phylon* and the author.

The Black Code, the cruelties of slavery, the occasional revolts, the exploitation of the freedman—all subjects largely ignored by the historians of his day—are presented without apology, defense, or distortion. Only the Civil War and Reconstruction, which would have required a book in themselves, are omitted. With this exception, the history is a prose summation of all that Cable wrote in his fiction about a subject which at one time was regarded as almost his personal literary property. The scenes of his stories and many of his major characters are easily recognized in the colorful incidents and historical figures in the book, so typical of all the author's work in its thorough scholarship, humanitarian approach, political progressivism, and Victorian moralism.

Cable's treatment of and relationship to the Creole is a major subject outside the province of this study but, since his many quadroon characters are depicted as closer to the Creole physically, culturally, and psychologically than to the Negro (in which case the identity is considered to be only that of an unjustly similar status), the subject requires passing attention here.

It is frequently supposed that Cable intentionally glamorized the Creoles and that his revelations of the discreditable aspects of their character and society were accidental or incidental. One modern writer comments: "only the virtues are really portrayed, evil being dismissed with platitudes."[5] Such a view, all too common, is not supported by the non-fiction and is not a reasonable conclusion from a careful reading of the fiction. On the contrary, Cable seems to have been concerned only with presenting the Creoles as they really were and must have known his unflattering portrait would not win their approval. While he recognized that Creole society was charmingly picturesque and may have had a romantic affection for it in an abstract way, he deplored its decadence and bestowed on it little respect. If he praised its quaint virtues, he did not condone its shortcomings and he distinctly condemned its vices. Evidently he considered Creole resentment to his work natural and unimportant. He made no effort to appease it.

An excellent instance of disregard for Creole approval can be seen in his definition of the term:

> What is a Creole? Even in Louisiana the question would be variously answered. The title did not here first belong to the descendants of Spanish, but of French settlers. But such a meaning implied a certain excellence of origin, and so came early to include any native, of French or Spanish descent by either parent, whose non-alliance with the slave race entitled him to social rank. Later, the term was adopted by—not conceded to—the natives of mixed blood, and is still so used among themselves. . . . Besides French and Spanish, there are even, for convenience of speech, "colored" Creoles; but there are no Italian, or Sicilian, nor any English, Scotch, Irish, or "Yankee" Creoles, unless of parentage married into, and themselves thoroughly proselyted in, Creole society. Neither Spanish nor American domination has taken from the Creoles their French vernacular. This, also, is part of the title; and, in fine, there seems to be no more serviceable definition of the Creoles of Louisiana than this: that they are the French-speaking, native portion of the ruling class.
>
> There is no need to distinguish between the higher and humbler grades of those from whom they sprang. A few settlers only were persons of rank and station. Many were the children of casket-girls, and many were of such stock as society pronounces less than nothing. . . .[6]

Creoles protested that in all Cable's stories there is only one Creole hero, Honoré Grandissime. Unabashed, the author continued to restrict his heroes to American Southerners—and continued to use Creole heroines. For Cable, this practice was justified, if not necessitated, by his evaluation of Creole character:

> The women were fair, symmetrical, with pleasing features, lively, expressive eyes, well-rounded throats, and superb hair; vivacious, decorous, exceedingly tasteful in dress, . . . They were much superior to the men in quickness of wit, and excelled them in amiability and in many other good qualities. . . . [The men] are said to have been coarse, boastful, vain; and they were, also, deficient in energy and application, without well-directed ambition, unskilful in handicraft—doubtless through negligence only—and totally wanting in that community feeling which begets the study of reciprocal rights and obligations, and reveals the individual's advantage in the promotion of the common interest. Hence, the Creoles were fonder of pleasant fictions regarding the salubrity, beauty, good order, and advantages of their town, than of measures to justify their assumptions. With African slavery they were, of course, licentious, and they were always ready for the duelling-ground; yet it need not seem surprising that a people so beset by evil influences from every direction were generally unconscious of a reprehensible state of affairs, and preserved their self-respect and a proud belief in their moral excellence.[7]

The Creole charge that the author "conveyed to Eastern readers the idea that the Creoles have a strain of Negro blood"[8] may have been based as much on his authoritative non-fiction as on his stories. While such stories as "'Tite Poulette" and "Madame Delphine" were more widely known, the non-fiction was more outspoken.

> The creoles of New Orleans and the surrounding delta are a handsome, graceful, intelligent race, of a decidedly Gallic type; though softened in features, speech, and carriage, and somewhat relaxed in physical and mental energies by the enervating influences that blow from the West Indies and the Spanish Main. Their better class does not offer to the eye that unpleasant evidence of gross admixture of race which distinguishes those Latin-American communities around the borders of the adjacent seas; and the name they have borrowed from those regions does not necessarily imply *any more than it excludes*, a departure from a pure double line of Latin descent.[9]

The same analytic approach which Cable applies to the Creole in his non-fiction is shown in his picture of the Negro. He does not gloss over ignorance and indolence of slaves or licentiousness and caste reasoning of quadroons. Though he understands the extenuating circumstances involved, Cable makes no sentimental apology.

> The coloured population [of New Orleans], notwithstanding the presence among it of that noted quadroon class which has enjoyed a certain legal freedom for many generations, has not greatly improved since the date of emancipation. A conventional system of caste cuts them off from the stimulating hope of attaining social rank and confines them closely to servile employments. The probability seems to be that their decided elevation must wait upon their acquisition of material wealth, an achievement which the conditions mentioned and some inherent deficiencies of race tend to make extremely difficult.[10]

Cable was well aware that the "legal freedom" the quadroon caste had experienced for many generations was largely a fiction.

> A poor freedom it was, indeed: To have f.m.c. or f.w.c. tacked in small letters upon one's name perforce and by law, that all might know that the bearer was not a real freeman or freewoman, but only a free man (or woman) of color,—a title that could not be indicated by capital initials; to be the unlawful mates of luxurious bachelors, and take their pay in muslins, embroideries, prunella, and good living, taking with them the loathing of honest women and the salacious derision of the blackmoor; . . . to fall heir to property by sufferance, not by law; to be taxed for public education and not allowed to give that education to one's own children, to be shut out of all occupations that the master class could reconcile with the vague title of gentleman; to live in the knowledge that the law pronounced "death or imprisonment at hard labor for life" against whoever should be guilty of "writing, printing, publishing, or distributing anything having a tendency to create discontent among the free colored population": that it threatened death against whosoever should utter such things in private conversation. . . .[11]

Though Cable's emphasis in his fiction is usually on the quadroon, his knowledge of the Negro slave, the field hand, was exceptionally detailed and extensive.

> These [field hands] came in troops [to the Place Congo]. See them; . . . tall, well-knit Senegalese from Cape Verde, black as ebony, with intelligent, kindly eyes and long, straight, shapely noses; Mandingoes, from the Gambia River, lighter of color, of cruder form, and a cunning that shows in the countenance; whose enslavement seems especially a shame, their nation the "merchants of Africa," dwelling in towns, industrious, thrifty, skilled in commerce and husbandry, and expert in the working of metals, even to silver and gold; and Foulahs, playfully miscalled "Poulards,"—fat chickens,—of goodly stature, and with a perceptible rose tint in the cheeks; and Sosos, famous warriors, dexterous with the African targe; and in contrast to these, with small ears, thick eyebrows, bright eyes, flat, upturned noses, shining skin, wide mouths and white teeth, the negroes of Guinea, true and unmixed, from the Gold Coast, the Slave Coast, and the Cape of Palms—not from the Grain Coast; the English had that trade. See them come! Popoes, Cotocolies, Fidas, Socoes, Agwas, short, copper-colored Mines—what havoc the slavers did make!— and from interior Africa others equally proud and warlike: fierce Nagoes and Fonds; tawny Awassas; Iboes, so light-colored that one could not tell them from mulattoes but for their national tattooing; and the half-civilized and quick-witted, but ferocious Arada, the original Voodoo worshiper. . . .[12]

The Creoles of Louisiana and *Strange True Stories of Louisiana*, the volume of stories which Cable collected and edited and from which so many later novelists and popular historians have culled exotic plot incidents and characters, contain many references to the cruelties of slavery and the sadistic punishments inflicted on the spirited blacks who tried to escape from bondage or revolt against it. And however much he bemoaned the status of the quadroon, Cable knew that the field hand's legal position was far worse:

> Even the requirement of the law was only that he should not have less than a barrel of corn—nothing else,—a month, nor get more than thirty lashes to the twenty-four hours.[13]

But it was not Cable's candid analysis of Creole society nor his persistent condemnation of slavery as morally wrong and politically inexpedient that led to his vilification by the American South. "His descriptions of the Creoles had been received with but mild remonstrances; his merciless scourging of the institution of slavery had been read with surprising calmness; but when he rebelled against what he considered unjust treatment of the black man today, a wave of bitter indignation swept over the entire Southern States."[14] The three articles with which Cable's rebellion began, "The Convict Lease System in the Southern States," "The Freedman's Case in Equity," and "The Silent South," all of which first appeared in *Century*, were collected and published as *The Silent South* in 1885. The Civil Rights Act, a detailed, positive measure intended to make the Fourteenth Amendment effective, had been invalidated by the U.S. Supreme Court in 1883 and the South had established absolute white supremacy. Cable's book, and particularly the title essay, "was a broadminded and brilliantly reasoned protest against the reinstitution of a kind of slavery through segregation."[15] The extreme Southern resentment which was aroused by Cable's militant arguments has abated little over the years, largely because his remarks were so vigorous and so advanced that they are still pertinent to the situation in the South. They are still quoted by those who urge the Negro's integration in the American democracy.[16]

In "The Freedman's Case in Equity," Cable speaks of the freedmen as "six millions of people from one of the most debased races on the globe"[17] (a judgment he was later to qualify), but he pleads for a change in the South's traditional sentiments.

> First, then, what are these sentiments? Foremost among them stands the idea that he [the Negro] is of necessity an alien. He was brought to our shores a naked, brutish, unclean, captive, pagan savage, to be and remain a kind of connecting link between man and the beasts of burden. . . . As a social factor he was intended to be as purely zero as the brute at the other end of the plow-line. The occasional mingling of his blood with that of the white man worked no change in sentiment; . . . Generations of American nativity made no difference; his children and his children's children were born in sight of our door, yet the old notion held fast. He increased to vast numbers, but it never wavered. He accepted our dress, language, religion, all the fundamentals of our civilization, and became forever expatriated from his own land; still he remained to us, an alien. Our sentiment went blind. It did not see that gradually, here by force and there by choice, he was fulfilling a host of conditions that earned at least a solemn moral right to that naturalization which no one at first had dreamed of giving him. Frequently he even bought back the freedom of which he had been robbed, became a tax-payer, and at times an educator of his children at his own expense; but the old idea of alienism passed laws to banish him, his wife, and children by thousands from the State, and threw him into loathsome jails as a common felon for returning to his nativeland.[18]

In "The Silent South," an extension of his arguments and a reply to Southerners who accused him of advocating social equality, Cable says: "Social equality is a fool's dream. The present writer wants quite as little of it as the most fervent traditionalist of the most fervent South."[19] He speaks of the foolishness of forcibly holding apart by segregation "two races which really have no social affinity at all."[20] He points out that what he had advocated was civil rights, not social rights.

> This attitude [the South's determination to limit the Negro to second class citizenship] in us, with our persistent mistaking his civil rights for social claims, this was the tap-root of the whole trouble. For neither would *his* self respect yield; and not because he was so unintelligent and base, but because he was so intelligent and aspiring as, in his poor way, he was, did he make this the cause of political estrangement. . . .[21]

Cable ridicules the Democratic party's inconsistent attitude on the Negro and says that no party or class has the right "to fasten arbitrarily upon any other class of citizens a *civil status* from which no merit of intelligence, virtue, or possessions can earn extraction."[22]

> It is widely admitted that we are vastly the superior race in everything—as a race. But is every colored man inferior to every white man in character, intelligence, and property? Is there no "responsible and steadfast element" at all among a people who furnish 16,000 school-teachers and are assessed for $91,000,000 worth of taxable property? Are there no poor and irresponsible whites? So, the color line and the line of character, intelligence, and property frequently cross each other. . . .[23]

"The Convict Lease System in the Southern States," an extension of the attack on Southern prisons and asylums which Cable had begun in *Dr. Sevier*, his second novel, is partly a comparison of the length and type of sentences and the general treatment of Negro and white criminals. Cable demonstrates that the Negro's punishment is often unjustly severe, simply because he is a Negro.

A modern Southern scholar states that although Cable admitted Northern mistreatment of the Negro he did not attack that injustice with the crusader's zeal which he applied to similar instances in the South.[24] Such charges were hurled at Cable in his own time and he replied:

> The North, the East, the West, shall never find in me a champion of any error in them. If I do not enlarge upon the presence of race prejudice there, it is because I see their best people recognizing, lamenting, and steadily crowding out the wicked error. Moreover, I find but half a million dark sufferers from this error in all the North. There are twelve times that number in the South. Meanwhile I see in the South the seat of the contagion, and her intelligent but deluded people alternately denying and boasting its presence, and openly proposing to perpetuate it, against the peace of the nation and their own good name, happiness and prosperity.[25]

In *The Negro Question*, a collection of political essays published in 1890, Cable further altered his views on Negro inferiority. He says in the article which gives the book its title: "For all that is known the black is 'an inferior race,' though how, or how permanently inferior, remains unproved."[26] This is probably Cable's best single essay on the Negro. It indicates a sound knowledge of the causes of the Civil War and presents a clear analysis of the reconstruction period, a notable intellectual achievement for a man who as a youth had served with conviction and distinction as a Confederate soldier.

But in this essay Cable does not argue the old issues; his concern here is with the plight of the Negro in the South *after* Reconstruction. He observes that "Emancipation had destroyed private, but it had not disturbed public subjugation. The ex-slave was not a free man; he was only a free negro."[27] He calls discrimination "a permanent ignominious distinction on account of ancestry, made in public, by strangers and in the enjoyment of common public rights . . . an insult or an injury"[28] whether or not it involves bodily discomfort, since separate accommodations cannot be equal. And he concludes that Negroes "are learning one of the worst lessons class rule can teach them—exclusive, even morbid, pre-occupation in their rights as a class, and inattention to the general affairs of their communities, their States and the Nation."[29]

Cable's social consciousness, his recognition that the Negro was not alone in being exploited and under-privileged, is evident in "National Aid to Southern Schools."

> I do not consider the education of the lower masses in the South [which he advocates in this article] a cure for all the ills of Southern society, but I fail to see how they can be cured without it. . . .[30]

He establishes the essential identity of the plight of the Negro and the poor white:

> Whatever we say with regard to illiteracy of blacks in the South applies to the illiteracy of whites also, since they are both fruit of the same tree, whose root drew its nourishment from a moral error [slavery] as wide as the nation.[31]

In "What Shall the Negro Do?" Cable continues his attack on segregation:

> But the Negro's grievance is, that the discriminations against him are more and more unbearable the better public citizen he is or tries to be; that they are impediments not to the grovelings of his lower nature, but to the aspirations of his higher; that as long as he is content to travel and lodge as a ragamuffin, frequent the vilest places of amusement, laze about the streets, shun the public library and the best churches and colleges, and neglect every political duty of his citizenship, no white man could be much freer than he finds himself; but that the farther he rises above such life as this the more he is galled and tormented with ignominious discriminations made against him as a public citizen, both in custom and by law; and finally, that as to his mother, his wife, his sister, his daughter, these encouragements to ignoble, and discouragements to nobler life are only crueler in their case than in his own.[32]

"What Makes the Color Line?" concedes virtues to the Negro's political activity during Reconstruction and scoffs at those who feared that, given the right to do so, he would vote along purely racial lines.

> The Negroes never did and do not now draw a strict color line in politics. Even in reconstruction days, when everything favored Negro supremacy, the Negroes generally entrusted the public offices of county and State to white men. And, speaking for Virginia, even as late in 1878–82, when the party of which the Negroes were the main strength had absolute control of the State, almost every office, from United States Senator to clerks in the State Capitol, was given to white men, and white men were elected to Congress, and to the State Legislature, by unquestioned Negro majorities.[33]

"The Southern Struggle for Pure Government" elaborates on the good intentions and many successes of the Reconstruction governments and on the failure of the conservative governments which displaced them. Cable stresses the similarity of interests of Negroes and poor whites and urges improved educational facilities for all the South's poor.

The above excerpts from *The Negro Question* do not fully represent the logical, penetrating detail with which Cable treated the subject. The strength of his arguments, the extent of his research, and the validity of his contentions can only be suggested here. The essays show Cable to have been a far-sighted liberal much in advance of the general political thought of his day, a lonely and uncomfortable inheritor of the spirit and ideology of the abolitionists.

Cable spent his youth and early manhood in the South and he studied the region and the Negro thoroughly. His knowledge was not limited to the Creole Louisiana which he portrayed so effectively. That other aspects of the Southern scene receive so little stress in his fiction results from his inability to suit such robust materials to his limited, delicate technique. Cable's non-fiction treatment of Reconstruction is far superior to that he attempted in *John March, Southerner*, one of the earliest novels on the period. But every contention he advanced in his political essays is at least implied in his stories and novels. "All that he . . . said in 'The Silent South' and 'The Negro Question' is potentially present in his fiction."[34]

Cable's concern for the Negro is moral and intellectual; his conversion to a progressive point of view was slow and had little or nothing to do with his emotional reaction to the black man. His unpublished article, "My Politics,"[35] traces the gradual emancipation from the racial attitudes of his native South, and the logical development and growth of a democratic spirit can be followed very readily in his fiction and political writings. His interest in the Negro led to a sympathetic understanding of the exploitation of the poor white and the immigrant. He wrote acute articles about the plight of these peoples and, through the Home-Culture Club which he organized in Northampton and headed for many years, he exerted personal efforts to integrate the immigrant into American culture. But there is no indication that he felt an emotional attachment for them, anymore than he did for the Negro, and he made relatively little use of them in his fiction.

Whether Cable's realistic picture of Negro life in his fiction is motivated most by the crusader's zeal, the intellectual's dispassionate insight, or the humanitarian's benevolence, it is clear that it has its basis in careful observation, study, and unprejudiced analysis, most explicitly evidenced in his historical and political writing.

Notes

1. *The Cambridge History of American Literature* (New York: Macmillan, 1944), II, 383.

2. *The Negro in American Fiction* (Washington: Associates in Negro Education, 1937), p. 67.

3. For the treatment of Cable's portrayal of Negro life see Charles Philip Butcher, *George W.*

Cable: Early Realist of Negro Life (Unpublished M. A. thesis) (Washington: Howard University, 1947). Winifred Lee Bonfoey's study, *George Washington Cable's Treatment of the Negro* (Unpublished M. A. thesis) (Durham, N. C.: Duke University, 1937), ignores the portrayal of quadroons and octoroons, evidently assuming that they are not Negroes, and omits reference to nonfiction and to five novels and some short stories which contain Negro characters. The work is argumentative rather than revealing.

4. Cable's qualifications as a historian were attacked in his day, particularly by the Creoles, apparently without legitimate justification. Practically all the derogatory remarks made about Creoles in *The Creoles of Louisiana* had been made by other men, including Creoles, and went unattacked. "Cable alone united all uncomplimentary opinions." Rosary Vera Nix, *Creole vs. Cable: or Creoles of Louisiana and George Washington Cable* (Unpublished M. A. thesis) (New York: Columbia University, 1936), pp. 64–65.

Cable was one of the twelve members, including Gayarré, who incorporated the Louisiana Historical Society in 1877. (It seems to have been organized about 1836.) His name was still on the society's rolls in 1888. Cecile Willink, "The Louisiana Historical Society Fifty Years Ago," *Louisiana Historical Quarterly,* 7 (October, 1924), 667–71.

5. W. Adolphe Roberts, *Lake Pontchartrain* (New York: Bobbs-Merrill, 1946), p. 281.

6. *The Creoles of Louisiana* (New York: Charles Scribner's Sons, 1884), pp. 41–42.

7. *The Creoles of Louisiana*, p. 139.

8. Alexander Nicholas DeMenil, *The Literature of the Louisiana Territory* (St. Louis, Mo.: St. Louis News, 1904), p. 217.

9. "New Orleans," *Encyclopedia Britannica* (9th ed., 1890), 17, 404. Italics mine. In all other cases the italics are those of the author.

Although Cable was vilified in his time for writing about intermarriage and miscegenation and was charged with implying that "the Creoles have a strain of Negro blood," he is widely quoted— and mis-quoted—today to support the contention that the term Creole "is never used in connection with persons of mixed white-and-Negro blood." See Hamilton Basso, "Boom Town, Dream Town," *Holiday,* 3 (February, 1948), 31.

10. "New Orleans," *Encyclopedia Britannica*, p. 405.

11. "Creole Slave Songs," *Century Magazine,* 31 (April, 1886), 811. The title of this article should not be understood as referring to slaves who were themselves Creole; no such implication was intended. "At length the spirit of commerce saw the money value of so honored a title [i.e. Creole], and broadened its meaning to take in any creature or thing of variety or manufacture peculiar to Louisiana that might become an object of sale: as Creole ponies, chickens, cows, shoes, eggs, wagons, baskets, cabbages, Negroes, etc." *The Creoles of Louisiana*, pp. 41–42.

Hamilton Basso, using the above as a basic point of departure, modernizes the contention "There are Creole Negroes, however, so-called because they speak a French patois evolved by their ancestors, and there are also Creole onions, tomatoes, oranges, and horses." "Boom Town, Dream Town."

12. "The Dance in Place Congo," *Century Magazine,* 31 (February, 1886), 522. This article, like "Creole Slave Songs," is primarily devoted to Creole slave songs and contains both words and music of several pieces from Cable's collection. He sang some of these songs on his reading tours. He understood the importance of studying and preserving these examples of folk culture; he recommended that other scholars continue his work on Creole slave songs and dialect and make similar studies of other folk groups in the nation. Cable's two articles have been starting points and references for much of the important work done in folk culture in recent years.

13. "The Dance in Place Congo."

14. Carl Holliday, *A History of Southern Literature* (New York: Neale Publishing Co., 1906), p. 378.

15. [Thomas Sancton], "A Note on Cable and His Times," *Survey Graphic,* 36 (January, 1947), 28.

16. See Isabel Cable Manes, ed., *A Southerner Looks at Negro Discrimination: Selected Writings of George W. Cable* (New York: International Publishers, 1946) and "A Voice from the Past—1885," excerpts from "The Silent South" by George W. Cable, *Survey Graphic*, 36 (January, 1947), 27–28.

17. *The Silent South* (New York: Charles Scribner's Sons, 1885), p. 3.

18. *The Silent South*, pp. 6–7.

19. *The Silent South*, p. 52.

20. *The Silent South*, p. 52.

21. *The Silent South*, p. 47.

22. *The Silent South*, p. 54.

23. *The Silent South*, p. 29.

24. Thomas Griffith Pugh, *George W. Cable: A Critical Biography* (Unpublished Ph.D. dissertation) (Nashville, Tenn.: Vanderbilt University, 1944), p. 220.

25. "Is It Sectional or National?" Open Letter, *Century Magazine*, 32 (October, 1886), 963.

26. *The Negro Question* (New York: Charles Scribner's Sons, 1890), p. 11. The essays observe no uniformity in treating "Negro" as a proper noun. Sometimes it is capitalized, sometimes it is not. This practice was common in the period.

27. *The Negro Question*, p. 34.

28. *The Negro Question*, p. 10.

29. *The Negro Question*, p. 51.

30. *The Negro Question*, p. 63.

31. *The Negro Question*, p. 65.

32. *The Negro Question*, p. 67–68.

33. *The Negro Question*, p. 113.

34. Henry C. Vedder, *American Writers of To-Day* (New York: Silver, Burdette, 1894), p. 270.

35. Quoted in Lucy Leffingwell Cable Bikle, *George W. Cable: His Life and Letters* (New York: Charles Scribner's Sons, 1928), pp. 155–65; passim.

George W. Cable, Novelist and Reformer

Arlin Turner°

Of George W. Cable's dozen volumes of fiction, the first three are on a plane of excellence which he never reached again. His literary reputation rests primarily on these three books, all published by 1884—the eight stories collected into *Old Creole Days* and two novels of New Orleans, *The Grandissimes* and *Dr. Sevier*. In explaining the deterioration of his literary art in the fiction he published in the next three decades, historians of American literature are likely to say in substance that before 1884 Cable wrote a volume of excellent stories and two powerful novels; then he became embroiled in social controversy, and the reformer destroyed the artist.

The story of Cable's career as a novelist and as a reformer does not wholly support this assertion. If in telling the story an attempt is made to relate the quality of his fiction to the varying intensity of his zeal for reform over a period of forty-five years, it provides a comment on several aspects of the novelist's relations to his times. Cable was an active reformer much of his life; he succeeded in some of his efforts and failed in others; everything he wrote was consciously didactic, and some of his fiction was first and avowedly social criticism. Some of his stories and one of his novels approached greatness; others fell far short.

Cable was a reformer by temperament and by deliberate intention long before writing his first story. In the grim, caustic years after Appomattox he witnessed at close hand in New Orleans a social and political order in upheaval. According to his statement later in life, his views crystallized in this period of turmoil and tense struggle for survival. He possessed a religious devotion and a sympathy for the debased and dispossessed which prompted him to begin working in his church and its mission school, where the poor of the city were instructed in cleanliness, cooking, and sewing as well as in Christianity. Two years as newspaper reporter and columnist added to his knowledge of the issues being fought out in the South and intensified his determination to crusade for general social betterment. He developed the habit of reducing every question to ethical considerations; while others debated technicalities of legality or constitutionality, he sought the ethical and moral answers; he thought it would be

° Reprinted from *South Atlantic Quarterly*, 48 (October, 1949), 539–45.

foolish to contend that laws or constitutions could not be brought into line. Thus, in a time when the very sills of the Southern social, economic, and political structure were awash, he did not hesitate to question inherited attitudes and established institutions.

At the same time Cable had occasion to study and write newspaper articles on early New Orleans. He came to see all history as of one pattern; in old newspapers and documents in the archives he followed the development of traditions and beliefs still powerful in the South. All combined to produce in him by the early 1870's a consuming resentment of what he considered to be great moral wrongs fostered by cherished institutions and attitudes. In consequence, he spliced together the history of his region, both before and after the war, not at all as might have been expected of a twice-wounded Confederate soldier and the son of a slaveholder, but instead as one sincerely contrite for the wrongs of the society to which he belonged and eager to right those wrongs by conscious effort.

With these thoughts and feelings boiling within him, Cable began writing stories. He was aware from the beginning of the attractive materials he had within his reach and was groping for an artistic method of employing those materials; but we have his own word for it that he wrote his first story out of compelling moral indignation. The fact that the reader of "'Tite Poulette," for example, or "Madame Delphine," may not realize that such intense feeling lay back of them is not a denial of the feeling but rather a testimony to the author's skill in fusing the social criticism and the essential elements of the stories.

Into the fabric of T' ₂ Grandissimes, his second book and his best novel, Cable wove much the se   e resentment and the same protest, with but slightly less subtlety than in the stories. Central in the novel is the episode of Bras Coupé, which as a separate story Richard Watson Gilder had thought "too unmitigatedly unpleasant" for Scribner's Monthly. Though this tragic story of an African prince in slavery is only an episode, not integral to the plot, it is the key to the meaning of the whole novel; it invokes a backdrop of tragic wrong against which the characters, including quadroons and free men of color, act out their roles in the plot.

Pained as he was in contemplating the past of the Negro in America and the future that appeared to be in the making for him, eager as he was to acknowledge the wrongs and to condemn attitudes which left no room for redress, Cable realized there was no ready solution of the intricate problems involved. Hence it must have pleased him to discover through a term of grand jury duty an area in which he could crusade for social betterment without attacking the baffling questions related to the freedmen. He found staggering abuses in the prisons and asylums of New Orleans and launched at once into a program for relieving them. In this effort, which used up much of his time for two years, he found himself supported actively by the city newspapers and by hundreds of citizens, who were willing to follow his leading and to spend both money and energy on the program. He had the satisfaction of seeing unexpectedly sweeping accomplishments, of receiving enthusiastic acclaim locally and recognition nationally. From this local project Cable was drawn, as he had not intended to be, into a study of the convict lease system then in vogue in the Southern states. He read a paper on the subject before a meeting of the National Conference of Charities and later published it in the *Century Magazine*.

Dr. Sevier, Cable's second novel, was planned and written in the years when prison reform absorbed his thought. He began it as a novelette which would assail the medievalism of the New Orleans jails. After it had grown into a novel and other matter had crowded the treatment of prison life into a few chapters, Cable still thought of it as a prison story. The preliminary drafts of the novel together with the correspondence between the author and his editors show an obsession with concrete reforms not discernible in the book as it was finally published, though the didactic purpose is apparent throughout. It seems remarkable, in fact, that the book became anything more than a reform tract. The prompting Cable had from his publishers was partly responsible, no doubt, but he had already shown himself able to give to the specific and immediate a universal significance without lessening the force of his ethical purpose.

Thus by 1884 Cable's literary achievement was considerable. Besides opening up a new vein of local materials, he had brought literary realism to the South. He had employed the actual, highly varied speech of the different racial and national mixtures so effectively that he had overcome the prejudices of both editors and readers against dialect. He had broken with tradition in writing of the lower classes of society and in broaching the problems related to the presence of the Negro race. Furthermore, he had shown himself the master of a delicate, finished style, perfectly suited to the half-whimsical and yet keenly perceptive manner in which he studied his characters. The books had won both popular and critical approval. To the reviewers his style and his character delineation suggested the French novelists; his handling of social problems invited comparison with Turgenev; the indirection of his narrative method suggested Hawthorne. On Cable's first platform appearance in Boston he received more "exclusively distinguished attention," as one reporter put it, than Matthew Arnold had recently been given there. The editor of the *Century Magazine* once said that he considered Cable a more valuable contributor than Howells or Henry James; a critic in England and another in France judged his art superior to that of either.

Early in 1885 Cable took a step to which he had been led by his study of the convict lease system: he published an essay entitled "The Freedman's Case in Equity," an uncompromising argument for the civil rights of Negroes supported by references to court and prison records. There followed a controversy, which made heavy demands on his attention for several years and which had significant effects on his life and thinking, leaving only stolen time for the novels and stories his publishers urged him to write. In spite of warnings as to the probable consequences, Cable felt impelled to publish the essay. He argued only for equal rights in the courts, but with unmistakable overtones of moral judgment; of course the implications were much broader. Some of his readers, at least the journalists, saw threats to what they considered to be the foundations of Southern society.

The flood of accusation and invective inspired by the essay can only with difficulty be conceived today. Cable was the target for abuse such as the South has leveled at no one else except perhaps John Brown and "Beast" Butler. He knew, nevertheless, that his opinions were shared by many of his friends and acquaintances, whether they acknowledged them or not, and he believed he spoke for many others. Until 1890 he used every means at his disposal to discuss different aspects of what was then called the Southern problem. His final and most elaborate attempt was through the Open Letter Club, which he organized with the aim of publishing from time to time a symposium on some Southern topic by leading citizens of the region. At the outset two dozen prominent men joined in the scheme, and hundreds showed an interest in reading the discussions. Before long, however, the members realized that they would suffer because of the association with Cable; sentiment in the Southern press was still frantically hostile.

Thus Cable found himself without a means of reaching the South directly; the lecture platform was closed to him, and his editors did not welcome more controversial essays. He had always thought of his fiction as an agent of good; now he undertook to freight a novel with the reform message he had no other means of presenting. *John March, Southerner*, which resulted, is perhaps his least artistic novel. Instead of a powerful, realistic novel like *The Grandissimes*, with concepts of right and wrong introduced through indirection and implication, Cable drew out to five hundred pages an intricate balancing of partial right against partial wrong in the postwar South, the scales being tipped finally to support his own views of the problems.

With this book Cable withdrew from the Southern controversy, though not bitter or without hope, even though some of the causes he had espoused seemed to be lost: in the few years preceding, the ballot had been effectively restricted; the crop-lien system had been perfected and fortified by laws; in some states there had been retrenchment in public education. He continued to support a few educational undertakings in the South and to speak out occasionally but never with the righteous indignation of the earlier years. At Northampton, Massachusetts, his home after 1885, he founded and for over thirty years worked in a series of enterprises for social betterment. They raised no controversies and rewarded his efforts with flattering success. But he visited New Orleans almost yearly, and his books continued to deal with the South. His publishers, begrudging the years he had given to polemics, urged him to write more stories and novels like the first ones. He made the attempt and produced half a dozen books between 1900 and 1918—but none equal to *Old Creole Days* or *The Grandissimes*, though *The Cavalier* in 1901 sold a hundred thousand copies in a few weeks and had a reasonably successful run on the stage.

Cable wrote these last books with the same delicate craftsmanship he had shown from the beginning. They have the same finished style, the same authentic dialect, the same reality of detail built on observation and research. Yet they have neither the charm nor the strength of his early books. It may be that his removal from New Orleans was partly accountable or that, like the other delineators of a particular region, he was unable to impart freshness to any stories after the first few. But Cable was far more than the reporter of a locality: from first to last he showed qualities rarely encountered among the local colorists.

It is not adequate to say that Cable became more reformer than novelist. This is true of one novel, *John March, Southerner*, but in those which followed he carefully avoided the positive attack on social injustice which characterized his early writings. In this fact, indeed, seems to lie a major explanation of the shortcomings of the later books. A novelist whose entire life and work had been interwoven with social conflict now pulled back, no less positive in his attitudes, but determined to avoid the sort of controversy which had raged about him since the publication of his first Creole stories. He could see that he had often antagonized when he hoped to convince, and he wondered, no doubt, whether the gain might not have been greater if he had spoken of right and wrong in less absolute terms. The revision in his attitude toward his work is apparent when two of his essays are placed side by side. In one, entitled "My Politics," written in 1889 but not published because his editors considered it too personal, he defended his views on laws and customs, attitudes and events which he thought violated democratic and Christian principles. The other essay, published in 1915 as "My Philosophy," is so generalized that it fails to identify the particular issues he had debated with such vigor a quarter of a century earlier. Another example: Cable's early fiction is filled with implicit condemnation of caste and class as he observed them in the stratification of society around him. But later, when he organized study clubs at Northampton, conceived mainly to benefit the mill workers, he gave assurance that no attempt would be made to tear down class barriers. He had abandoned frontal attacks on entrenched attitudes and institutions.

Cable was especially sensitive to the attacks aimed at him from New Orleans, and most of all to the attacks of the Creoles, for he believed he had pictured them accurately and fairly, as some of the Creoles themselves thought also, and he knew he had drawn them with affection. For thirty years he smarted under their accusations before he received in 1915 a pleasing token of their changed attitude. Then in his last novel, *Lovers of Louisiana*, he wrote again of the Creoles and the Americans. This time he was scrupulously careful to balance the virtues of each and to leave slight possibility of resentment. He did here with the Creole question what in the other late novels he had attempted to do with all aspects of the Southern question: to heal old wounds and placate an entire population.

Cable created no villains; the evil confronting his characters derives always from some element in the social order. In consequence of his desire to make peace with Southern society in his last years, he abandoned or at least mollified the only forces of evil he had ever used. As a result his last books are well executed historical romances, with plots which often turn on intrigue, motivated by a fortuitous miscarriage of noble intentions.

Cable's novels, then, illustrate three moods and three manners of the social critic: In his first books a burning humanitarianism and a pained awareness of social wrong elevated what otherwise might have been only charming local color stories into moving, realistic fiction. In one novel an overpowering concern for immediate social problems resulted in a tract for the times. Others, in which the author consciously suppressed his positive convictions in deference to militant prejudices, display most of the excellences of his best writing but lack the intensity of purpose which in his early novels gives reality to the characters and compelling significance to the action.

"Jadis"

Arlin Turner°

Edward King remarked afterward, when he was called the discoverer of George W. Cable, that rather "Cable discovered himself, and would have dawned upon the world had there never been any 'Great South' scribes in New Orleans, to hear his mellifluous reading of his delightful sketches."[1] Cable was always eager, though, to credit King with introducing him to the Eastern publishers.

King came to New Orleans early in 1873. With an illustrator, J. Wells Champney, he was beginning eighteen months of travel on which to base a series of articles on "The Great South" for *Scribner's Monthly Magazine*. While recording voluminous facts, King also interpreted and judged. He came south with an open mind, inclined to be sympathetic, and before leaving Louisiana had decided he could recommend the South to the sympathy and generosity of his Northern readers, and to their sense of justice. He and Champney were delighted with New Orleans. They found in the Vieux Carré much of what they had both seen in Europe, but they saw more than carnival and gaiety and romantic past. In fact King broached most of the questions the people had uppermost in their minds. He opened his article: "Louisiana to-day is Paradise Lost. In twenty years it may be Paradise Regained. . . . It is the battle of race with race, of the picturesque and unjust civilization of the past with the prosaic and leveling civilization of the present." The former aristocrats, of the plantations and of the city, Creoles and Americans, told him of property worth half its former value, of the lack of capital for even the meagerest rebuilding, of interest rates from thirty to sixty per cent, of confiscatory taxes. A prominent Creole historian, Charles Gayarré, obviously, told him that "among his immense acquaintance, he did not know a single person who would not leave the state if means were at hand."

All were eager to explain that the former slaves would not work, that one state legislature had included fifty-five Negro members who could not read or write. Of the populace King wrote that "each and every foreign type moves in a special current of its own, mingling little with the American." Again, "It is also astonishing to see how little the ordinary American citizen of New Orleans knows of his French neighbors; how ill he appreciates them. It is hard for him to talk five minutes about them without saying, 'Well, we have a non-progressive

° Reprinted from *George W. Cable: A Biography* (Durham, N.C.: Duke University Press, 1956), pp. 52–64.

element here; it will not be converted.' Having said which, he will perhaps paint in glowing colors the virtues and excellences of his French neighbors, though he cannot forgive them for taking so little interest in public affairs"[2]—as if King had read books of Cable's not yet written. But he had talked with Cable and others, both Creoles and Americans.

What King's papers accomplished cannot be said exactly. Readers of the articles—in the magazine from July, 1873, to December, 1874, or in the thick volume of the next year, or in the two printings in England—found in them the first extended treatment of the South under the Reconstruction government. Looking backward from 1914, Cable wrote to F. L. Pattee that he thought the papers had no effect on the Southern literary awakening, that the two were merely coincidental.[3] Yet the papers prepared readers and editors for literary use of Southern materials and thus opened the way for Southern writers. Within the next ten years every important magazine made some effort to encourage writing in and about the South. The effect of the "Great South" undertaking on Cable's literary fortune was direct.

King found in Cable an abundance of both facts and interpretations. To Cable the visitors represented high literary and artistic accomplishment, though King was only twenty-five and Champney thirty. After leaving a factory to become a newspaper reporter, King had been to Europe twice, had published a book, was a contributor to Scribner's Monthly, and talked eagerly of the fiction and poetry he was writing. Champney's beginning had been similarly modest, as a wood-engraver's apprentice, and later he had been twice to Europe for study. They visited in Cable's home and bounced his two children on their knees. They went with him to the Cotton Exchange, met his employers, and caught his enthusiasm for the old city. On the eve of their departure, he read them the stories he had been writing and laying away, known only within his family. They were so impressed with the stories and his modest dedication to his writing that they were certain he deserved help in making a start. King, the voluble spokesman of the pair, took some of the stories away with him and in the following months kept up a stream of letters to his new friend, who had agreed to supply additional information for the Louisiana articles and to read proof on them.

King had taken with him "Bibi," the tragic story, in broad outline a true story, of an African prince in American slavery, a story no one outside the author's immediate family had read. On March 25 it already had "waltzed away to New York," to Richard Watson Gilder, associate editor of Scribner's Monthly, but its fate was not settled for weeks. In the letter King wrote on that day he added: "Fear not, O Cable, for your fame is sure if you continue to make Bibis." And on April 24, " 'Bibi' rode me as a nightmare last night." On May 9 he wrote again: "Bless you, my dear friend, if they don't print it, someone else will. But I am jogging their weak memories. I am deluging them with reproaches. . . . But I am only a worm crawling before the Scribnerian throne. Still, I plead poor Bibi's cause. . . . My heart goes out to you earnestly in your striving; and all the more because I know you will succeed."

King's pleading and his reproaches did not save "Bibi." Gilder rejected it on May 19, as other editors were to do afterward, all perhaps for the reason given by George Parsons Lathrop, at the *Atlantic Monthly:* "on account of the unmitigatedly distressful effect of the story."[4] Rejected a second time by Gilder on January 2, 1875, after it had been revised and he had held it a full year, the story was not published until it became the episode of Bras Coupé in Cable's first novel, *The Grandissimes.*

Meanwhile another story was on its way to the Scribnerian throne. King had taken " 'Sieur George" with him also, and after returning it for revision he forwarded it early in May and himself reached New York toward the middle of July, in time to make a direct plea to Gilder, as he had planned to do for "Bibi." A week later, July 22, he wrote Cable: "The battle is won. 'Monsieur George' is accepted, and will be published in *Scribner. . . .* I read the story myself to the editor, who liked it; it trembled in the balance a day, and then Oh ye gods! was accepted! I fancy I can see you waltzing around the office of the venerable cotton brokers, shouting the war-cry of future conquest! Courage!"[5] King's skill in reading the Creole dialect may be doubted, but not his relish for it. Like Mark Twain, William Dean Howells, and others afterward, he spoke in Creole, he said, and he scattered Creole expressions through his letters.

King's efforts did not lessen after " 'Sieur George" had been accepted. For several years he was Cable's unofficial agent in New York, arguing his case in the Scribner office, forwarding rejected stories to other editors, and urging him to work slowly, submit nothing below his best, and especially guard his health. He recommended Cable to other editors, and in Paris six years later persuaded the editor of the *Parisian* to make him an offer for some of his writings.[6] It was King who first urged him to move east, to write a novel, and to consider translating his stories into French. But as important as his tangible assistance or his advice, was the exuberance of his encouragement. "I am now ready to admit . . . that you are a genius," he wrote late in 1873. "Now I hope you will labor up from this level, and never, like Harte, drop below it! Still you have the satisfaction of knowing that there are but few who can touch the level where you stand now. Be strong! O my friend—BE STRONG!!!" A few months later, "One who has so thoroughly the artistic feeling should always make his methods as artistic as possible. How you grow!"

Robert Underwood Johnson, who was assistant editor of *Scribner's* in 1873, wrote long afterward that it was "a fresh and gentle southwest wind that blew into the office" when " 'Sieur George" arrived and that the editors believed in Cable from the start.[7] Though Gilder had rejected the first story and needed two months and King's pleading to persuade him to accept the next, after reading it in proof he wrote the new author on August 29:

> I feel moved to say that "we" hope you know that you have the markings of one of the best story-writers of the day. All you want to do is to appreciate yourself. You will do much better than " 'Sieur George" . . . . Go to work in good earnest and high faith in yourself—work as religiously as if you had already Bret Harte's reputation—& perhaps you may have one as lasting.[8]

Those who read " 'Sieur George" at the Scribner office in the spring of 1873 or in the October number of the magazine were introduced to old New Orleans, which they were to know in the following years as Cable's province. They were led along the *banquettes* of the French Quarter, under the balconies balustraded with intricate iron-work; they stopped to peer into the flowered courtyards or caught teasing glimpses through the sap-green shutters that might be cautiously ajar but never open wide; they paused, as it were, across the street from a dilapidated old house and heard from the author an enchanting tale of *jadis*, once upon a time, when the house and the street had known better days. A reviewer in the *Picayune* of October 5, 1873, when the story had just appeared in the magazine, said that local readers would recognize it at once "as a genuine story of New Orleans."

'Sieur George lived at the corner of Royal and St. Peter streets in a house which Lafcadio Hearn found still resisting change ten years after the story was published and which is pointed out today as 'Sieur George's House,[9] but Cable placed it no more exactly than "in the heart of New Orleans." It is a story of the olden time; street names are of less moment than the "gray stucco peeling off in broad patches," giving "a solemn look of gentility in rags, . . . like a faded fop who pretends to be looking for employment," the "masses of cobwebbed iron," the "square court within, hung with many lines of wet clothes, its sides hugged by rotten staircases that seem vainly trying to clamber out of the rubbish."

The story is told with the indefiniteness appropriate to a street where decayed old men or dark-eyed young women slip through half-opened doors, leaving the observer to wonder what is inside and what stories the mildewed walls could tell. For fifty years 'Sieur George came and went, known by no other name to the reader or to the landlord, Kookoo. The author wanders in and out of the old house, reporting a snatch of conversation or a glimpse of the hair trunk always kept in the rooms, telling of 'Sieur George setting out for the Mexican War, or climbing the stairs with a faltering tread. With such indirect touches the thread of the story is unwound: 'Sieur George has spent fifty years losing and attempting to regain his own fortune and that entrusted to him which should have gone to support a friend's daughter left to his care, and later a granddaughter. His disintegration has paralleled the decay of the house, and finally when he can no longer pay the rent he is glimpsed picking his way to the bounds of the city, where he will sleep in the tall grass. He has always meant well, has intended the best for the daughter of his friend and later her daughter. At the last he has a new combination and is sure that with ten dollars he could win. The hair trunk full to the brim of worthless lottery tickets has taught him nothing.

The *Scribner's* editors thought the story confused, and in deference to their objections several sentences and a final paragraph were added after the first printing. They expected a plot with definite complication, suspense, and resolution, and so were hardly prepared for a story achieving its effects through lightness of touch, half-revelation, and suggestion. Readers of Nathaniel Hawthorne's stories had met the same difficulty. In fact, the method of " 'Sieur

George" is reminiscent of Hawthorne in the location of the action in a hazily defined past, real in atmosphere rather than circumstantial details, and in the reliance on hints and speculation instead of direct assertion. And too, the trunk of lottery tickets recalls Hawthorne's chest of worthless currency in "Peter Goldthwaite's Treasure." Though Cable's attention was not mainly on plot, he was yet uncertain what methods were most suitable to his purposes and what liberties he might take in constructing a story. In consequence " 'Sieur George" employs artificial concealment and contrivance of plot that suggest an author attempting to stay within a narrative method unsuited to his materials.

Yet the reader is not troubled by the half-heard conversations and the glimpses of the hair trunk, for with the first sentence he enters a fairy land of *jadis* and is caught up by the gentle movement of the story, as if loitering on the streets of the old city, stopping here before a courtyard, there before a shop window, and yet urged on to see what is next. The air of anticipation grows as the story takes turns as unexpected and as revealing as those in the narrow streets—twenty years passed, or 'Sieur George appeared in full regimentals, off to Mexico, or he climbed the stairs with a baby in his arms. The sense of expectancy, the surprise at every step, the effects felt but hardly noticed hold the reader's interest.

" 'Sieur George" is in a style which in every sentence, especially in the abundant figurative language, reflects the author's fondness for whimsical turns of thought and expression. If this trait seems at first strained, after a page or two its delicate, ironic turns become integral to the place and the action of the characters. The trunk and the house and the street become symbols, not subtle in themselves, but subtle in the handling and in the way their meanings enter the reader's awareness. The flavor of the dialect is unobtrusive but unmistakable in its effect. Through the simple French phrases and the occasional Gallicized pronunciations the reader is reminded that the people are French and talk in French, but the best effects come from such expressions as "he addresses to him a few remarks," by which the language is suggested without a burdensome transcription.

After Cable's first story had been accepted, his editors asked repeatedly for others. In the next three years he submitted ten more stories, of which six were published in *Scribner's*, three were rejected and apparently destroyed, and one was published in *Appletons' Journal*.

The second story, "Belles Demoiselles Plantation," in *Scribner's* for April, 1874, avoids the hiatuses of plot and the straining for suspense of " 'Sieur George," and it has excellences only partly realized in the first story. It concentrates on the essentials and yet is richer in suggestion. Lafcadio Hearn thought it the most singular of Cable's stories.

The plot is of the simplest and is only the vehicle for the character study. It tells of Colonel De Charleu and Old De Carlos, each descended in a slender line from the count who came to Louisiana long ago an agent of the French king. De Carlos, descended from a Choctaw woman, the count's wife for the nonce, and with other undesignated mixtures of blood, clung to his inheritance, a block of dilapidated buildings in the heart of New Orleans. De Charleu, of purest blood, had inherited the most beautiful plantation in Louisiana, where he lived with his seven daughters. Wishing to build also the finest house in the city and forgetting in cavalier fashion that the plantation was already mortgaged to De Carlos for more than it was worth, he proposed to buy his distant relative's property. De Carlos would not sell but would make an even exchange, for thus he would not relinquish his claim, as he saw it, on the original count's blood. An exchange was unthinkable to De Charleu until he discovered that the river was eating inexorably toward his house, and then he agreed. As both looked on, the noble mansion slipped into the river, taking with it the seven beautiful daughters. In De Charleu's periods of consciousness before he died a year later he insisted the trade had not been completed; his kinsman of Choctaw blood, his faithful nurse during the year, insisted they had traded. Loyalty to blood finally would not allow either to cheat the other.

The character trait at the center of the story is generalized for the Creoles as a whole, to the displeasure, understandably, of some of them who read the story: "One thing I never knew a Creole to do. He will not utterly go back on his ties of blood, no matter what sort of knots those ties may be. For one reason, he is never ashamed of his or his father's sins; and for another—he will tell you—he is 'all heart.'" Pride of descent and loyalty to blood are as strong in De Carlos, Injun Charlie as he is called, as it is in De Charleu, surrounded by his *belles demoiselles* and boundless splendor. De Charleu says once, "And we had both been bad enough in our times, eh, Charlie?"—not with the facile implications that would be expected in Bret Harte, but simply to testify to the bonds between them. He has no compunction for the luxurious idleness of his life, for "his name was fame enough."

The delicate relations between the two kinsmen are revealed in a touch here and a hint there. They converse in English, which hobbles and stumbles from unfamiliarity, as a reminder that intimacy is impossible. Neither uses profanity in the presence of the other for the same reason. Yet they discover in the presence of calamity the loyalty each owes the other.

In the glimpses of the *demoiselles*, dancing past the windows or smothering their papa in kisses, Cable approaches the portraits of young Creole women that were to ornament his later stories. The women in "'Sieur George" stay far in the background; here they flit in and out of the story, figures of grace, frivolity, and charm. The French they speak is refined, of course, and is suggested by a few French phrases and locutions, but when they mention Injun Charlie, they switch to English—"something is going to took place"; "too blame clever, me, dat's de troub'." Cable was exploring the use of dialect. He had learned that without burdening the reader he could give the flavor of the Creoles' speech in either French or English. His inclination was to strive for the literal accuracy of full transcription, but he realized that some compromise must be made, and his editors cautioned him to simplify the dialect.

The original of the Belles Demoiselles plantation was tumbled down and overgrown in Cable's time, but as in the story, it had been passed down through generations of one family, unnamed, he says, because "the old Creoles never forgive a public mention." Lafcadio Hearn found it a few years later still recognizable from Cable's description, though on the opposite side of the river, and he saw evidence that it would in time meet the destruction Cable had postulated for it.

The third story printed, " 'Tite Poulette," in *Scribner's* for October, 1874, was probably one of the first Cable wrote and possibly a reworking of the sketch in the *Picayune* entitled "A Life-Ebbing Monography." Along with "Bibi," it grew from his sympathy for the Negro race as he had become aware of it in the early history. In narrative method it suggests " 'Sieur George." There is less reliance on half-revelation for suspense, but there is some of the same kittenish playing of revelation against concealment, as when we are told that the wig-maker whispered something about Madame John. The passage continues: "She was the best yellow-fever nurse in a thousand yards round; but that is not what the wig-maker said." Still, this whimsicality has an unexpected appropriateness. The glimpses of characters or of shadowy interiors and the accidentally overheard remarks are the threads from which the fabric is woven that has a clear, simple design when completed.

The story suggests in a few quick touches the essentials of the system under which the quadroon women lived in early New Orleans. Zalli, white as a water lily and black-eyed, had been taken by her mother to the quadroon balls. There she had met Monsieur John, who had treated her generously and at his death had left her well provided; but after loss in a bank failure she and 'Tite Poulette, white as she and vastly more beautiful, have made their living by occasional dancing lessons and a little needlework. Now 'Tite Poulette "has seventeen," as the admiring young Creoles say, an age when she should, as the cycle demands, attend the balls and there make an arrangement. Madame John, forced to dance at the Salle de Condé but careful to keep 'Tite Poulette away, dreams of a white marriage for her and decries bitterly the law which prohibits it. But the young woman has no protest—"God made us. He made us just as we are; not more white, not more black."

The full meaning of their purgatory is realized only when Kristian Koppig, a Dutch clerk, declares his love and begs 'Tite Poulette to marry him. She stands immobile except for the flow of tears and the words, "It is against the law." Then, in a turn which the reader does not expect but through fleeting hints has been prepared to accept, Madame John produces papers to prove that 'Tite Poulette is not her daughter but was left to her when her parents died after landing from Spain. In the dignified beauty of the two women, the bitter protest of Madame John and the resigned acceptance of 'Tite Poulette, the story is a moving plea for the quadroon caste. The author apparently wished not to identify the system with the Creoles solely. Though the manager of the Salle de Condé is Monsieur de la Rue and the bewitching "smiles and grace, smiles and grace" at the ball are French, the system belongs to the time and place, not to one part of the population.

The action is set in real houses on Dumaine Street—one of which is known today as Madame John's Legacy—and the coming and going on the narrow sidewalks lends a compelling sense of actuality. Koppig is an awkward piece of stage furniture, but he is useful to the story as a source of humor and as a newcomer to the scene who can speak from an unencumbered conscience. It is with the two women, the first women Cable drew full-scale, that he achieves his greatest success. Through glimpses of their faces at the window and snippets of their dialogue, he suggests without full delineation their feelings and their speech "in the unceasing French way."

"Jean-ah Poquelin," published in May, 1875, impressed Cable's editors as the best he had yet written. It was a favorite with Mark Twain, who liked to read aloud the Creole-English of the title character.[10] It illustrates what H. H. Boyesen later told Cable was most valuable in his books, the portrayal of two civilizations in conflict. The Creole and the American civilizations are suggested, in essence, as they stood delicately balanced at the point where the future course was faintly discernible. The old and the new are side by side: Jean's decaying old house on the bank of the abandoned canal and the straight gravel road bordered by new cottages. To balance Jean, with his mysterious past of smuggling and slave-trading, is White, an efficient young clerk. Jean is one of the old Creoles who, one of the Americans says, "would liever live in a crawfish hole than to have a neighbor."

But there is more to the picture. The development company which finds Jean's padlocked enclosure in its way has no motive but profit. The members of the party who threaten Jean are drunk and have no more commendable motive than to torment him because he prefers to be left alone. When they realize, finally, that he has died at the end of seven years of caring for his half-brother, a leper, and has guarded the isolation of his house in order to save him from the Terre aux Lépreux, they stand uncovered and stunned at the climactic moment when the black mute shoulders Jean's coffin and turns down the path through the swamp to the land of the lepers, followed by the leper-white brother.

"Jean-ah Poquelin" shows Cable maturing in his fictional method. It has his usual compression and heightening through suggestion and quick turns, but there is greater naturalness than he had yet achieved. The author stays outside Jean's padlocked grounds, maintains that point of view, avoids speculations by secondary characters. The impact of the final revelation is breath-taking, though the reader then realizes that details earlier have pointed to the outcome. The dramatic intensity is the greater for the dignity—and the horror—of the tableau at the edge of the woods. "Jean-ah Poquelin" left no doubt that a fiction writer with uncommon dramatic power had appeared.

The story has a substantial base of actuality. In his boyhood Cable had seen the streets pushed from the high ground near the river into the swamp back of the city. When he wrote the story, plantation homes still stood in swamps that had once been indigo or sugar cane fields. Jean's house seems to have had as a model that of a "childless, wifeless, companionless old man," "Doctor" Gravier, which early in the nineteenth century stood on the bank of Poydras Canal. Cable described this old man in his article "The Great South Gate," later a part of *The Creoles of Louisiana,* and Hearn, who surely checked his surmises with the author, suggested that both the house and Gravier appear in the story.

"Madame Délicieuse," printed in August, 1875, is one of the most delicate, most whimsically gay of Cable's stories. Its plot is airy and offsets in charm anything it may lack in plausibility. Old General Villivicencio's disowning his son because he would not become a soldier is convincing only because this is a story of long ago and the General personifies archaic Creole pride and imperiousness. The love affair of the son and Madame Délicieuse is fantasy, but it is acceptable, for before it is revealed, the reader is at home in the remote *jadis.*

The setting is on Royal Street, appropriately, for Madame Délicieuse and the General belong at the center of the Vieux Carré. But the street and the houses are less important than in " 'Sieur George" or " 'Tite Poulette"—the atmosphere is set rather by the bevy of Creole ladies on a balcony waving handkerchiefs and receiving kisses thrown by the veterans of 1815 marching in an Eighth of January parade. An election in which a few days later the old and the new will measure strength, a threatened duel that descends into farce—all is keyed to the conniving and coaxing of a clever and beautiful woman to bend a haughty old man to her will. When all is resolved amid embracing and kissing and they pass out into Royal Street, they are met by the rare odor of orange blossoms.

The story is almost entirely in dialogue; the language is French, of course, and is rendered in good English except for occasional archaisms and French idioms. The characters are Creoles of refinement, admirable and lovable in all their foibles, and a reviewer in the New Orleans *Times* of June 1, 1879, thought they could not fail to please the Creole readers. The General belongs to a past which refuses to admit that it is past, but his hatred of the *Américains* and his love of the old order are as natural to him as breathing and do not deny him kindness, generosity, and fairness any more than his pride keeps him from acknowledging finally the bravery of his son.

In several respects the "Café des Exilés," in *Scribner's* of March, 1876, differs from the other stories. The characters are refugees with multifarious backgrounds, brought together by their homesickness and their purpose of smuggling arms to the Antilles. There are two threads of the plot and a storyteller is employed who recounts what he has been told by the chief character. Yet it is recognizably a Cable story.

Again the story is built solidly into its background. The Café des Exilés, actually on Rampart Street, was moved to Burgundy in the story, and the refugees from Cuba, San Domingo, and the other islands came directly from history. The story focuses on four characters and leaves the others, each with his particular confused past, to form a backdrop for the rivalry of two of them for the love of Pauline, daughter of the owner of the Café. There are instances of double or triple areas of understanding, depending on how much the different characters know of the rivalry for Pauline and the plans for smuggling. Cable obviously enjoys working out the intricate complication, but he does not employ intricacy for its own sake; he succeeds, rather, in narrating a story of conspiracy and intrigue with a directness that sacrifices nothing of suspense. The dialect is troublesome more than in any of the earlier stories, for the dialogue includes varying mixtures of Irish, French, Spanish, and Italian, but after a page or two the reader begins to feel at ease with the speech.

Of all Cable's stories "Posson Jone' " had widest and most distinguished commendation in his lifetime. It answered for Charles Dudley Warner the question of realism against idealism: it showed him that actual life, even low life, can be heightened to gain an idealistic effect.[11] Edmund Gosse, reading it in England, saw in its delineation of races and nationalities sure promise of a great novelist.[12] It is ironic that these judgments were passed on a story which had been hawked from one editor to another before it found a publisher. Rejected at *Scribner's* it went to the New York *Times*, the *Galaxy*, and later *Harper's Magazine*. H. M. Alden, editor of *Harper's*, returned it on July 28, 1875, with the comment: "The disagreeable aspects of human nature are made prominent, & the story leaves an unpleasant impression on the mind of the reader." The stories in *Harper's*, he added in a letter of August 9, "must be of a pleasant character &, as a rule, must be love-tales." Finally "the little parson story," as Gilder called it, found a place in *Appletons' Journal* for April 1, 1876.

"Posson Jone' " does not have the delicacy or the rich suggestion usual with Cable. It is broad comedy, presented in bold strokes of extravagant action and characters that approach caricature. Yet nowhere did he demonstrate a surer hand, and nowhere did he achieve more truly delightful effects. Posson Jone', the giant bumpkin preacher from the West Florida parishes, in New Orleans on business with five hundred dollars belonging to "Smyrny" Church, could not encounter a more antithetical person than Jules St. Ange, nor one who would welcome the encounter more. For Jules and his body servant Baptiste are out of funds. The episodes are hilarious in which Jules and the parson visit gambling parlors and saloons and then, when Jones has become drunk, attend the buffalo and tiger fight at Congo Square. Jones talks in a stream of "lingual curiosities" of the backwoods which barely exceed in curiousness Jules's own manipulations of the English language. The scene at Congo Square, where Jones preaches to the throng and then hugs the tiger to his chest and pursues the buffalo, talking all the while of Daniel in the "buffler's" den, leads as a matter of course to the scene of Jones in jail and another at Bayou St. John as he embarks for home, a saddened Christian ("which I hope I can still say I am one"). Jules has arranged his release from the *calaboza* and now offers to replace, with his own winnings in a card game, the money of Smyrna Church which has mysteriously disappeared. Jones refuses, and as he kneels on the boat vowing his humility before God, Colossus, his slave, returns the lost money, which he slipped away earlier for safekeeping. Jules, impressed by the "so fighting an' moz rilligious man as I never saw," pays his debts with his winnings and goes "to his father an honest man."

The supporting materials are in keeping with the broad comedy. The time is soon after 1800, when the streets are filled with Kentucky flatboatmen, sailors from the ports of the world, and refugees from the West Indies. Congo Square, back of the old palisaded city, the site of the slave orgies of dance and song and of Cayetano's famous circus, is the scene of the tiger and buffalo fight. The characters of Jules and Jones are as clear-cut as any others Cable drew in his stories, and at the level of the servants the contrasts between the two worlds represented are effectively reinforced.

These seven stories had reached the publishers by November of 1875. After that Cable sent nothing for three years. The pay for the stories, about seventy dollars each, was negligible in relation to the time they required. He had been able to finish them only by hiring an assistant in his office and holding himself to a killing schedule. Furthermore, not all of his work had been accepted. Two stories, "Dr. Goldenbow" and "Hortensia," were rejected by *Scribner's* in the fall of 1874, at least partly because, Cable said afterward in "My Politics," they had political implications. Another, "Ba'm o' Gilly," was rejected the next year. These stories seem not to have been preserved. Cable had reached a pause. It had been his hope to leave the counting room and give himself wholly to literature, but he could not unless he found a way to make writing pay better.

Notes

1. L. L. C. Biklé, *George W. Cable: His Life and Letters* (New York: Charles Scribner's Sons, 1928), p. 51.

2. Edward King, *The Great South* (Hartford: American Publishing, 1875), pp. 17 ff.

3. In Biklé, p. 47.

4. In Biklé, p. 48.

5. In Biklé, pp. 46–47.

6. C. S. Wasson to Cable, April 4, 1879.

7. *Remembered Yesterdays* (Boston: Little, Brown, 1923), p. 122.

8. In Biklé, p. 49.

9. In an article on "The Scenes of Cable's Romances," *Century*, 27 (November, 1883), 40–47, Hearn identified and described the landmarks of Cable's writings published to that time. 'Sieur George's and seven other houses still standing and associated with Cable's stories are described in Stanley Clisby Arthur's *Old New Orleans* (New Orleans: Harmanson, 1936).

10. Howells wrote after almost half a century (*The Great Modern American Stories*, New York: Boni and Liveright, 1920, p. xi) that he could not read this story "without hearing the voice of Mark Twain in reading its most dramatic phrases with his tragic pleasure" in the defiance of the old slave-trader. Howells made a similar comment in *Literary Friends and Acquaintance* (New York: Harper, 1900), pp. 403–4.

11. "On Mr. Cable's Readings," *Century*, 26 (June, 1883), 311–12.

12. A review in the *Saturday Review*, 52 (August 20, 1881), 238.

[Introduction to *The Grandissimes*]

Newton Arvin[*]

When the editors of *Scribner's Monthly*, in 1879, accepted the manuscript of *The Grandissimes*, and began publishing it serially in the November issue, they were well aware of the freshness and distinction of their young author's work, but they could hardly have foreseen how far the novel would ultimately throw its beams. They had already published several short stories by its author, a young New Orleans accountant and part-time journalist, George Washington Cable, who had been "discovered" and drawn out—living as he did, in those harsh post bellum days, at so great a remove from the literary center—by another *Scribner's* author, Edward King, who had gone to New Orleans in the mid-seventies to do a series of articles on the new South. Cable's stories had been collected, earlier in 1879, in a volume entitled *Old Creole Days*, and *The Grandissimes* was to be published as a volume in the following year. It may not have been perfectly evident then, but in a quiet way the novel made a sharp break with the central tradition of Southern fiction, as it then was and was long to be; it pointed forward to a kind of thing that was to assert itself only after several decades. This is what led Hamilton Basso to say, some years ago, that Cable was the first writer to question the validity of the aristocratic tradition in Southern fiction—the "spiritual godfather," as he said, of more recent writers such as Ellen Glasgow, Thomas Wolfe, and William Faulkner. There is a sense in which, as Mr. Basso said, Cable may be said to have been the first of the "Southern realists."

The phrase, to be sure, requires a good deal of qualification, with Cable as with Faulkner, and even a fairly responsive reader might understandably come away from *The Grandissimes* with a sense of having been breathing the warm, soft air of the romantic, and even the sentimental, rather than the colder and more energizing atmosphere of realism. At a quick glance the novel does certainly *look* romantic. The central ganglion of the action is a bitter feud between two old, proud, aristocratic families—a feud for which the author himself finds a romantic analogy in the strife of Shakespeare's Capulets and Montagues. As for the time of the action, it is, and was even for Cable, a by no means immedi-

---

[*] Reprinted from *The Grandissimes: A Story of Creole Life* (New York: Sagamore Press, 1957), pp. v–xi.

ate past; it may have been what James called a "visitable past," but the opening years of the nineteenth century, at the moment when Napoleon had just ceded Louisiana to the United States, were already bathed, in the seventies and eighties, in a haze of romantic and even glamorous remoteness. And if the time of the action has this quality, what is to be said of the scene?—old New Orleans, still essentially the little eighteenth-century city, dominated by French and Spanish Creole families, and abounding in elements of the picturesque to which one can no longer even allude without falling into the clichés of colorfulness and charm. The story gets under way at a masked ball in the old Théâtre St. Philippe, and something of the effect of a masquerade—of the courtly, the costumed, the masked, the choreographic—is never wholly absent from the action.

It is true, moreover, that, to the sensibility of a later generation, there is a distasteful streak of sentimentality in much of Cable's work—of that peculiarly sweetish and effeminate sentimentality that throws one off in so much of the fiction of the period, including even Howells's and Mark Twain's. Cable himself once said: "Great is sentiment"; and though he went on to say that *sentimentality* is "despicable," being "at best but a feeling after feeling," the truth is that his own sensibility had been infected, on one side, by the dreadfully ladylike "feeling after feeling" of which even the great writers of the age were guilty. Howells drooled mawkishly over the two Nancanou ladies, Aurore and Clotilde, in *The Grandissimes*—Aurore, he said, "is one of the most delicious creations I ever knew"—but to our taste Cable's treatment of them is unendurably coy, arch, and, as Mencken once said of these writers, "kittenish." Even the great and terrible story of Bras-Coupé—the core around which the book grew—ends on a note of false and untrue feeling that for a moment seems almost to unman its power.

All these things are true, and yet the fact is that Cable had a complex and curiously contradictory nature; the duality of his mind is accountable for both what is weak and what is unmistakably strong in his work as a whole and in his best novel, *The Grandissimes*, in particular. He was capable of "feeling after feeling," as he was capable of making the utmost of every romantic tone and hue in local color, but he was also an extraordinarily sharp-eyed, quick-glancing, astute observer of ordinary social reality, with a strongly developed critical sense, a love of the thoroughly documented fact, and a habit of tough resistance to the conventional and traditional version of things.

The result is that, both on superficial and on deeper levels, *The Grandissimes* is a singularly searching and veracious rendering of the life it represents. Cable's scene may be a romantic one in a certain sense, but the fidelity of his depiction of it is painstakingly and even literally, perhaps too literally, accurate. Lafcadio Hearn, who ought to have known, testified to the "sharp originality" of Cable's descriptions, and in an article in the *Century Magazine* went so far as to identify the particular houses in New Orleans that Cable had used as settings in *Old Creole Days*; he could undoubtedly have performed a similar service for the buildings in *The Grandissimes*. And so with the speech of

Cable's Creole and Negro characters: his passion for faithful and realistic precision was so intense as to carry him, here, beyond the limits of what the literary art can profitably do, and led him, in the use of dialect, to cultivate a laborious and literal accuracy that comes close to destroying the imaginative sense of human reality. Randolph Bourne once spoke of Cable's "phonetic atrocities": readers of *The Grandissimes*, picking their way through some of the speeches of Aurore Nancanou or Raoul Innerarity or Clemence the *marchande des calas*, will agree that the phrase is not an unjust one.

Mistaken as all this was, it is a small price to pay for the great qualities of *The Grandissimes* as a piece of social and historical realism—the qualities Edmund Wilson had in mind in calling Cable "essentially a sociologist." The phrase points to only one pole of the work, but certainly Cable's primary aim in the novel was to paint a full, truthful, critical picture of a social and regional scene. On the surface this scene is Creole society in New Orleans in the first decade of the century, but it is evident enough to a careful reader that the New Orleans of *The Grandissimes* is the South pretty much as a whole, not only in 1803 but in Cable's own time too. Indeed he himself furnished the clue to this in an entry in his diary: "*The Grandissimes*," he said, "contained as plain a protest against the times in which it was written as against the earlier times in which its scenes were set." A Northerner must speak with all possible humility here, but in that perspective it is difficult not to feel that Cable's representation of the Creole social character, his free and unsparing treatment of its vices and his tenderness for its high virtues, is, in every sense but the literal one, a representation of the South in the mid-century—the South of the fifties, of the War, and of Reconstruction.

The guilt of the Civil War was a divided one, if ever guilt was, but we are not speaking, nor was Cable writing, about the sins of the North: his subject is the Southern temper, and it is evident that he is criticizing his own people in his delineation of the Creole spirit, and particularly of the Grandissimes'—that Creole dynasty which embodies the best and the worst of the old Southern ethos, as the Atridae embodied, for the Greek tragic poets, the best and the worst of *their* inherited ethos. The best and the worst was their pride—that pride that at one pole took the form of arrogance, bluster, swagger, and disdain, and at the other pole took the form of a generous and magnanimous self-respect. Honoré Grandissime, the "white Honoré," expresses one half of this antithesis in his colloquy with the young Yankee pharmacist Frowenfeld: "Did you ever hear of a more perfect specimen of Creole pride? That is the way with all of them. Show me any Creole, or any number of Creoles, in any contest, and right down at the foundation of it all, I will find you this same preposterous, apathetic, fantastic, suicidal pride. It is as lethargic and ferocious as an alligator."

Honoré is speaking here, to be sure, of some of the De Grapions, not of the Grandissimes, their hereditary enemies; but Cable himself, we need have no doubt, is taking this dramatic mode of criticizing that whole aspect of the Southern temper that made real compromise or conciliation impossible in the forties and fifties, and that led in the end to the suicidal steps of secession and rebellion. Nor is this all. It is Southern writers themselves, especially since Cable's time, who have told us in effect how constant and tragic a role has always been played in Southern life by violence. And Cable, here, is their ancestor. "Charming" as much of the business of The Grandissimes is, the novel abounds, almost like a work of Faulkner's, in the imagery of violence. The action, as we have seen, has its center in a family feud—a feud that is itself an emblem of the enmity between the sections—and the feud had its source in a duel, a duel in which a De Grapion had been shot and killed by a Grandissime. This blood guilt was later deepened and darkened when another Grandissime, Agricole Fusilier, shoots and kills, over another insult, the husband of another De Grapion. These duels seem emblematic of a sectional war that had some of its roots in irrationality and hot temper, and there is a transparent symbolism in the passage in which the Yankee Frowenfeld persuades the aged Agricole to refrain from still another duel, this time with a cousin of his own, and to seek a reconciliation by peaceful means. It is at least a wishful gesture of a symbolically political nature.

Meanwhile the novel has been pervaded by the growling of suppressed, or the roar of open, violence. An aged gentleman is set upon in a dark street and knifed in the arm; his presumed assailant is shot and wounded in the shoulder. A mob of Creoles, enraged by a Yankee shopkeeper's liberal sentiments, attacks and wrecks his shop. An old Negro woman is cut down from the tree on which she has been nearly lynched, allowed to save herself by running away if she can, and then shot and killed as she attempts to flee. A principal character is finally given his death wound, stabbed thrice in the back, by an embittered relative. Most notably of all, most grandly and terribly, the magnificent Bras-Coupé, the African chief turned Negro slave, having struck down in a moment of anger his white master, and having been hunted down in his lair in the swamp, has been punished under the old Code Noir by being flogged and hamstrung, as well as by having his ears cut off. It was this ferocious tale, composed first as a short story, and rejected by G. P. Lathrop for the Atlantic as "unmitigatedly distressful," "to and around which," as Cable later said, "the whole larger work is built." Violence, in short, is at the very heart of The Grandissimes.

Violence—and the tension of relations between the races. The feud between Grandissimes and De Grapions, and even that other feud between the Creoles and the new American territorial government, is as nothing to the hostility, the never-absent, unevadable, obsessive hostility, between white and Negro. Hostility, yes, but one of a sort that can be felt only by human beings whose lives are as intimately, as inextricably, bound together as those of brother and brother, or cousin and cousin. Such was the hostility between North and South in the days before and after the War, and such, in all but the literal sense, was that between the Grandissimes and the De Grapions. The three forms that human antagonism takes in the novel—familial, political, racial—are all seen as involving a confusion of emotions, attraction as well as repulsion, closeness as well as division, love as well as hatred. The central token of this is the relation between the "two Honorés" (their names are identical)—the white Honoré, the Creole gentleman, and the quadroon Honoré, his declassed and alienated half-brother. There is a curious anticipation, in this pairing, of the intense and almost amorous relation between Henry Sutpen and his mulatto half-brother, Charles Bon, in Faulkner's *Absalom, Absalom!* as there is an anticipation in the essentially sisterly relation between Aurore Nancanou and the quadroon Palmyre of the essentially brotherly relation between Bayard Sartoris and Ringo in *The Unvanquished*. Like Faulkner, Cable had an intuition of the inescapable and profound dependence upon each other—a dependence like that of inimical brothers—of the two races.

In moral insights such as this, and in his transcendence of the literal and factual, his indirection and his sense of metaphor, Cable took a long step beyond the sociological realism with which he has been justly credited. "It is not sight the story-teller needs," he once wrote, "but second sight. . . . Not actual experience, not actual observation, but the haunted heart; that is what makes the true artist of every sort." His own heart was haunted—haunted by the spectre of sectional hatreds and bitternesses, and by the spectre of racial strife—and this was what made him so much more than one more local-color short-story writer and more, too, than one more prosaic realist. *The Grandissimes* ends, like *The Tempest*, in a marriage that betokens a permanent reconciliation between families: Cable was not far off, historically, in hinting thus at a reconciliation between the sections. As for the races, a step is taken that seems to promise a similar reconciliation. But Cable, like Faulkner, was too veracious a writer to delude himself with the image of an easy and premature solution, and the end of *that* is failure and tragedy. It would be a very long time before a truthful writer could depict any other.

George W. Cable and
Two Sources of Jazz

Hugh L. Smith°

The effect of the Creole song on jazz has been noted in nearly every historical jazz study. Goffin, Borneman, Blesh and Finkelstein are among those who have treated the matter, while Marshall Stearns' comment in *The Story of Jazz* is a recent example: "As might be expected, the French influence is perhaps the greatest European influence on New Orleans jazz. It merged with rhumba rhythms to produce Creole songs. . . ."[1]

George Washington Cable, the great New Orleans novelist, was a literary figure who sought out Creole songs with a collector's zeal and used them repeatedly in his novels; he also sang them from the lecture platform in just about every section of America and even in England. Cable showed as well an avid interest in a better known jazz source, that of slave songs, rhythms and dances. Employing the transcendent powers of observation necessary to an important novelist, he wrote of Creole and slave music in both fiction and magazine articles in such a way as to suggest, and even stress, musical qualities which were later to become of interest to jazz as inherent elements of jazz.

Cable was a writer who in his time was thought by some critics to be the equal of Nathaniel Hawthorne, and he still enjoys a prominent position among the local colorists of American literature. Recent biographical studies by Arlin Turner and Philip Butcher indicate, in fact, a resurgence of interest in Cable.

Cable's observations of the early musical performances by slaves in New Orleans' Congo Square, as they appeared in his 1886 *Century* magazine article "The Dance in Place Congo," are a commonly quoted source in jazz scholarship. He also wrote a study of slave songs for *Century* in which he divided this genre into love songs, voodoo songs, the lay, the dirge, and songs of the woods and water. The article reproduced the music to several of these songs and even went so far as to comment on the social implications of the lyrics, which in one instance contrasted the octoroon mistresses of white gentlemen with the slaves who served and played music for their entertainment:

> Yellow girl goes to the ball;
> Nigger lights her to the hall.
> Fiddler man!
> Now what is that to you?
> Say what is that to you,
> Fiddler man!

° Reprinted from *Second Line*, 11 (January–February, 1960), 1, 3–5, 19.

185

"It was much to him; but it might as well have been little. What could he do?" Cable adds, going ahead to explain that such lyrics were looked upon by whites as meaningless nonsense.[2] It has since become commonplace for jazz writers to acknowledge and discuss the ambiguous social criticism in jazz (especially blues) lyrics as evolved from the songs of the Southern Negro. Cable's section on voodoo songs furnishes another example of his interest in a characteristic area of New Orleans music which is still to be felt in jazz today, for voodoo terms like "goofer dust" and "root man" (one who sells roots to cast spells with) have continued to appear in songs, particularly blues again, by such unsophisticated performers as Cripple Clarence Lofton and such businesslike units as the Buddy Johnson band. Voodoo, of course, is still a power in New Orleans and Harlem at least.

The spell, whether voodoo or not, that early New Orleans music cast over Cable is apparent in his fiction. *The Grandissimes*, most highly regarded of Cable's novels today, presents one scene based upon the Calinda, a voodoo dance which Stearns says was connected with the zombiism of Haiti. Cable was fascinated by these musical dances with their Creole-French lyrics, and he pictures them as being performed by both slaves and their Creole masters, connecting the Negro and French musical cultures. In this instance the song accompanying the dance is being employed to satirize the younger Honoré Grandissime, who has been guilty that day of publicly associating on friendly terms with the United States-appointed "Yankee governor" who is to rule New Orleans under the Louisiana Purchase. Cable actually employs the Calinda as a kind of Greek chorus in the structure of this section of the novel to dramatize the unreasoning displeasure of the Creole reaction to the doings of the afternoon:

> Certain of the Muses were abroad that night. Faintly audible to the apothecary of the Rue Royale through that deserted stillness which is yet the marked peculiarity of New Orleans streets by night, came from a neighboring slave-yard the monotonous chant and machine-like tune-beat of an African dance. There our lately met *marchande* . . . led the ancient Calinda dance and that well-known song of derision, in whose ever multiplying stanzas the helpless satire of a feeble race still continues to celebrate the personal failings of each newly prominent figure among the dominant caste. There was a new distich to the song tonight, signifying that the pride of the Grandissimes must find his friends now among the Yankees:
> Miché Hon'ré, allé! h-allé!
> Trouve to zamis parmi les Yankis.
> Dance calinda, bou-joum! bou-joum!
> Dance calinda, bou-joum! bou-joum![3]

It is an amusing oddity that Cable goes on to describe the effect of the music on the listener, his protagonist Joseph Frowenfeld, with a term that has come to be synonymous with jazz: "The cathedral clock struck twelve and was answered again from the convent tower; and as the notes died away he suddenly became aware that the weird, drowsy throb of the African song and dance had been swinging drowsily in his brain for an unknown lapse of time."

When the young apothecary Frowenfeld visits the Grandissime mansion

Cable uses the African song and dance once more. Before Frowenfeld's departure some gesture of hospitable entertainment is felt to be necessary, and Cousin Raoul, the artistic member of the family, chants while the ill-fated slave Clemence performs an African dance:

> Raoul began to sing and Clemence instantly to pace and turn, posture, bow, respond to the song, start, swing, straighten, stamp, wheel, lift her hand, stoop, twist, walk, whirl, tip-toe with crossed ankles, smite her palms, march, circle, leap—an endless improvisation of rhythmic motion to this modulated responsive chant. . . .[4]

There follows a series of calls and replies between Raoul and Clemence, reproduced by Cable in the Creole dialect, which suggests something of the folk-mythology of the African leader and group response shouts, often mentioned as an influence on jazz solo and ensemble patterns.

The same scene stresses the African rhythmic force in this performance: "Frowenfeld was not so greatly amused as the ladies thought he should have been, and was told that this was not a fair indication of what he would see if there were ten dancers instead of one."

It is Raoul's custom to entertain his family with both Creole and Negro songs, and Cable repeatedly includes the lyrics in Creole dialect. There are even two instances in *The Grandissimes* in which Cable the musician takes precedence over the novelist. Raoul is asked to sing a Negro boat song "which they sing as a signal to those on shore" when they go out "into the bayous at night, stealing pigs and chickens!" Cable furnishes the actual musical notation to this song as well as the lyrics. Rudi Blesh and others have made a good deal of the Negro's use of ambiguity in his songs for purposes of communication, signalling, and protection to himself.

The notation device is used again in chapter XXIX when Don Jose, suffering bad crops, receives the cheering news that a new crop—sugar cane—has just been introduced into Louisiana, and that it is immune to the worms that have been destroying his indigo.

> "Oh, Senor, it will make you strong again to see these fields all cane and the long rows of negroes and negresses cutting it, while they sing their song of those droll African numerals, counting the canes they cut," and the bearer of good tidings sang them for very joy.[5]

This time Cable divides the lyrics into syllables below each note as in ordinary sheet music.

Cable applies this same unusual technique in another novel, *Bonaventure*, in which he reproduces a wedding song of the Acadian district of Louisiana.[6] His readers can thus perform his novels on the piano to some small extent, reproducing for themselves some of the musical atmosphere he tries to convey. But it is through his interest in the poetic ambiguity of the Negro's songs, in the music and rhythms of his dances, and in the Creole contribution to New Orleans music that we are reminded of a captivating novelist who was clearly aware that original music was churning in New Orleans during the nineteenth century. Though Cable died a very old man in 1925 before he began to be quoted by jazz critics, it seems doubtful that he would be at all dismayed by the attention that has been lavished on New Orleans music since his day, however sophisticated it may have become since the times of which he wrote.

Notes

1. Marshall Stearns, *The Story of Jazz* (New York: Oxford University Press, 1956), p. 73.

2. George W. Cable, "Creole Slave Songs," *Century Magazine*, 31 (April, 1886), 808.

3. George W. Cable, *The Grandissimes* (New York: Charles Scribner's Sons, 1929), pp. 121–22.

4. *The Grandissimes*, p. 404.

5. *The Grandissimes*, p. 245.

6. George W. Cable, *Bonaventure* (New York: International Association of Newspapers and Authors, 1901), p. 63.

Of Time and the River:
"Ancestral Nonsense" vs.
Inherited Guilt in Cable's
"Belles Demoiselles Plantation"

Howard W. Fulweiler[*]

. . . I hope to show, therefore, that a specifically literary approach to the work of an American writer—in this case, George Washington Cable—may add something to our general understanding of what Parrington called the "main currents of American thought."

In his New Orleans tale, "Belles Demoiselles Plantation," George Washington Cable describes the psychological compulsions that bind the the aristocratic Colonel de Charleu and his half-caste kinsman, Injin Charlie, to their respective family homes as "ancestral nonsense."[1] We are not entirely surprised at reading such a comment from the platform companion of that mytho-clastic realist, Mark Twain. Ironic commentary on the romantic idealism of the south comes as naturally to the local colorist Cable as it does to Mark Twain in the local color portions of *Life on the Mississippi*. The pragmatic and provisional quality of later nineteenth-century American thought, as it appears in the realistic modes of Twain, James, Howells or genre writers like Mary E. Wilkins Freeman and Sarah Orne Jewett, is often shared by Cable. Recent re-evaluation of Cable's fiction has been especially fruitful in demonstrating just this aspect of his work. Two perceptive essays by Louis Rubin and Edmund Wilson ably connect Cable to his own milieu and even suggest his relationship to serious contemporary southern regionalists, especially Faulkner.[2] Both Rubin and Wilson have particularly emphasized Cable's realism and the astonishing astuteness and courage of his social criticism of the post-Civil War South. This approach, however, has caused them to neglect the more commonly read local color stories of *Old Creole Days*. It has also caused them to overlook, I believe, some of the literary qualities in Cable's work which give it added dimension beyond social criticism on the one hand or the bizarre romanticism of so much local color on the other.

Richard Chase has described Cable's novel, *The Grandissimes*, as a "strongly realistic social novel" which "becomes at the same time a poetic melodrama."[3] This intriguing, if paradoxical, generalization points in the di-

[*]Reprinted from *Midcontinent American Studies Journal*, 7 (Fall, 1966), 53-59.

rection I think further Cable criticism should move. As an example of the kind of criticism Cable needs, I should like to take one of his most often anthologized stories, "Belles Demoiselles Plantation," and subject it to a critical close reading. Once we see what in fact we have in a representative story we may be better able to clarify our general concepts of Cable both as realistic social critic and as romanticist.

Since Lafcadio Hearn remarked in 1883 that "Belles Demoiselles Plantation" was the "most singular tale" in Cable's *Old Creole Days*, criticism has been uniformly respectful of the story's charm, but has offered little explanation of its artistic success.[4] This story, however, is more than charming. Its continued popularity is not the result of Cable's "love of mystification," or his treatment of "quaint" regional eccentricities. Instead, a mature control of plot, character and symbolism gives it a powerful unity of theme, which raises it above the topical slickness of so much local color fiction.

The theme of "Belles Demoiselles Plantation" is composed of two parts which are closely and intricately related. The first and more apparent aspect of the theme is mutability, the precariousness of human institutions and distinctions—social, racial or economic. The second, and perhaps more important aspect for Cable, the Presbyterian Sunday School teacher, is the Biblical drama of judgment, the inevitable justice of Providence, Whose agents are mutability and nature: time and the river. Added to this seemingly romantic theme is the subtly ironic tone of the narrator, the pragmatic and provisional commentator whose "common sense" realism deftly highlights the "ancestral nonsense" in the rigid attitudes of the protagonist and antagonist of the story. The tale achieves its peculiar quality of richness and depth by its craftsmanlike tension between a romantic theme of ancestral guilt and mutability and a sensitive, if ironic and pragmatic, point of view—a point of view almost Jamesian in its sense of the ongoing, unfolding quality of experience.

Judgment in "Belles Demoiselles Plantation," as in so much American literature, early and late, is exacted not only for the sins of the present generation, but also for the sins of past generations. Early in the story Cable tells us with a characteristic deadpan irony that the first Count de Charleu had left his Choctaw wife behind when he was recalled to France "to explain the lucky accident of his commissariat having burned down with his account-books inside." The Count's excuses were accepted for this almost Faulknerian accident, and he was rewarded by a grant of land. Cable then introduces the ancestral guilt of the De Charleu family ironically: "A man cannot remember every thing! In a fit of forgetfulness he married a French gentlewoman, rich and beautiful and 'brought her out.' " The artistry of the narration is apparent in its evenly balanced tension. Although Cable treats the concept of ancestral guilt ironically, he nevertheless takes the fact of guilt quite seriously. His irony shifts to a mordant indictment of the Count's indifference in the next sentence: "However, 'All's well that ends well;' a famine had been in the colony, and the Choctaw Comptesse had starved, leaving nought but a half-caste orphan family lurking on the edge of the settlement." From this first crime, which resulted in

the founding of the De Charleu dynasty, Cable carefully unfolds the consequences, the pragmatic results of the crime. He shows how the inevitable
working of judgment, operating in time, destroys the external values—money,
prestige, family, property—that the first Count and his descendants so
cherished.

Since the first Count sacrificed his integrity for prestige, for the continu-
ance of his "name" in all its feudal inconsequence, Cable comments indirectly
on the results of this act by a subtly modulated ironic symbolism. The fragility
of the legitimate branch of the family increases, as we see it rise, "generation
after generation, tall, branchless, slender, palm-like." This symbolic attenua-
tion of the masculine strength of the house finally flowers "with all the rare
beauty of a century-plant"—which blooms only once before death—in the
present Colonel's daughters. The "name," therefore, of which the Colonel is so
proud cannot, despite his day-dreams, be passed on. As time destroys the male
vitality of the legitimate branch of the family, so also the other branch, with the
sole exception of the childless Charlie, "diminished to a mere strand by in-
judicious alliances, and deaths in the gutters . . . was extinct." Similarly, the De
Charleu inheritance is slowly worn away by constant attrition from the Mississippi River.

> The Count's grant had once been a long Pointe, round which the Mississippi used to
> whirl, and seethe, and foam, that it was horrid to behold. Big whirlpools would open
> and wheel about in the savage eddies under the low bank, and close up again, and
> others open, and spin, and disappear.

The analogy between the action of the river, whose surface is constantly affected by its buried depths, and the buried past of the De Charleus is suggested
in Cable's imagery.

> Great circles of muddy surface would boil up from hundreds of feet below, and gloss
> over, and seem to float away,—sink, come back again under water, and with only a
> soft hiss surge up again, and again drift off, and vanish. Every few minutes the loamy
> bank would tip down a great load of earth upon its besieger, and fall back a foot—
> sometimes a yard—and the writhing river would press after, until at last the Pointe
> was quite swallowed up.

Until his final recognition of the truth, Colonel De Charleu avoids confron-
tation with the realities of time and judgment. Although his own plantation is
heavily mortgaged, the old man confidently plans to buy and rebuild the decayed property of De Carlos, the last descendant of the Count and his Indian
wife. Cable skillfully develops the contrast between external appearance and
inner reality. As the river quietly erodes the foundation upon which De Charleu's outer facade of wealth and position is displayed, so inner corruptions gnaw
secretly underneath the seemingly unchanged appearance of the man. "He had
had his vices—all his life; but had borne them, as his race do, with a serenity of
conscience and a cleanness of mouth that left no outward blemish on the surface
of the gentleman." Moral emptiness underlies the Colonel's aristocratic shell as
sterility and death lurk behind the final bloom of the century plant. Even De

Charleu's Creole virtue, that he "will not utterly go back on the ties of blood," is ironically related to his moral insensitivity and the ancestral guilt of his family. "He is never ashamed," Cable tells us of the Creole, "of his or his father's sins." Under the courtly exterior, there is only pride and self-love. Cable's incisive realism removes the mask of southern gentility. "With all his courtesy and bounty, and a hospitality which seemed to be entertaining angels, he was bitter-proud and penurious, and deep down in his hard-finished heart loved nothing but himself, his name, and his motherless children." One remembers, as no doubt the Bible scholar Cable remembered, that it was Lot, the inhabitant of Sodom, who entertained angels before judgment was executed on his home, and his daughters were rendered motherless.

The intricate dialectic between romantic theme and realistic point of view is further intensified as Cable continues to unfold his narrative. His realistic, though comic, treatment of the aristocratic Colonel's ludicrous and pathetic attempt to bolster his decaying external identity by acquiring Injin Charlie's house in town balances with delicate irony the transcendent theme of the story against the humorous *facts* of the situation. Although the attempts of the two old men—one of them deaf—to speak English are comic, mutability and judgment are always present, modifying and transforming the quality of the humor.

> "Eh, well Charlie!"—the Colonel raised his voice to suit his kinsman's deafness,—"how is those times with my friend Charlie?"
> "Eh?" said Charlie distractedly.
> "Is that goin' well with my friend Charlie?"
> "In de house,—call her,"—making a pretence of rising.
> "*Non, non!* I don't want,"—the speaker paused to breathe—"ow is collection.?"
> "Oh!" said Charlie, "everyday he make me more poorer!"
> "What do you hask for it?" asked the planter indifferently, designating the house by a wave of his whip.

This comic scene is finally terminated by what is both a significant revelation of character and an important turning point in the story.

> "I'll trade with you!" said Charlie.
> The Colonel was tempted. "'Ow'l you trade?" he asked.
> "My house for yours!"

Angered, the Colonel closes the interview. In the careful unraveling of the drama, the Colonel has been offered a choice: he has been given the opportunity to acknowledge the common humanity he shares with his kinsman, a brotherhood symbolized by the two inherited houses. This is the common humanity the first Count De Charleu denied in order to have a "name." The Colonel, like his ancestor, refuses to acknowledge his human brotherhood with De Carlos and in so doing refuses self-recognition as well.

The beginning of De Charleu's self-recognition comes some months after he has refused Charlie's final offer to trade his city block for the plantation house. Sitting on the levee, he muses on the emptiness of his past life, paralyzed and made useless by "pride," "gaming," and "voluptuous ease." Nevertheless, "his house still stood, his sweet-smelling fields were still fruitful, his name was fame enough; and yonder and yonder, among the trees and flowers, like angels walking in Eden, were the seven goddesses of his only worship." As the Colonel begins to perceive the attrition of time and vice on his personality, he turns complacently to the external possessions that have hitherto been his substitute for character—house, name, property, daughters. At this moment he hears a slight sound which brings him to his feet. "There came a single plashing sound, like some great beast slipping into the river, and little waves in a wide semicircle came out from under the bank and spread over the water." The bank upon which his house stands, the material foundation of his life, which had seemed so solid, has begun to cave in. Like Henry James's John Marcher, the Colonel has always avoided contact with the real substance of life until, with feral stealth, it slips into his life "like some great beast." Yet this first revelation does not cause a moral awakening in De Charleu; he only sees with brutal clarity the reality of time and decay.

At the threat of losing his property, in which he has always based his sense of identity, De Charleu's moral collapse becomes complete, and he hurries frantically back to town to trade his house for Old Charlie's block. It is not until the two men return to look at the property, that he finally has a true vision of himself; he recognizes that he is about "to betray his own blood," that he does share a common humanity with Charlie which he is ready to violate. Although he warns Charlie, time and the river are inexorable. The thoughtless super-ficiality and the self-seeking pride of the De Charleus, with their dependence upon externals, are judged. "Belles Demoiselles, the realm of maiden beauty, the home of merriment, the house of dancing, all in the tremor and glow of pleasure suddenly sunk, with one short, wild wail of terror—sunk, sunk, down, down, down, into the merciless, unfathomable flood of the Mississippi." If Cable has suggested God's punishment of Sodom and Gomorrah early in the story, he suggests finally His judgment of the contemporaries of Noah.

By this final symbolic action of the river Cable fuses his two themes into one. The river, as type and metaphor of time and mutability, the ever-flowing substance that has joined together the generations of the De Charleus and now washes them away, emerges as the agent of divine justice.

What conclusions are we to draw then from our close reading of this local color sketch? Before we come to conclusions, there are some questions that must be answered. Our reading shows clearly, it seems to me, that Cable is making use of the universal themes of mutability, sin, guilt and judgment presented in romantic, idealistic and sometimes gothic modes in the earlier fiction of Poe, Hawthorne or Melville. Does this mean that Cable's story is simply a continua-tion of the romantic symbolism of the earlier nineteenth century? Not exactly. Our reading seems to show differences and modifications as striking as the likenesses. Cable's delicate control of narrative point of view, his ironic balancing of pragmatic and unsentimental comment with romantic theme, and his sense of the ongoing, unfolding quality of experience relate him to the tradition of critical realism.

What general conclusions may we arrive at, then? Perhaps the work of Cable's friend and colleague, that sometime local colorist and frontier humorist, Mark Twain, may be instructive. It is a continual source of paradox that the elemental themes of a book like *Huckleberry Finn* have made inevitable mythic and romantic interpretations of Twain, a conscious, even self-conscious realist. In "Belles Demoiselles Plantation" we have a similar fusion of realistic technique with romantic theme. Does not our close reading, perhaps, make it possible to see Cable as more than an intelligent and socially aware critic of his own time or as a quaint romancer of superficial eccentricities? Do we not see another link in the chain of American literary history? I would like to suggest that in the realistically handled unravelling of the fate of the last of the De Charleus we may perhaps see even more clearly a stage in development from the openly romantic treatment of mutability, guilt and retribution in, say, "The Fall of the House of Usher" or *The House of the Seven Gables* toward the realistic myth of Yoknapatawpha County in the twentieth century. And is it not just this sort of concrete example of change, this fusion of traditions, that both illuminates and validates *our* concept of what Parrington might have termed a "main current" of American Thought.

Notes

1. All quotations from "Belles Demoiselles Plantation" are taken from *Old Creole Days* (New York: Charles Scribner's Sons, 1897), pp. 121-45.

2. See Edmund Wilson, *Patriotic Gore: Studies in the Literature of the American Civil War* (New York: Oxford University Press, 1962), pp. 548–87, and Louis D. Rubin, Jr., *The Faraway Country: Writers of the Modern South* (Seattle: University of Washington Press, 1963), pp. 21-42.

3. Richard Chase, *The American Novel and Its Tradition* (Garden City, N.Y.: Doubleday, 1957), p. 176.

4. Arlin Turner writes that the "plot is of the simplest and is only the vehicle for the character study," *George W. Cable: A Biography* (Durham, N.C.: Duke University Press, 1956), p. 58. Carlos Baker, writing of Cable's fiction in general, notices a "gentle love of mystification, a diffusion—not of syntax but of total effect—which seems to be the chief source of Cable's charm," *Literary History of the United States*, eds. Spiller, Thorp, Johnson and Canby (New York: Macillan, 1948), II, p. 857. In his generally laudatory essay on *The Grandissimes*, Richard Chase speaks of Cable as a "local colorist who wrote quaint, pathetic and humorous tales," p. 167.

The Division of the Heart: Cable's *The Grandissimes*

Louis D. Rubin, Jr.[*]

In an important sense, George W. Cable's *The Grandissimes* (1880) may be said to be the first "modern" Southern novel. For if the modern Southern novel has been characterized by its uncompromising attempt to deal honestly with the complexity of Southern racial experience, then *The Grandissimes* was the first important work of fiction written by a Southerner in which that intention is manifested. In this respect, Cable opened up the path along which Ellen Glasgow, William Faulkner, Thomas Wolfe, Robert Penn Warren, Eudora Welty, William Styron and others would follow. In unmistakable and uncompromising terms, he dealt with that most pervasive of all Southern social issues, the race question and the role of the Negro in society. If the loss of the Civil War had at last freed the Southern writer from the need to defend Southern racial attitudes, it was Cable who first took advantage of the new freedom.

In its own day *The Grandissimes* was highly praised, and its author compared, and not unfavorably, to Nathaniel Hawthorne himself. Along with *Old Creole Days*, the volume of short stories that was his first published book, the novel seemed to augur a brilliant career for the young ex-Confederate cavalry-man and cotton house clerk now come into national literary prominence. Unfortunately, that promise was never borne out. Cable went on to write seven more novels and numerous short stories before his death in 1925, but nothing that he did was ever to surpass, or even to equal, the literary achievement of his first two books.

To explain why Cable failed to develop beyond his first work is more than can be attempted in the confines of a single essay. It involves complex questions of time and place, his relationship to the South and to the Genteel Tradition that dominated American letters during the latter years of the nineteenth century, and, most importantly of all, his own complicated and sometimes even contradictory personality. All the same, if we look carefully at *The Grandissimes*, both in terms of its successes and its shortcomings, we may discover some clues to the answer.

"I meant," Cable wrote later in his life, "to make *The Grandissimes* as truly a political work as it ever has been called. . . . I was still very slowly and

[*]Reprinted from *Southern Literary Journal*, 1 (Spring, 1969), 27-47.

painfully guessing out the riddle of our Southern question." And again, "I wrote as near to truth and justice as I knew how, upon questions that I saw must be settled by calm debate and cannot be settled by force or silence; questions that will have to be settled thus by the Southern white man in his own conscience before even the North and South can finally settle it between them. This was part of my politics and as a citizen I wrote." But Cable's novel was more than a disquisition on race; it was also the picture of a society in transition, very much a *Kulturroman* as his friend the novelist H. H. Boyesen had predicted. And although set in New Orleans in 1803, just after the Louisiana Territory had been purchased by the United States from France, its implications were very much for post-Civil War Louisiana.

What seems most striking about *The Grandissimes* today is its rich social texture. Though the story had its romantic elements, in particular the conventional love story plot of the day, more than almost any other Southern novel of its time it was, to use the distinction set forth by Hawthorne in his Preface to *The House of the Seven Gables*, a Novel, as opposed to a Romance, in that it presumed to deal with the "probable and ordinary course of man's experience" rather than the fanciful, the Marvellous. Not of course that it is a work of Howellsian realism, and still less does it resemble the kind of faithfulness to everyday life of a Sinclair Lewis or a Sherwood Anderson. But its essential fidelity is to the here and now. The dynamics of the story arise from the problems of caste and class, the human beings are portrayed to a remarkable degree as they exist in everyday life. Cable's chief concern is with social problems, and the weaving of a dense social fabric, in which what transpires among the characters is presented as part of a complex community existence, is absolutely necessary to the meaning of the novel. We see Creoles, *Américains*, quadroons, Negroes at work and at play, in their homes and on the streets, of balls, receptions, feasts, eating meals, making love, in illness and in health, jesting, talking, quarreling, scheming, going about their lives from day to day. There is plenty of adventure and excitement, of course, and not a little violence—a riot, a lynching, a murder, several stabbings, even a suicide. Yet such events arise out of the patterns of community life for the most part, and exist not for their own sake alone but as the heightened representation of the ultimate tendencies of community life.

To readers of the day, for whom Creoles, quadroons, and life in a semi-tropical city in the early years of the century were strange and fascinating, the life depicted in *The Grandissimes* doubtless seemed romantic and exotic indeed. In particular the dialect that Cable's French-speaking Creoles used to converse in the English language with Americans was singularly droll; not only Mark Twain but others of Cable's literary friends zestfully savored its quaintness and delighted in talking to each other in Creole English. Cable was intensely interested in language, and his recreation of Creole speech was the product of close observation and considerable literary labor. When the Boston *Literary World* had criticized the way that the Creoles talked in "Jean-ah Poquelin," Cable had written to protest that he thought the accusation "does me real injustice. If I may do so I assure you that scarce a day has passed since the publication of 'Jean-ah Poquelin' that I am not told by persons who have been accustomed to hear the 'dialect' from their earliest days, and many of whom speak it, that I have rendered it capitally. . . ." Cable was quite careful to have his Creole characters speak in such fashion only when talking with Americans. Their conversations among themselves were reported in mostly flawless English. In his careful attention to the way in which his people talked, and his considerable reliance upon dialogue to develop his story, Cable resembled another American novelist whose work he perhaps had never read at the time, Henry James. And at its best, Cable's representation of the social scene, with its texture of dialogue and description, is reminiscent of James's fiction.

The events of *The Grandissimes* take place within no more than a year's time. The novel opens at a ball given in September of 1803, and closes in September of the year following. Its central character is one Joseph Frowenfeld, a young German who has come to Louisiana to make his fortune in the very year that the territory was sold by Napoleon to Thomas Jefferson. Frowenfeld sets himself up as a pharmacist, and begins to learn the ways of the Creoles and of the few *Américains* who are in the city. He becomes acquainted with the proud and powerful Grandissime family, whose ancestry dates from the earliest days of the province and from Bourbon France before that. The family's leader is Honoré Grandissime, a vigorous and thoughtful man in his thirties. Old Agricola Fusilier, Honoré's uncle, is proud, martial, the epitome of Grandissime pride and an exemplar of the Creole temperament at its most fiercely passionate and atavistic.

Frowenfeld is befriended by old Agricola, however, and also wins the friendship of Honoré, with whom he discusses the problems of caste and class and of Creole adjustment to the coming of American hegemony. He also makes the acquaintance of his landlord, likewise named Honoré, Grandissime, and he finds out that the two Honorés are half-brothers, sons of the same father but one by a white mother and the other by a quadroon. The two had attended school together in Paris, and it was to the quadroon Honoré that most of the father's considerable wealth had been left. Because the older Honoré, known as "f.m.c."—free man of color—is of mixed blood, however, he is not recognized by the family, and is considered beyond the pale of white society. The clash of the close blood ties of the two Honoré Grandissimes and the separation by race that the society requires constitutes the main dramatic struggle of the novel.

There is, however, a love plot, which Cable has woven into the problem of caste. Among Joseph Frowenfeld's clients are Aurore de Grapion-Nancanou, in her thirties and still very attractive, and her daughter Clotilde. Aurore's husband had gambled with Agricola Fusilier, lost his plantation, fought a duel with Agricola, and been killed. Their plantation now owned by the Grandissimes, the Nancanous live in genteel but extreme poverty. Honoré Grandissime has long been in love with Aurore, and Frowenfeld soon falls in love with Clotilde. But Honoré is loved by a quadroon, Palmyre Philosophe, and she in her turn is loved by Honoré's brother, Honoré Grandissime f.m.c.

The resultant overlapping triangle is further complicated by the passionate hatred borne by Palmyre for Agricola Fusilier, which goes back to the time of Bras-Coupé, a Negro slave. Written originally as a short story, the Bras-Coupé narrative was incorporated into *The Grandissimes* as a story within the story, and as such it represents an effective thematic presentation of the issue of Negro slavery that is at the novel's heart. An African prince, Bras-Coupé had been brought as a slave to the plantation of a Spaniard, Don José, and betrothed to Palmyre by her owner, Agricola Fusilier. Palmyre already detested Agricola, and his willingness to give her to the huge African, whom she admired but did not love, only infuriated her the more. The wedding, which the Creoles all considered a joke because it involved Negroes, took place as part of the ceremony in which Bras-Coupé's owner Don José was being wed to Honoré Grandissime's sister, but it was not consummated, because when Bras-Coupé, drunk on wine, was refused another drink by Don José, he knocked him down and ran away. The huge slave lived in the swamps, with all attempts to capture him failing, while the voodoo curse he had placed on Don José's establishment was followed by Don José's taking sick and dying and his plantation and crops deteriorating. Finally Bras-Coupé was captured when drunk, while he danced in Congo Square outside the city. He was whipped, mutilated, and hamstrung at the order of the dying Don José, just as the law decreed for a slave who struck his master. Before he died, however, Bras-Coupé lifted the curse on the now-dead Don José's child. Then, when asked by a priest "Do you know where you are going?," the huge slave murmured "To—Africa," and died.

Palmyre Philosophe's continued hate for Agricola Fusilier causes her to attempt to put a voodoo curse upon him, and she employs a Negro cake vendor, Clemence, to place various voodoo talismans about Agricola's house. Meanwhile, Honoré Grandissime, whom Palmyre loves in vain, has decided to make recompense to Aurore de Grapion for the loss of her plantation to Agricola. To do so, he endangers his financial well being, and therefore that of the Grandissime family. Both because of that and because of his decision, in which he is encouraged by Joseph Frowenfeld, that the caste system that puts him and his brother asunder is wrong, he enters into a business partnership with Honoré Grandissime f.m.c., to be known as Grandissime Brothers. In thus officially recognizing his kinship to his half-caste brother, he earns the dismay of the family and the outrage of Agricola Fusilier.

Meanwhile the cake vendor Clemence is captured as she goes to Agricola Fusilier's house to place a voodoo fetish there, at the behest of Palmyre, and she is taken out by the whites and shot to death. Then, as Agricola Fusilier talks with Joseph Frowenfeld in the Druggist's shop, Honoré Grandissime f.m.c. enters. The enraged Agricola orders him to remove his hat, and when the half-caste refuses, attacks him, whereupon the half-caste stabs Agricola, who dies shortly thereafter. Honoré f.m.c. and Palmyre flee to Paris, but still in love with the white Honoré, Palmyre refuses the f.m.c.'s hand, and the half-caste takes his own life by diving into the harbor at Bordeaux. As for the white Honoré, he is accepted in marriage by Aurore de Grapion, while Frowenfeld himself marries the daughter Clotilde.

The elaborate family relationships of the Grandissimes are unraveled only slowly by Joseph Frowenfeld, as he comes to learn the nature and the customs of New Orleans society, and it is his deepening discovery of the situation, with its overtones of caste, injustice, and clashing concepts of honor, that provides the narrative development of the novel. Of German parentage, but reared in America, Frowenfeld represents the coming of the Anglo-American ways to Creole Louisiana. A scientist, without prejudices of caste, Frowenfeld is characterized by an innocence that enables him to judge the attitudes and the ways of Creole society objectively, and though he is made out as being somewhat naive and rather too quick to view complex questions of custom, caste, and habit in terms of abstract moral principles, it is plain that Frowenfeld's opinions represent Cable's, and that his lack of commitment to Creole society renders him able to judge it by superior moral standards. Thus Honoré Grandissime, who recognizes this, instinctively turns to Frowenfeld for advice and support in his problems, and the counsel he receives from Frowenfeld is always disinterestedly moral.

But if *The Grandissimes* was designed to be a *Kulturroman*, a novel of the clash between two societies, it must be noted from the outset that Cable's own conscious position in the matter is *not* as disinterested artist bent on showing the accommodations forced upon both sides and the values inherent in the opposing social ideas. For although Cable makes a few gestures to the effect that Frowenfeld is naive, overly given to theory, too innocent of human perception, and so forth, there is really very little attention paid to Frowenfeld's own liabilities. What Frowenfeld must learn is never any new moral perspectives, but only a more detailed knowledge of the society he has come to join. Nothing that Frowenfeld does find out about the society serves to change in any way his views or the judgments he makes; what he discovers only confirms and clarifies his principles, which he never questions, and which Cable also never questions. Thus Cable's viewpoint is not so much *of* Frowenfeld as it is *through* and *with* Frowenfeld.

Arlin Turner has noted the relevance of the novel to the problems of post-Civil War New Orleans, and the probability that Cable was well aware of this. The Creoles of Louisiana, at the time of its acquisition by the United States, faced the necessity of coming to terms with a government imposed upon them and not of their own choosing, and they saw in that government a threat to their own institutions and rights. Similarly the New Orleans of the years following the Civil War had a government imposed upon it by force, and pledged, in theory at least, to political and social principles very much at odds with those of the society thus subjected. In both instances, what was being forced upon New Orleans from the outside was, as Cable saw it, a government based upon ideals of liberty and attitudes of progress which ran counter to established prejudices and which demanded new and more enlightened responses. And in making the problems of race and caste the central theme of his novel of the Louisiana of 1803, Cable was dealing with the single most controversial and inflammatory issue of post-Civil War Louisiana life.

Cable's original impulse for writing the story which became the Bras-

Coupé episode had come from his having encountered the restrictive provisions of the ante-bellum laws for punishment of Negroes. Cable transferred this concern to the larger scope of the novel, and the episode of Bras-Coupé is made into the novel's principal thematic motif. The violation of the Negro's humanity involved in his enslavement is dramatically symbolized by the depiction of the tall, handsome African prince standing regally among the Creoles, and the curse he pronounces upon his owner's plantation when he is mistreated signifies the blight that the South brought upon itself and its lands by the moral crime of human slavery. The callous willingness of the whites to flout Bras-Coupé's dignity and integrity by staging the mock wedding of the slave with the unwilling Palmyre is a measure of the white South's insensitivity to the Negro's humanity, and the acquiescence of the Catholic priest who performs the ceremony in the violation is emblematic of the failure of Southern Christianity to perceive the moral wrong of slavery and caste. Properly treated, respected as a human being, Bras-Coupé could have been of tremendous help to the whites in their agricultural enterprise—and Cable makes a point of showing how the material advantages even of slave life exceeded anything that Bras-Coupé had known in his African savagery. But by their inhuman, unfeeling exploitation of him, Bras-Coupé was converted into an implacable enemy by his Creole owners, and his vengeance causes the death of his owner even while he is himself dying. His final words, in which he expresses his yearning for his African home, signify his desire for freedom above all else. The inescapably brutal nature of the whole transaction, the savagery whereby the African is subdued and forced into the status of slave, constituted a powerful indictment of the racial injustice and suppression which lay at the base of New Orleans—and Southern—society.

The wrong done to Bras-Coupé is emblematic of the basic corruption that runs through Creole New Orleans, and it is precisely the same attitudes that could acquiesce in the enslavement and mutilation of Bras-Coupé, that permit the humiliation of Honoré Grandissime f.m.c. Significantly, it is Agricola Fusilier who plays a leading role in both transactions. That fiery, passionate old Creole had been willing to give Palmyre to be Bras-Coupé's bride, had resisted all the efforts of the white Honoré to bring about a reconciliation between Bras-Coupé's owner and the slave who was hiding out in the swamps, had insisted upon the whipping and mutilation of the captured Bras-Coupé in accordance with the provisions of the *Code Noir*. It was he who refused to recognize his nephew Honoré's acceptance of his half-brother the f.m.c., and by assaulting the f.m.c. had brought about his own death and the flight of the f.m.c. to France. In his terrible pride, his furious insistence upon purity of race at the expense of justice and of blood ties, his invincible belligerence and his championing of Creole rights and Creole virtue, Agricola Fusilier typifies the unreasoning atavism of the Creoles, and by inference, of the white South.

Yet such are Cable's insight and artistry that the basic characterization of the fiery old Creole is by no means totally unsympathetic. For Cable recognizes the pathos and dignity of the proud old man, the heroic quality of his misguided loyalty to Creole tradition and his zeal in a miserable cause, and the warmth of his friendship as well as of his hatred. The deathbed scene, in which the mortally wounded old Creole struggles for words with which to imbue his kinsmen with his own lifelong prejudices and loyalties, is one of the most moving in the novel. Feeling his grasp slipping on a world in which his own fixed principles and goals seem to be commanding less and less respect, he tries to rally the young men to their defense. "Oh, Honoré," he pleads with his nephew, "you and the Yankees—you and—all—going wrong—education—masses— weaken—caste—indiscr—quarrels settl'—by affidav—Oh! Honoré." To his friend Frowenfeld he says, "Joseph, son, I do not see you. Beware, my son, of the doctrine of equal rights—a bottomless iniquity. Master and man—arch and pier—arch above—pier below." Then, at the very last, "Agamemnon! Valentine! Honoré! patriots! protect the race! Beware of the"—

that sentence escaped him. He seemed to fancy himself haranguing a crowd; made another struggle for intelligence, tried once, twice, to speak, and the third time succeeded:

"Louis-Louisian—a—for—ever!" and lay still. They put those two words on his tomb.

Here, as indeed throughout the novel, the artistry of Cable takes precedence over the politics and is responsible for so much of the success of *The Grandissimes*. For it is impossible, more so perhaps than Cable had consciously intended, not to admire the old man's conviction and his resolution. If, as is likely, Cable intended for Agricola Fusilier to represent not simply a passionate old man, and not merely the embodiment of Creole virtues and vices, but of those of the South itself, then his very name, signifying the planter and the soldier, is quite appropriate. For Cable himself, the onetime trooper of the Fourth Mississippi Cavalry, C.S.A., had long since come to feel that he and his countrymen had fought bravely and well for a cause that was unjust, and that the South's passionate bellicosity, however heroic in battle, represented a primitive, unreasoned defiance of the moral imperatives of the nineteenth century.

In any event, it is what Cable was able to do with Agricola Fusilier that makes his novel so compelling an examination of his society. For it enabled him to portray Creole society with considerable fondness and sympathy even while he was engaged in searching out its essential defects, and to save his novel from becoming a didactic censuring of Creole deficiencies alone. There was no conscious doubt in his mind as to where, between the Creoles and the newly arriving Anglo-Americans, the chief virtues lay. With the notable exception of old Fusilier, Cable's Creoles were generally portrayed as possessing important positive virtues only to the extent that they were atypical of their race. Honoré Grandissime is seriously disturbed over the racial views of a society which would force him to deny his kinship with his half-brother; he will not adopt the short-sighted policy of refusing to take part in the new American government being imposed on New Orleans; he does not share the Creole contempt for mercantile pursuits; and he places justice above both expedience and pride by restoring to the Nancanous the value of the plantation that Agricola Fusilier had won in a game of chance.

Agricola's own refusal to give up the Nancanou plantation had been dictated not by its financial worth, but by the imputation that he had won it unfairly. He had written to the widow and offered to restore the estate, if she would only state in writing her belief that the stakes had been won fairly; if not, he would be compelled to retain the plantation in vindication of his honor. It is Honoré's salvation that he perceives the emptiness and falsehood of what even Charlie Keene had considered necessary Creole honor. And in the letter in which he restores the property, Honoré Grandissime appends these words: "*Not for love of woman, but in the name of justice and the fear of God.*"

In contrast to the idealistic Frowenfeld, however, Honoré is aware of the difficulties involved in reforming conditions in New Orleans. In an early conversation with Frowenfeld, he remarks, gesturing toward a path in the fields, "Now, Mr. Frowenfeld, you see? One man walks where he sees another's track; that is what makes a path; but you want a man, instead of passing around this prickly bush, to lay hold of it with his naked hands and pull it up by the roots." To which Frowenfeld replies, "But a man armed with the truth is far from being barehanded."

Quite expectedly, Honoré's conduct, in the affair of the Nancanou estate, in his willingness to cooperate with the American governor Claiborne, and in his public recognition of his kinship with the half-breed f.m.c. implied in his use of the name *Grandissime Brothers* for his firm, arouses intense hostility among his family. Their dilemma is cruel, because in gaining for his firm the considerable financial resources of the f.m.c., Honoré has rescued the family fortunes from considerable imperilment. As Raoul Innerarity, Frowenfeld's devoted clerk and member of the Grandissime family, tells Doctor Keene, "H-only for 'is money we would 'ave catch' dat quadroon gen'leman an' put some tar and fedder."

Except for Honoré Grandissime, the Nancanous, and perhaps Agricola Fusilier, most of the other Creoles in *The Grandissimes*, like those in *Old Creole Days*, are portrayed, on the conscious level at least, with a mixture of condescending good humor and moral scorn. The best of them is Raoul Innerarity, who as Frowenfeld's clerk comes to admire and trust his immigrant employer even though he does not understand Frowenfeld's odd opinions on race and society. Innerarity is attractive and amusing because of his quaintness, vanity, and hedonism. It is he who proposes that Frowenfeld exhibit and sell for him in his store window the painting of "Louisiana rif-using to hanter de h-Union!" which so amuses and appals Frowenfeld, and becomes for him the symbol of Creole dilettantism in the fine arts. Raoul is one of Cable's prime comic characters, the best perhaps of all the minor portraitures that adorn the rich texture of Creole life that contributes so much to the charm and the firmness of Cable's literary art.

As for most of the other Creoles, they are vain, boastful, sensual, and given to violence. Enraged over Honoré's "betrayal," incensed at the presence of the

American governor and his agents, harangued by Agricola, they go off in a rage and take revenge on the first convenient object, which happens to be Frowenfeld's store; holding back the loyal Raoul Innerarity so that he cannot interfere, they sack the druggist's establishment. Again, having trapped the calas-vendor Clemence at midnight as she creeps through the woods to do Palmyre's bidding and plant another voodoo talisman on Aricola's property, they form into a lynch mob and prepare to hang the terrified old Negro woman. As if in mercy, they remove the noose, and tell her to run for her life; as she scuttles off, one of them shoots her in the back.

Thus in *The Grandissimes* Cable joined to the unflattering picture of the Creoles as seen in *Old Creole Days* a direct castigation of their racial attitudes. The Creoles are depicted not only as being sensual, backward, morally lax; they are strident racists as well, and they embody the spirit of the lynch mob. Through the person of the old cake-vendor Clemence, Cable delivers himself of some direct criticisms of racism. He shows how Clemence must pick her way warily among the whites, and masquerade her opinions in order to keep from starving to death. He demonstrates the fatuity of white assumption about Negro attitudes. When someone tells her that "you niggers don't know when you are happy," she replies, "Dass so, Mawse—*c'est vrai, oui!* . . . we donno no mo'n white folks!" And she tells Charlie Keene, "white folks is werry kine. Dey wants us to b'lieb we happy—dey *wants to b'lieb* we is. W'y, you know, dey 'bleeged to b'lieb it—for' dey own cyumfut. 'Tis de sem weh wid de preache's; dey buil' we ow own sep'ate meet'n-houses; dey b'leebs us lak it de bess, an' dey *knows* dey lak it de bess." Her independence, her ostensibly good-humored insolence, do not go unnoticed, however, and when the opportunity comes, as it does when she is trapped while bearing Palmyre's voodoo fetishes, Creole revenge is swift. The scene in which the old Negro is killed is one of Cable's most effective; the very lack of didactic intrusion makes it a powerful indictment of lynching.

It should be noted that Cable's dislike and disapproval of the Creoles do not extend to their women. Though occasionally he enters a sarcastic remark, as for example about the compassion of the Creole women being exhibited in their desire that the Negro woman Clemence be given only "a sound whipping" for having been caught bearing the voodoo objects toward Agricola Fusilier's house, Cable generally portrays Creole ladies as soft, tender, and financially impractical. The essence of their femininity comes in their innocence of the real world; the Nancanous are wholly incompetent to take care of their financial problems, and are easily led. Whatever they lack in business acumen, however, they more than make up for in their beauty and their devotion to true love. What in male Creoles would be portrayed as faults are for Creole ladies part of their charm. The Nancanous, for example, are highly superstitious, but their faith in charms and folk remedies is made into an emblem of an impracticality that adds to their femininity. Their inability to comprehend the philosophical pronouncements of Frowenfeld only increases their feminine appeal. As women, they feel rather than think; their emotions are their chief concern, and they live for love.

In portraying the Nancanous, of course, Cable was creating his heroines in the accepted stereotype of the romance form, and since their chief function in *The Grandissimes*, as in most of his other fiction, is to advance the love story plot, they are circumscribed by the needs of the story line. But Cable's males, in *The Grandissimes* at least, are not thus limited by their roles in the love story plot, and so it will not do to explain their limitations of intellect and the general recessiveness of Cable's female Creoles as being due to plot function alone. Rather, they are indicative of the kind of attraction that the sensuous and the voluptuous held for Cable; that he conceived of Creole women as so very feminine, and so sensuously appealing in their helplessness and impracticality, is an index to his ambivalent attitude toward the Creoles. His conscious disapproval of so much that the Creoles stand for is accompanied by a considerable delight in the sensuous, languorous ways of the Creoles; as an artist he is drawn to their impracticality, their hedonism, their love of ease and their addiction to creature comfort. This comes out not only in the manner in which Cable designs his heroines, but in numerous other ways. However much his own Calvinist upbringing may have taught him to regard dancing as a sin, for example, his delight in describing the masquerade ball that opens the novel is clear. His depiction of the Grandissime women gathered together for their fête de grand-père shows a connoisseur's eye for feminine beauty. Nor is Cable's awareness of female loveliness restricted to pure-blooded Creoles; he is adept in his description of quadroon beauty. And if the Nancanous are soft and helpless, not so the beautiful Palmyre Philosophe. She is sensual, svelte, predatory; Cable uses the word "feline" to describe her appearance and her disposition. The scene in which Joseph Frowenfeld goes to her quarters to tend her wound in place of the ill Doctor Keene, and administers to her as she lies in her bed, is full of a repressed sexuality made only more smouldering by Cable's claim that Frowenfeld, almost alone of the men she knows, does not look upon the quadroon women as a sexual object. The description of Frowenfeld's emotions upon leaving Palmyre Philosophe is striking:

> It was many an hour after he had backed out into the trivial remains of the rainstorm before he could replace with more tranquillizing images the vision of the philosophe reclining among her pillows, in the act of making that uneasy movement of her fingers upon the collar button of her robe, which women make when they are uncertain about the perfection of their dishabille, and giving her inaudible adieu with the majesty of an empress.

In such scenes, and in others such as the several descriptions of Aurore and Clotilde Nancanou in their bedroom at night, Cable clearly exhibits both his talent for and delight in the voluptuous.

But if an eye for sensuous beauty is very much a part of Cable's art, it is emphatically not made into an aspect of Joseph Frowenfeld's character. That young man is almost unbelievably high minded and out of touch with the baser realities of world around him. In the passage just quoted, in which Joseph leaves the presence of Palmyre Philosophe, it is unlikely that Cable meant consciously to imply that Frowenfeld was attracted by the physical beauty of the quadroon;

what ostensibly disturbs the pharmacist is the plight of the woman, who because of her Negro blood is automatically considered "as legitimate prey" for all Creole males. Frowenfeld's moral rectitude pointedly distinguishes him from almost all the Creole males, and it is depicted as an aspect of his Northern European, which is to say, his German, but in effect his Anglo-American, Protestant nature. So much so that it comes with something of a shock to realize that an important part of what, after all, takes place in *The Grandissimes* is that this high minded, shy, studious young immigrant has come to New Orleans and within a single year's time has not only become a highly successful businessman, but has won the hand of a lovely Creole heiress in whose veins flow, as Charlie Keene put it early in the novel, the "best blood of the Province; good as the Grandissimes." For someone who disapproves of ancestry-worship, social caste, and sordid materialism, Frowenfeld would seem to have done quite well for himself both socially and financially. If it is an inner grace that Frowenfeld possesses, then in true Calvinist fashion the outward sign would seem to have been made manifest in his acquisition of the things of this world.

To suggest such a meaning to *The Grandissimes* is startling, to say the least, for none of the rhetoric of the novel seems to run in that direction. The design of the book, after all, is to show the triumph of non-Creole virtue and the evils of both racism and caste. That its hero, having come to see the pervasive cruelty of Creole racial attitudes and the emptiness of Creole boasts of social caste, should end by marrying a Creole heiress, would seem an odd way to confirm what he has learned, however, for it might tend to suggest a very different conclusion, to the effect that true success consisted of securing a high place in just that Creole society that has ostensibly been so condemned.

In the letter that Cable had written to the editor of the Boston *Literary World* in 1875 to defend the authenticity of his Creole dialect in "Jean-ah Poquelin," Cable had concluded his defense with a strange claim: "Though it does not absolutely prove anything I will add that I am a creole myself, living today in sight of the house where I was born." That the lie therein told was told for the purpose of convincing the editor of the authority with which he portrayed Creole dialect seems clear; but even so, it is an interesting matter. To assert, in private correspondence with a Boston editor who would surely not know the claim was false, membership in a society of which he is publicly so censorious, and of whose many differences from his own society he was so very conscious, would seem to indicate less actual disapproval of Creole society than Cable appeared to feel. And when we remember, too, that Joseph Frowenfeld, who is so clearly Cable's surrogate in the novel, is rewarded by winning the hand of a Creole heiress of high social position, and we keep in mind the obvious unconscious attraction that Creole life and Creole ways actually held for Cable, we might well question just what George W. Cable's attitude toward the Creoles of New Orleans was. It would seem to be rather more complex than one might at first glance suspect.

Certainly Cable was sincere when he castigated Creole lethargy and smugness, and there can be little doubt of his strong conviction as to the cruelty of

Creole racial attitudes; within the next few years he was to brave the censure of not only the Creoles but the entire white South in order to speak the truth as he saw it. Yet all the same, cannot one perhaps detect evidence of a certain amount of envy of the Creoles as well—the desire, surely not consciously held, to gain a place in the very Creole society he professed to disprove of, and which might, because suppressed, manifest itself in an intensified zeal for denouncing the attitudes and pretensions of that society? But if this is so, it must be emphasized that whatever secret attractions that Creole ways may have held for Cable were almost entirely unconscious. Nothing that Frowenfeld says, and very little that he thinks, would indicate the presence of such an attraction.

Throughout *The Grandissimes*, Frowenfeld is not a character who is ever subjected to much critical scrutiny by his author. Cable assumes that Frowenfeld's motives are of the highest, and his only sin is a certain amount of naiveté, a tendency to go off into theoretical abstractions and pronounce moral judgments a bit too readily. "My-de'-seh," Honoré Grandissime tells Frowenfeld at one point, "you mus' *crack* the egg, not smash it!" Frowenfeld may at times be somewhat too hasty and tactless, but Frowenfeld is *right*, in Cable's view.

For Frowenfeld there was, ultimately, success, love, the hand and heart of a Creole heiress. We see him out walking along the levee arm-in-arm with Clotilde Nancanou; they exchange confidences, "no part of which was heard by alien ears," and the lovely Creole tells her "lately accepted lover" how long she has loved him. Frowenfeld is indeed an alien no more; he has been accepted into Creole society, insofar as winning the hand of an authentic De Grapion-Nancanou, and having for his closest friend and now his step-father Honoré Grandissime himself may be said to constitute acceptance. Yet the novel itself has been, ostensibly at least, unconcerned with Frowenfeld's social mobility, so that when we think about what Frowenfeld has been able to accomplish in Creole society, we are quite startled. Not only has it not been explained, but we have not been made conscious that Frowenfeld *had* any ambitions of this sort. He seems entirely innocent of the whole business.

What, one might wonder, would a writer such as Marcel Proust have made of Frowenfeld's ascendency? And how would Proust, for example, or Henry James perhaps, have looked upon the apparently quite inexplicable way in which proud, caste-conscious Agricola Fusilier is made immediately to take up the immigrant pharmacist Joseph Frowenfeld and become his friend and champion?[1] What is clear is that Cable himself fails completely to study Frowenfeld in terms of the remarkable social mobility that he displays. His *Kulturroman* describes in great depth the impact of Anglo-American culture upon the Creoles, but almost nothing of the reverse of the process. The latter transaction we can only surmise. In place of what might have been a fascinating delineation of the manner in which an outsider responds to the attractions of a richly complex, formidable but ultimately vulnerable society, we are given only the high minded but wooden and lifeless characterization of Joseph Frowenfeld.

It is this, I think, that prevents *The Grandissimes*, for all its undoubted excellence of social texture and its unflinching realistic dramatization of the evils of caste and of racism, from being a novel of the first rank. In the best of Clemens, Hawthorne, Melville, one finds no such area of experience within the story so completely neglected. Because of this neglect, the love plot of *The Grandissimes* remains a romantic stereotype, and the author's strictures on Creole society, because not examined in terms of motive, tend toward didacticism. Cable's New York editors were quite right in insisting as they did that he cut down on some of the preaching. But what his editors did not recognize, and so could not tell Cable, was that the reason *why* the author was being didactic was that, instead of examining his character's motives, he was letting the pharmacist serve, uncritically and directly, as surrogate for himself. For the most part the characterization of Joseph Frowenfeld seemed quite adequate to Cable's editors, and the sentimental (because partly unmotivated) love plot whereby the story is resolved and in part structured quite acceptable. Both character and plot fitted the requirements, and suited the aesthetics, of popular serialized fiction well enough. Cable's editor Robert Underwood Johnson complained only that Frowenfeld sometimes seemed too saintly; he ought to have lost control of himself sufficiently to have knocked Sylvestre Grandissime down when the little Creole slapped him: "As it is, don't you see you are doing just what you don't want to do—making goodness seem unattributable because not mixed with enough humanity—human frailty if you will." But of what the frailty should have consisted, Johnson did not say. For Joseph Frowenfeld to have envied some of the social glamor of the Creoles of Louisiana, to have been attracted at least partially by the sensuality of their ways, to have exhibited, in short, just a trifle of the motivations of a social climber, would have hardly suited a magazine hero of the Genteel Tradition.

What is missing, in short, from this novel is enough *introspection*. For if Frowenfeld represents Cable, then what happens to Frowenfeld bears considerable relationship to its author. And what happens to Frowenfeld is at considerable variance from the kind of person he ostensibly is. The obvious attraction that Creole society, and some of the values of that society, held for Cable is not reflected in what Cable *says* Frowenfeld is, but it is very much reflected in what Frowenfeld *does*. There is no evidence that Cable himself ever recognized the discrepancy. He was unable to apprehend—and whether consciously or on the level of fictional characterization it does not finally matter—the mixed motives and clashing sensibilities within himself.

Throughout the course of a long life and literary career, the same sharp division would always be present. On the one hand there was the social critic, far in advance of his time, who felt deep outrage at the injustice and humiliation forced upon the recently-freed Negro throughout Southern society, and who embarked on a heroic but futile campaign on the lecture platform and in his writings to awaken the conscience of his region and the nation to the way in which the freedman was being denied his civil rights. On the other hand there was the artist who relished the savor of Creole ways, delighted in the social milieu, admired its distinction and distinctiveness, and zestfully rendered the rich textural fabric of Southern society.

He never brought the two impulses together, never attempted to realize and to delineate the contradictions and cruxes involved in their presence within a single sensibility, his own. The result was that something is absent at the heart of his fiction, so that it remains divided. Plot and characterization, form and meaning, never come properly together, for the sensibility that should join them is missing from all his principal characterizations. It was only within himself that he could have found the necessary reconciliation, for it was there that it existed. He never found it, because he never looked there. The result was that *The Grandissimes*, George W. Cable's best novel, a work of social observation of Southern society unsurpassed in its time, and the first novel by a Southerner to deal seriously with the relationships of white and Negro, remains even so a deeply flawed work.

Notes

1. As a fictional character, Agricola Fusilier has some lines that are worthy of the Baron de Charlus, as when he declares that "Hah! sir, I know men in this city who would rather eat a dog than speak English! *I* speak it, but I also speak Choctaw."

French-English Literary Dialect in *The Grandissimes*

William Evans*

By the time George Washington Cable wrote *The Grandissimes*, in 1879, use of the French language in Louisiana was in decline. Like the French speech of England five hundred years before, it could still be heard and would continue to be heard, but its day of dominance was over. Unlike the French of medieval England, of course, this New-World French had been the native language of the European settlers of the area and had become firmly entrenched in the homes of simple and sophisticated alike. And even during the forty-odd years of Spanish rule in the latter eighteenth century, when Spanish was the official language, French actually prevailed—not only in the home, but also on most levels of communication.[1] It was only with the official arrival of the Americans in 1803—the period in which *The Grandissimes* is set—that the commanding position of Fench began to be seriously threatened. Nine years later, when the southern tip of the Louisiana Purchase became a state, the handwriting was clearly on the wall. Although laws were to be written and cases tried in both French and English for decades,[2] and although judicial announcements were to be published in French in the New Orleans papers for more than a hundred years afterwards,[3] it was obvious by 1812 that the intruding Americans had the authority and the numbers to make their language ultimately the dominant one. And it is equally obvious from contemporary documents, such as C.C. Robin's *Voyage to Louisiana*,[4] and from the pages of Cable's novel that the Creoles[5] of the period were not about to give up their linguistic heritage without a bitter struggle. It is significant, for example, that one of Cable's most outspoken Creoles in the novel, Agricola Fusilier, maintained that he knew "men in this city [New Orleans] who would rather eat a dog than speak English."[6] And even Cable's most captivating feminine character, the Creole Aurore de Grapion Nancanou, took a letter written to her in English and "held it out . . . as if she was lifting something alive by the back of the neck."[7]

It was out of this tangle of passionate hatred of the new and strange and American, and passionate attachment to the old and familiar and French, that Cable wove his novel of contrasts and clashes between Creole and American

*Reprinted from *American Speech*, 46 (Fall–Winter, 1971), 210–22.

and between Creole and Creole in the earliest days of American rule in Louisiana. And the same minute attention that he gave to the people and to the times, he gave also to their language—as reflected, however, in the speech of their descendants seventy-five years later.[8] Cable's close study of the speech of the Creoles of his day—especially their colorful blend of French and English— is suggested by his informal, but informative, comments on French-English phonology in his historical volume *The Creoles of Louisiana*. His observations here are somewhat impressionistic, to be sure, and are not always marked by a clear distinction between sound and symbol. The Creole, according to Cable, "makes a languorous *z* of all *s*'s and soft *c*'s except initials" and he "flattens long *i*, as if it were coming through cane-crushers."[9] But Cable is often perceptive underneath it all, and most of his comments in this discussion are graphically reflected in the pages of *The Grandissimes*.

PHONOLOGY

The major phonological characteristics of the literary dialect of *The Grandissimes*, from the point of view of a speaker of standard English, include alteration of consonants, variation in vowels, and some apparent change in prosodic patterns. The consonant alterations usually involve final consonants, which are either lost or modified in various ways. The dental stops /t/ and /d/, for example, tend to disappear in final clusters (*innocent/innocen', and/an'*). In the final unstressed syllables of words like *impossible* and *people*, the liquid /l/ tends to be lost and, from the English viewpoint, the syllable as well— though for the French speaker this would presumably be simplification of a consonant cluster (*impossible/impossib', people/peop'*). Preconsonantal and final /r/ tends to disappear also, not only in final unstressed syllables, but in both stressed and unstressed syllables, whatever their position (*for/fo', father/ fatheh, retards/retahds, merchant/mehchant*). There are a few initial losses: the initial fricative /h/, in both words and syllables, often tends to disappear (*head/'ead, behind/be'ine*) but, on the other hand, is frequently added in words beginning with vowels (*ask/ hask*). And in the initial sequence /hw/ that occurs historically in words like *what* and *where*, the first element /h/ also tends to disappear (*what/w'at, where/w'ere*). However, the fricatives /f/ and /s/ and stops /p/, /t/, and /k/ in final position after vowels are not lost, but tend to become voiced (*if/iv, yes/yez, shop/shob, not/nod, knock/knog*). Replacement of the velar nasal /ŋ/ by the dental nasal /n/ is frequent in final position (*crying/cryne, anything/annyt'in'*). Sometimes prevocalic /r/ presumably becomes more characteristically French, as indicated by an orthographic *h* (*recollect/rhecollect, preserved/prheserved, cherishing/cherhishing*). The dental fricatives /θ/ and /ð/ usually appear as the corresponding stops /t/ and /d/ (*month/mont', something/somet'ing, think/t'ink; with/ wid, other/odder, those/doze*).

Variations in vowels are also relatively frequent in the novel, but they are confined largely to front vowels. The high-front and mid-front tense vowels /i/ and /ɛ/ often change—again from the English point of view—to the corresponding lax vowels /ɪ/ and /ɛ/. Instead of *please* and *fever*, for instance, we find *pliz* and *fivver;* and instead of *slave* and *make,* we find *slev* and *mek.* Occasionally the reverse occurs: the vowels /ɪ/ and /ɛ/ appear as /i/ and /e/. Hence, we may find *ees* and *tale* instead of *is* and *tell,* but not often. Somewhat more frequently, the vowel /ɛ/ will appear as /χ/, but usually before nasal consonants (*send/sand, enter/hanter*). Finally, the vowel /ai/ often occurs presumably as /ɑ/ (*I/ah, cry/crah, write/wrat*). Apparently this is what Cable was referring to in his description of "long i" flattened as if it were coming through cane-crushers.

Cable's representation of the prosodic aspects of his French-English dialect is somewhat limited—partly, of course, because of the limitations of English spelling. But he is able to suggest certain variations in stress—and sometimes in transition as well. On occasion, he uses the fairly obvious convention of italics, sometimes in conjunction with respelling: *certainly* emerges once, for example, as *certainlee,* with the last syllable italicized and respelled, presumably to indicate final stress. More often, however he avoids italics and settles primarily on respelling, sometimes with a hypen, to indicate an unusual stress. Primary stress seems often to be on the first syllable of a word that historically has it elsewhere. *Refer* and *relation,* for example, tend to appear as *riffer* and *rillation,* presumably /'rɪfər/ and /'rɪlešən/. *Because* is spelled *bicause,* presumably /'bɪkəz/, in similar fashion, except that a hyphen appears instead of a repeated consonant; with this device, Cable is able to suggest even more clearly the alteration of syllable boundaries that is presumably also reflected in *riffer* and *rillation.*

GRAMMAR

Besides the loss, replacement, and occasional addition of consonants and the changes in front vowels and in stress and transition patterns, Cable's French-English in *The Grandissimes* is also characterized by grammatical variations that set it off from conventional English. Notable among these are inflectional losses in verbs and nouns and syntactic differences involving determiners, pronouns, adjectives, and larger grammatical units. The present/past/past-participle distinction in irregular verbs is often lost, typically in favor of the present form ("who *struck* him"/"oo *strigue* 'im," "he got his head *struck*"/" 'e godd his 'ead *strigue*"). The preterit and past participle dental suffix of regular verbs tends to disappear ("he *betrayed*"/"he *betray*'," "I am *amazed*"/"I am *amaze*' "); the same is true of he third-person singular present indicative suffix -*s* of all verbs ("he *says*"/"he *say*' "). And in like fashion, the noun occurs without the customary plural -*s* ("the *weeds*"/"de *weed*' ").

Determiners vary significantly—both the definite article and the indefinite article. What would presumably be *the* in conventional English often becomes *that* or *those* in French-English ("You was in *dad* shob," "to hass all *doze* question' "). And what would normally be *a* or *an* sometimes becomes *one* ("Ah cannod be *one* Toussaint l'Ouverture"). Notable too is the use of an emphatic pronoun, usually a repeated first-person singular form in the objective case ("I would say dad, *me*, fo' time' a day"). The descriptive adjective is sometimes converted to a substantive in instances where the English adjective is not convertible ("Clotilde is sudge a *foolish*").

But one of the most striking syntactical variations is the tendency toward a declarative form in questions, both *yes/no* and *wh-* questions. The *yes/no* questions are syntactically indistinguishable from English echo questions, in which the interrogative meaning is conveyed by intonation rather than syntactic change ("You want a clerk?" "You was in dad shob of 'Sieur Frowenfel'?"). But they are noticeable in being usual for *yes/no* questions in the dialect, whereas they are only occasional in English. The *wh-* questions, on the other hand, are distinctly unconventional syntactically, since for them the lack of subject-verb inversion or of the auxiliary *do* is not a grammatical option in English ("W'ere you was, *chérie?*" "*Wad 'e said?*" "*W'ere you lef you' hat?*").

SOURCES OF THE DIALECT

Most of the grammatical variations in Cable's French-English, like the phonological ones, are understandable in view of the differences between the two languages: a speaker of French learning English with relatively little systematic instruction might be expected to say *innocen'* rather than *innocent, fivver* rather than *fever,* or "he *say'* " instead of "he *says,*" and the like.[10] And a speaker of French in southern Louisiana would be susceptible to such tendencies as the loss of *r,* a characteristic that is widespread, though not universal, in the English of this area and of much of the rest of the South.[11] Hence, French and English would appear to be the major contributing elements in the dialect, and French-English would seem to be an appropriate name for it.

Some of the characteristics of this French-English, however, such as those reflected in *innocen'* and "he *say',*" also occur in other dialects spoken in southern Louisiana—in some varieties of black English, for example. Hence, there are other possible sources for some aspects of Cable's literary dialect. The Creole historian Charles Gayarré suggested as much when he insisted that Cable made his Creoles speak in what was, according to Gayarré, the "broken, mutilated africanized English of the black man."[12] And it is also possible that there was some influence from what might be termed the "black French" of Louisiana—more often called the "patois nègre," the "gombo dialect," or, rather ambiguously, the "Creole dialect." For example, preconsonantal *r* is also characteristically absent in this patois, as well as in much black English. Influence from black English or the patois would be difficult to demonstrate, however.[13] The Creoles of Louisiana were as fiercely proud of their linguistic heritage as they were of other aspects of their cultural tradition. French continued to be their principal language, even down to Cable's time. It would seem natural that this prestige speech—along with standard southern English—should exert the strongest impact on their acquisition of another tongue, particularly a tongue to talk to the Americans with. Furthermore, a number of the most frequently recurring characteristics of Cable's dialect occur also in other literary representations of French-English, far removed from nineteenth-century New Orleans in place or time, or both. Much of the phonological and inflectional simplification already discussed is also found, for example in the literary dialect of the poet William Drummond, writing in Quebec at the turn of the century, and in that of the playwrights George Farquhar and Thomas Shadwell, writing in England two centuries earlier.[14] In both instances, the influence of black English and the patois nègre would have been unlikely. Thus, while these dialects may have had a reinforcing influence on some aspects of the speech represented by Cable, it would seem reasonable to infer that the principal sources were the French of Louisiana Creoles and the English of the Americans with whom they had the most frequent contacts—in other words, relatively conventional French and English.

ACCURACY OF THE DIALECT

The charge has been made by some of Cable's critics that the speech he attributes to reputable Creoles—whether essentially French-English or not—is inappropriate and misleading socially. One critic felt, for example, that the dialect in *The Grandissimes* was an "artistic mistake" by which "accomplished women and cultured cavaliers" are made to talk "in a jargon unreal and impossible beyond conception in people of their class." He concluded that "no such lingo ever existed except in Mr. Cable's imagination, or as picked up in the French Market of New Orleans, among the most degraded of dagoes."[15] As already suggested, however, most of the characteristic variations in Cable's "lingo" are plausible for speakers of French in general, whatever their class. Furthermore, Cable typically distinguishes between French-English-speaking characters with different kinds of education and different degrees of proficiency in English. There are also a number of letters by contemporaries, some of them Creoles, who are perceptive and in a position to know, affirming that Cable's dialect is appropriate to his characters.[16] Finally, Cable has a chronological advantage in representing French-English speakers of three-quarters of a century earlier. However cultivated some of the Creoles may have been in their English speech in Cable's day—and there is evidence to suggest that some, like the highly educated historian Alcée Fortier, were not so cultivated as they liked to think[17]—the probability is that the Creoles of 1803, with less exposure to English, would have been much less polished in the language, particularly in view of the antipathy that many of them had toward anything associated with les Américains. In short, it seems likely that in *The Grandissimes* Cable represented the French-English dialect of a number of southern Louisiana Creoles, largely those of culture and accomplishment, in a reasonable, realistic manner.

LITERARY EFFECTIVENESS

The problem of how far to go in the direction of realistic detail, in fact, seems to have been a bothersome one during the writing of *The Grandissimes* and afterwards, if we are to judge from the comments of Cable's editors and critics and from the changes he made in the dialect in a subsequent revision.[18] The minute research that served him so well in gathering historical background for his fiction sometimes became a doubtful virtue in his handling of dialect. About literary artistry, Cable could say very dispassionately in the late 1890's, "It is probably always best that dialect should be sketched rather than photographed."[19] But even his staunchest advocates would probably admit that twenty years earlier he was sometimes using the camera too much and the crayon too little. At any rate, in *The Grandissimes* there is a great deal of difference in the density of the dialect in the speech of various characters, ranging from what one might call full-scale presentation in Aurore and Clotilde de Grapion Nancanou to the barely minimal touches in the white Honoré Grandissime, half-brother of the quadroon Honoré.[20]

Quite apart from the exotic charm that many critics and other readers have found in the speech of the two Nancanou women, mother and daughter, the abundance of dialect in their conversation is understandable in terms of much of the emphasis in the story. Among other things, *The Grandissimes* is a novel of ideas—advocating understanding, tolerance, and freedom for nationalities, races, and individuals. Although Aurore and Clotilde are far from expendable in the story as a whole, they are not the primary exponents of these ideas. Much of their dialogue is clearly less essential to plot and theme than that of the protagonists, the white Honoré Grandissime and an American nondialect speaker, Joseph Frowenfeld. Thus a reader is not likely to lose the thread of the story or the essence of Cable's thought even if he misses an occasional dialect word or sentence by Aurore or Clotilde. Furthermore, a substantial part of their dialogue is given in conventional English—Cable's way of representing their French speech and of making it clear that in keeping with their class and education they were quite capable and cultivated speakers of their native tongue.[21] Hence, a significant portion of their dialogue would present no problem to a reader.

In their French-English dialect speech Aurore and Clotilde are virtually indistinguishable, both of them exhibiting most of the features of sound and grammar already mentioned, and others in addition. The following selection is approximately representative:

> [Aurore] asked in English, which was equivalent to whispering:
> "W'ere you was, *chérie?*"
> "'Sieur Frowenfel'—" . . .
> "'E godd his 'ead strigue! 'Tis all knog in be'ine! 'E come in blidding—"
> "In w'ere?" cried Aurora.[22]
> "In 'is shob."
> "You was in dad shob of 'Sieur Frowenfel'?"
> "I wend ad 'is shob to pay doze rend."
> "How—you wend ad 'is shob to pay—"
> Clotilde produced the bracelet. The two looked at each other in silence for a moment, while Aurora took in without further explanation Clotilde's project and its failure.

"An' 'Sieur Frowenfel'—dey kill 'im? Ah! *ma chère*, fo' wad you mague me to hass all doze question?"

Clotilde gave a brief account of the matter, omitting only her conversation with Frowenfeld.

"*Mais*, oo strigue 'im?" demanded Aurora, impatiently.

"Addunno!" replied the other. "Bud I does know 'e is hinnocen'!"

A small scouting-party of tears reappeared on the edge of her eyes.

"Innocen' from wad?"

Aurora betrayed a twinkle of amusement.

"Hev'ryt'in', iv you pliz!" exclaimed Clotilde, with most uncalled for warmth.

"An' you crah bic-ause 'e is nod guiltie?" . . .

"*Mais*, anny'ow, tell me fo' wad you cryne?"

Clotilde gazed aside for a moment and then confronted her questioner consentingly.

"I tole 'im I knowed 'e war h-innocen'."

"*Eh, bien*, dad was h-only de poli-i-idenez. Wad 'e said?"

"'E said I din knowed 'im 'tall."

"An' you," exclaimed Aurora, "it is nod pozzyble dad you—"

"I tole 'im I know 'im bett'n 'e know annyt'in' 'boud id!"

The speaker dropped her face into her mother's lap.

"Ha, ha!" laughed Aurora, "an' wad of dad? I would say dad, me, fo' time' a day."[23]

Brief though it is, the passage reveals many of the common characteristics in the language of the two women. Their speech is not alike in every particular in this brief selection, of course, but their French-English dialogue elsewhere in the novel demonstrates that their language is represented as being of the same kind. While this dialectal closeness in two characters might be a defect in another novel, it seems to be defensible here—like the quantity and the density of their dialect speech. For Aurore and Clotilde are presented as hardly separable in appearance, in character, and in function. Joseph Frowenfeld says of them, "I can hardly understand that you are not sisters."[24] Though Clotilde is perhaps shier than her mother, and certainly less loquacious, they are both coy, coquettish, and yet charming—both irrepressible, unpredictable, and yet irresistible. And both have essentially the same role—to attract and captivate one of the two protagonists in the novel. In the ultimate marriages of Clotilde and Aurore—women as like in essence as in dialect—to the American Frowenfeld and the Creole Honoré Grandissime, respectively—men very different in cultural background—Cable seems to be embodying his optimistic desire for greater harmony is Louisiana between the French and the Americans, and between feuding factions within the French community itself.

Just as Clotilde is a natural reflection of Aurore, so the quadroon Honoré Grandissime is a natural foil for the Creole Honoré, who stands at the opposite end—the minimal end—of the dialect continuum. Although the quadroon has had virtually the same education as his white half-brother, his French-English dialect resembles that of Aurore and Clotilde, as his first remarks in the novel suggest:

One day . . . the landlord [the quadroon] . . . noticed in Joseph's hand a sprig of basil, and spoke of it.

"You ligue?"
The tenant did not understand.
"You—find—dad—nize?"
Frowenfeld . . . expressed a liking for its odor.
"I sand you," said the landlord.[25]

The quadroon's speech, like Aurore's, is marked by the same conversion of dental fricative /ð/ to the corresponding stop /d/, the change of /ɛ/ to /χ/, and the voicing of final stops like /t/ and /k/. His relatively dense French-English dialect presumably reflects less contact with the English-speaking Americans than his brother has had; he is characterized, in fact, as a shy, retiring individual. But his dialect speech is also recognizably different from Aurore's, sometimes in obvious ways, sometimes more subtly. This contrast is clearly indicated, for example, by the fact that in the conversation already quoted between Aurore and Clotilde, and in their speech generally, the pronoun *I* retains its conventional spelling. But in the speech of the quadroon, *I* often appears as *ah*. In fact, *ah* is the only form he uses in one of his encounters with Joseph Frowenfeld, where the pronoun occurs half a dozen times: "Ah lag to teg you apar'," "Ah was elevade in Pariz," "Ah wand you mague me one *ouangan*," "Ah ham nod whide, m'sieu'," "Ah ham de holdez son of Numa Grandissime," "Ah can nod spig Engliss."[26] In more subtle fashion, his speech also reflects the loss of preconsonantal /r/ and the loss of dental stops in final clusters, but much less frequently than in the speech of Aurore; and Aurore's tendency to stress words like *because* and *refuse* on the first syllable does not appear. On the other hand, the quadroon has a greater tendency (from the English speaker's point of view) to omit auxiliaries like *will* ("I sand you") and pronoun complements like *it* ("You ligue?").

In contrast to the withdrawn, introverted quadroon, the Creole Honoré is a merchant with extensive business and social contacts among the Americans, as well as the Creoles. The comparative lack of variation from conventional English in his dialogue is quite natural and understandable. For the most part, his speech is unmarked, except for the relatively consistent absence of preconsonantal /r/ and the presence, presumably, of a characteristically French /r/ in other positions:

My-de'-seh, rhecollect that to us the Grhandissime name is a trheasu'e. And what has prheserved it so long? Cherishing the unity of ow family; that has done it; that is how my fatheh did it. Just or-h unjust, good o' bad, needful o' not, done elsewhere-h o' not, I do not say; but it is a Crheole trhait.[27]

On rare occasions we find a few additional dialect characteristics, notably in one passage in which the Creole is talking with intense feeling about the color problem in Louisiana. There are at most a dozen examples reflecting things other than the peculiarities of /r/—most of them phonological, and most of them involving loss of final consonants (*mos'* and *thousan'*, for example). But this minor linguistic lapse is strikingly appropriate and effective and is underlined by Cable's comment, "He was so deep in earnest that he took no care of his English."[28] In the partial revision of *The Grandissimes* in 1883, dialect characteristics are systematically removed from the Creole's speech. An occasional *my-de'-seh* is retained, but, except for the variations in the emotional passage mentioned, practically everything else has been normalized:

> My-de'-seh, recollect that to us the Grandissime name is a treasure. And what has preserved it so long? Cherishing the unity of our family; that has done it; that is how my father did it. Just or unjust, good or bad, needful or not, done elsewhere or not, I do not say; but it is a Creole trait.[29]

Cable's motive seems clear enough. Although, for the most part, only the representation of the consonant /r/ was unconventional in the original edition, this difference would account for a sizable number of alterations of standard spelling in a paragraph or a page of dialogue—as the first quotation from the Creole suggests—and would have given a reader the impression of much more variation in speech than was actually represented.[30] Since the Creole Honoré is one of the two principal spokesmen for the author in the novel, Cable presumably felt that his character would have more dignity and that his ideas would be clearer and carry more weight in a closer approximation to conventional English. And, for most readers, he was probably right.

CONCLUSION

In *The Grandissimes*, then, Cable presents a French-English dialect that is probably a reasonably accurate reflection of the occasional speech of some southern Louisiana Creoles of the nineteenth century. It was a dialect, as Cable apparently realized, that could sometimes be vulnerable to criticism on various grounds. To unsympathetic readers like Charles Gayarré, the English of some of the Creole characters was not only "broken"; it was "mutilated." Nevertheless it was an English, a French-flavored English, that could be useful and effective in linking like characters together; in differentiating contrasting characters, and in distinguishing different moods in a given character. And it formed a significant part of Cable's attempt to preserve something of a unique and valuable, but declining, culture and to make the world aware of it.

[Received May 1973]

Notes

1. Edwin A. Davis, *Louisiana: The Pelican State*, 3d ed. (Baton Rouge: Louisiana State University Press, 1964), p. 104.

2. Davis, p. 131.

3. Reginald F. Trotter, Jr., "An Index of the *Comptes Rendus* of *l'Athénée Louisianais* and a General History of the Organization," Thesis Tulane, 1952, pp. 4–16, 18–19, and 31–32. Announcements of judicial proceedings were regularly published by the French newspapers of the state until prohibited by the Legislature in 1868. This privilege was restored to the French press of New Orleans a decade later, but finally withdrawn in 1916.

4. *Voyages dan l'Intérieur de la Louisiane* (Paris: F. Buisson, 1807), translated and abridged by Stuart O. Landry as *Voyage to Louisiana* (New Orleans: Pelican, 1966). Landry's translation includes a lengthy memorandum (pp. 163ff.) written by Robin, at the request of a number of

French-speaking Louisianians, on the importance of retaining French as the language of the territory.

5. *Creoles* here refers to the white descendants of the colonists who came directly (or occasionally by way of the Caribbean) to Louisiana from France—and, to some extent, from Spain—at various periods beginning at the end of the seventeenth century; the Creoles were people of prestige and spoke a dialect that was very closely akin to cultivated continental French (William A. Read, *Louisiana French*, rev. ed., Baton Rouge: Louisiana State University Press, 1963, p. xvii; August W. Rubrecht, "Regional Phonological Variants in Louisiana Speech," Diss. University of Florida, 1971, pp. 11ff.). Their attempt at English speech is sometimes referred to as *Creole* also (as noted, for example, by Arlin Turner in his edition of some of Cable's stories and articles, *Creoles and Cajuns: Stories of Old Louisiana*, Garden City, N.Y.: Doubleday, 1959, p. 8). But *French-English* is a less ambiguous term and probably fairly accurate as a description, as will be demonstrated later.

6. *The Grandissimes: A Story of Creole Life* (New York: Charles Scribner's Sons, 1880), p. 60. All subsequent references will be to this edition, except where otherwise indicated. The novel first appeared in serial form in *Scribner's Monthly*, beginning in the fall of 1879. The task of finding and examining manuscripts and editions of the book and other materials about it was made much easier because of the generous help of many people—among them, Connie Griffiths, who, as Director of Special Collections at the Howard Tilton Memorial Library of Tulane University, made available the excellent resources of the Cable Collection; Ray Browne and Larry Landrum, who, as curators, provided access to the increasingly valuable collection of Cable materials at Bowling Green State University; and Evangeline Lynch, who opened up the riches of the Louisiana Room at the Louisiana State University Library.

7. *The Grandissimes*, p. 83.

8. It seems clear, as Kjell Ekström points out, that Cable "made no attempt to reconstruct the English of the Creoles of the early nineteenth century but took the artistic liberty of putting into their mouths the English of contemporary Creoles" (*George Washington Cable: A Study of His Early Life and Work*, University of Uppsala Essays and Studies on American Language and Literature, Uppsala: A.B. Lundequistska Bokhandeln, 1950, p. 177).

9. *The Creoles of Louisiana* (New York: Charles Scribner's Sons, 1884), pp. 317–18. This "long *i*" would be rather difficult to pin down with any precision solely on the basis of Cable's description. However, in his actual respellings for this and other sounds in *The Grandissimes*, it is usually fairly clear what he intends. His respellings are those of a relatively acute, though not scientifically trained, observer of languages, particularly English and French. In my comments on pronunciation, the phonemic system is essentially that of Hans Kurath as set forth, for example, in his *Phonology and Prosody of Modern English* (Heidelberg: Carl Winter, 1964).

10. Specifically, the influence of the French phonemic system can easily account for the occurrence of *innocen'* and *fivver* in terms of the historical loss of many final consonants in French and the lack of a French phonemic contrast corresponding to that between the English /i/ and /ɪ/. Similarly, the occurrence of "he *say*' " can be readily accounted for by the lack of a third-person singular -s in French and, in fact, by the frequent absence in spoken French of any third-person singular and plural contrast, except with certain kinds of liaison. In like fashion, most of Cable's other variations in sound and grammar can be reasonably interpreted as a reflection of the attempt of speakers of French to communicate in English. Extremely useful in this sort of interpretation are discussions such as Claude M. Wise's chapter on French in North America in his *Applied Phonetics* (Englewood Cliffs, N.J.: Prentice-Hall, 1957), pp. 325–63. For few of the characteristics of Cable's French-English, such as the apparent shift of stress to the first syllable of words like *refer*, exact explanation is rather elusive. One would expect a shift in the opposite direction, where appropriate. Yet a possible parallel presents itself in the phenomenon of emphatic stress on various syllables in French as discussed, for example, by Pierre Delattre in "Comparing the Prosodic Features of English, German, Spanish and French," *International Review of Applied Linguistics*, 1 (1963), 199–205. Or the shift might perhaps be a kind of hypercorrection, the French speakers having noted the tendency toward initial stress in English in general and in similar words like *differ* and *suffer* in particular.

11. It seems quite evident that this loss of /r/ in Cable's dialect can be explained, not with respect to any French interference, but in terms of the particular variety of English that the French speakers were exposed to. Rubrecht ("Regional Variants," pp. 159–62 and 217ff.) provides some of the most recent evidence of the extent to which the loss of /r/ has penetrated southern Louisiana. Occasionally, on the other hand, one of Cable's variations—such as that in the vowel sound /ai/— appears to reflect both French and Louisiana English equally. Something approximating the /α/ phoneme might be anticipated, both because of the lack of a diphthongal sound /ai/ in French, and because of the variety of articulations of /ai/ including monophthongal ones in southern Louisiana (as noted also by Rubrecht, pp. 176–79).

12. Ekström, *George Washington Cable*, p. 176, n. 11. Needless to say, this hardly represents Cable's view of the matter.

13. In addition to the absence of /r/, or /t/ in final clusters, and of the -s verb inflection, much black English resembles Cable's French-English in other characteristics. These can be observed in the useful and illuminating discussion by Louise A. DeVere, "Black English: Problematic but Systematic," *South Atlantic Bulletin*, 36, no.3 (May, 1971), 38–46. But resemblance is not necessarily influence. The patois nègre has another feature, in addition to the lack of preconsonantal and final /r/, that is somewhat reminiscent of Cable's dialect—the absence of the copula (James F. Broussard, *Louisiana Creole Dialect*, Baton Rouge: Louisiana State University Press, 1942, pp. 2 and 14–15). Since much black English is also marked by this absence and since it is not characteristic of conventional French, there is perhaps a more tangible possibility of influence on Cable's dialect in this respect than in most others. Although the lack of the copula seems, on occasion, to be part of the French-English speech of some of Cable's characters, the trait is not found at all in the speech of the quadroon Honoré Grandissime, where it might be expected. Furthermore, about two-thirds of the examples in Cable's dialect occur with a present participle in what would be called a present progressive form in conventional English ("I goin' rad now"). It is not inconceivable that a French speaker might omit the copula in his attempt to reproduce a common English construction that he has often heard. In fact, in such sequences as "You lookin' verrie well" or even "You de bez man" (without a participle), the lack of the copula can be quite plausibly interpreted simply as loss of final or preconsonantal /r/. Finally, as Juanita V. Williamson has pointed out, the lack of a copula in Southern speech is not confined to black English ("Selected Features of Speech Black and White," *CLA Journal*, 13, June, 1970, 421, 424–25).

14. The French-English dialect of William Henry Drummond, an integral part of his *Collected Poems* (Toronto: McClelland and Stewart, 1926), does not appear to have been investigated in much detail. But the dialect efforts of Farquhar, Shadwell, and some other Restoration playwrights have been illuminated by Brother William F. Gruber, Jr. ("The Broken English of French Characters of Restoration Comedies: A Linguistic Analysis," Thesis, Louisiana State University, 1971).

15. "The Writing of George Washington Cable," *Critic* (January 2, 1893), n. pag.

16. Ekström, *George Washington Cable*, pp. 177–80.

17. Ekström, p. 179.

18. For example, Irwin Russell, an editorial assistant at Scribner's and a writer of dialect himself, frequently questioned the probability of some of Cable's carefully recorded linguistic details. Most reviewers of the first edition of the book had some difficulty with the dialect, some finding it tedious in its total effect. And the changes that Cable made in the dialect in the revision of 1883 were mostly in the direction of simplicity (Arlin Turner, *George W. Cable: A Biography*, Durham, N.C.: Duke University Press, 1956, pp. 96–101).

19. "Editor's Symposium," *Current Literature*, 22 (September, 1897), 193.

20. There is also a middle ground, exemplified by a few dialect-speaking characters in the novel in addition to the quadroon Honoré, notably a clerk with the unlikely name of Raoul Innerarity, whose speech, though decidedly dialectal, also differs from that of Aurore and Clotilde in a number of ways.

21. This is one effective rejoinder to those contemporaries who felt that cultivated Creoles were

being misrepresented as low life in Cable's writings.

22. Early in the book, Cable converts *Aurore* to *Aurora*, remarking that "it sounds so much pleasanter to anglicize her name" (p.88). The conversation as a whole needs some explanation. Through a misunderstanding, Frowenfeld had been hit on the head by a servant; and Clotilde witnessed the ensuing confusion because she had gone to his shop—a pharmacy and sometimes pawnshop—to raise money on a bracelet in order to pay the rent that the women owed to the quadroon Honoré Grandissime, who also happened to be Frowenfeld's landlord. Only partly concealed behind Clotilde's words is her growing affection for Frowenfeld. The situation is made even more complex by the fact that Clotilde, unknown to him, had helped to nurse Frowenfeld back to health after a nearly fatal bout with yellow fever in his earliest months in New Orleans.

23. *The Grandissimes*, pp. 276–78.

24. *The Grandissimes*, p. 117. Frowenfeld had been told of the actual relationship of the two women earlier in the story by the Creole Honoré Grandissime (p.70).

25. *The Grandissimes*, p. 53.

26. *The Grandissimes*, pp. 134–37. The first statement is an amusing example of Cable's occasional bilingual humor, but at the same time an expression that is quite appropriate to the dialect and understandable in the speaker. Presumably the quadroon's request reflects the French idiom *prendre quelqu'un à part* and means, as Frowenfeld recognizes, "to take someone aside." The *ouangan* referred to in the third statement is the quadroon's term for some sort of magical love potion or "poudre d'amour," as he later calls it (p. 140).

27. *The Grandissimes*, p. 289.

28. *The Grandissimes*, p. 201. This realistic intensification of dialect under emotional stress occurs also in the speech of the quadroon at one point (pp. 256–57) where he is speaking heatedly of Agricola Fusilier, the one person in the world for whom he has a passionate hatred. On this occasion, some words that otherwise have the conventional English high and mid-front lax vowels $/ɪ/$ and $/ɛ/$ in his speech appear with the corresponding tense vowels $/i/$ and $/e/$ (*didn't/deen, dead/dade*).

29. *The Grandissimes: A Story of Creole Life* (New York: Scribner's, 1888), p. 289. The 1883 edition was not available to me, but all subsequent reprintings have retained the dialect changes made in that year (Louis D. Rubin, *George Washington Cable. The Life and Times of a Southern Heretic*, New York: Pegasus 1969, p. 282).

30. The inadequacy of the English spelling system for representing dialect variations in pronunciation—combined with the probable inability of the Creole readers, like most readers, to sufficiently distinguish between spoken and written language—doubtless goes a long way to account for the violent reactions of such readers as Charles Gayarré to Cable's French-English dialect.

George Washington Cable's Creoles: Art and Reform in *The Grandissimes*

Elmo Howell°

In the generation following the Civil War, George Washington Cable was one of the most widely celebrated men of letters in the United States. Speaking at Smith College in the 1890's, James Barrie said that no American novelist, past or present, stood higher than the little man from Louisiana—he was vaguely thought of as Creole beyond his region—who had revealed a picturesque civilization in an obscure corner of the world. His fame was short-lived, however. The South was suspicious of him from the beginning, and by the turn of the century Cable's radical views on race and civil rights for Negroes had alienated much of his Northern audience. He continued to write, renouncing controversy at last for the romantic fiction his generation loved; but when he died in 1925, the Providence, Rhode Island *Journal* said that his death "struck a careless world as savoring of an anachronism." Of his more than twenty volumes none was in considerable demand, and "on the biographical shelves there is not a single complete study."[1]

But after almost a century of semi-oblivion, Cable is experiencing a "revival," which promises a wider audience than he enjoyed in his lifetime. Several of his works have been reissued in the last decade, and plans are under way for a new edition and publication of material hitherto unavailable to the general public. The Howard-Tilton Library of Tulane University, which has the bulk of Cable's papers, is agog with activity, with the results appearing in the journals and in book-length studies. The current interest centers in his social views. What he advocated only a few years after the Civil War is finally being realized. What seemed to the North daring and unacceptable at the end of the century—social equality and complete integration—appears no longer impossible, and Cable has become something of a prophet or seer who dared to speak before his time. This contemporary interest, of course, has little to do with literary merit, although most of the work is being done by literary scholars. Even *The Grandissimes* and *Old Creole Days*, on which his reputation is principally based, are made to appear important primarily as the prelude to his

°Reprinted form the *Mississippi Quarterly*, 26 (Winter, 1972–73), 42–53.

writings on race. "The strength of the early fiction," says Mr. Arlin Turner, one of the leaders in the Cable revival, "lies in the author's zeal in exposing evils . . . and his success in dramatizing social wrongs."[2]

The single-mindedness of the reformer leaves little time for merits purely literary, but with all his faults Cable is still an impressive artist, at least in the promise he shows in his early work. Even those who do not share his views acknowledge the charm of his sketches of Creole manners, which he, Anglo-Saxon and Presbyterian, could not approve. Born of a New England mother and brought up in a strict Puritan household, he never became a part of the excitement of the French Quarter, about which he knew so much and where he liked to stroll with his guests from out of town, like any other tourist. He kept aloof, and so his pages are lacking in that generous sentiment which comes from the author's identification with his subject. His approach is cerebral; his effect almost wholly visual. And yet with these limitations, the best of *The Grandissimes* is comparable with the best in American fiction. It is more than the political novel he intended. The Creoles cast their spell, which Puritan logic could not altogether exorcise, at least in the early years before he moved to the North. Along with *Old Creole Days*, it is his most impressive achievement, when the artist had not yet given way to the reformer.

The Grandissimes is a story about New Orleans in 1803, just after Louisiana is sold by France to the United States. The Creoles do not like the Cession, and diehards like Agricola Fusilier insist that the Yankee domination is only temporary and cry out for preservation of their distinctive manners, their language, their legal system, and even the slave trade, already outlawed in the United States. Against this background of cultural change, Cable tells the story of a dispute between two aristocratic Creole families and a final reconciliation in a romance and marriage. The protagonists, however, are not so interesting as the minor figures—the Creoles of lesser station, the mulattoes (including the half-brother to the hero), the Negroes newly out of African jungles, and the sprinkling of Americans who have just moved in. He presents a rich variety of Creole life: the quadroon balls, slave dances in Congo Square, voodoo, the code duello, hurricane and pestilence, the mixture of races and tongues and a carefully defined gradation of class and caste. The charm of the book lies in the profusion and intricacy of a way of life which was doomed in April of 1803, when the American flag was raised for the first time in the Place d'Armes.

Beyond the definite setting in time and place, one of the most satisfactory aspects of *The Grandissimes* is the author's feeling for the natural world of Louisiana—for its "delicious February," for the tropical swamps where Bras-Coupé found refuge, or for a garden in the Rue Royale. New Englanders—and Cable was always essentially a New Englander—have been drawn to the Southern natural scene, as to the social scene, without granting complete approval, as if in some insidious way the two are related. Before describing a luxuriant New Orleans garden, Harriet Beecher Stowe says that it was evidently arranged "to gratify a pictursque and voluptuous ideality."[3] Cable would not go so far, since his delight is genuine, at least in the Southern spring. "It was one of those afternoons in early March that make one wonder how the rest of the world avoids emigrating to Louisiana in a body." But the "Creole spring" is always early.

> The land was an inverted firmament of flowers. The birds were an innumerable, busy, joy-compelling multitude, darting and fluttering hither and thither, as one might imagine the babes do in heaven. The orange-groves were in blossom; their dark green boughs seemed snowed upon from a cloud of incense. . . . The magnolia was beginning to add to its dark and shining evergreen foliage, frequent sprays of pale new leaves and long, slender, buff buds of others yet to come.[4]

He is more reserved in his feeling for summer. The hurricane which breaks upon Bras-Coupé's wedding lets loose the violence which pursues the royal slave to the swamp, where the "noisome waters" and the "dull and loathsome" creatures of the "lifeless bayou" suggest the system of which the Negro is the victim (pp. 181–182). A summer evening in the Place d'Armes, while the shadows lengthen across the river and the swallows twitter overhead, lures one on to "the embrace of this seductive land"; and it is here that the "fashion and beauty" of the city take their pleasure, sublimely indifferent to the suffering on which their privilege is built (p. 332). "The climate is *too* comfortable," says Frowenfeld, Cable's spokesman in the novel, which partly explains why Creole society is "so sadly in arrears to the civilized world" (p. 142). In spite of his reservations, Cable's details are so lavish and intimate that it is hard to imagine him at home in later years among the elms and maples of his celebrated garden at Northampton. But his affinity for New England was complete and accounts perhaps in part for the freshness of his description of Louisiana, as though it were being seen for the first time by a visitor from another world.

His ambivalence concerning the natural world applies in at least one respect to the social order. He admires the Creole woman. One of the most delightful scenes in the novel, which at the same time betrays his weakness as an artist, is the visit of Joseph Frowenfeld, the author's surrogate, with Madame Aurora Nancanou and her daughter Clotilde. It is a social occasion, a time for small talk, but Frowenfeld with Puritan self-righteousness turns it into a Chautauqua lecture on the shortcomings of Creole character. The ladies, wonderfully feminine and complaisant, concur with opinions they do not share or understand and bid their visitor go on.

> "Doze Creole' is *lezzy*," said Aurora.
> "That is a hard word to apply to those who do not *consciously* deserve it," said Frowenfeld; "but if they could only wake up to the fact,—find it out themselves—"
> "Ceddenly," said Clotilde.
> " 'Sieur Frowenfel'," said Aurora, leaning her head on one side, "some pipple thing it is doze climade; 'ow you lag doze climade?"
> "I do not suppose," replied the visitor, "there is a more delightful climate in the world."
> "Ah-h-h!"—both ladies at once, in a low, gracious tone of acknowledgment. (p. 142)

Professor Louis D. Rubin, Jr., finds an inconsistency in Frowenfeld's stark ethics and his attraction to the Creole ladies and suggests that he is trying to raise himself socially when he marries the younger one. "When we think about what Frowenfeld has been able to accomplish in Creole society, we are quite startled."[5] But Frowenfeld is no "social climber," as Rubin suggests, but an iconoclast, whose aim is to supplant the Creole way of life with what he considers the superior Anglo-Saxon Protestant ethos. Like many another Northern reformer, in fiction and in real life, he feels the influence of Southern manners and makes love to Southern ladies, while managing at the same time to keep his Puritan ideal unscathed. He makes no bow in the house of Rimmon, since his wife, in good Creole fashion, will defer to her husband's principles. This lurking admiration, however, suggests a tension, which Cable the reformer could not afford to recognize. The lecture must go on, and so the novel is deprived of the wider relevance which a free play of the imagination would have given it.

But the ladies Nancanou are unusual among his Creole characters. For the most part, he dislikes and distrusts them, particularly the men, and cannot let them alone to act and think for themselves. His Northern readers liked to believe that he portrayed his people "with the kindest intentions and the broadest sympathy," just as they found his singing of Creole songs in his platform appearances "indescribably charming."[6] Some of them spring to life, like old Fusilier the Creole apologist, for example, only to be buried again in the necessities of the argument. Honoré Grandissime is Cable's emancipated Southerner, who advances radical views in race relations, much to his family's dismay. "Yesseh! 'e gone partner' wid dat quadroon" (p. 277). Bras-Coupé, the slave whom some readers make a central figure even though his story antedates the main action, is a tour-de-force, a contrived Oroonoko, thrown in to project Cable's horror of slavery. All of his characters, however multifarious and rich in suggestion, are circumscribed by his thesis and strictly speaking have no life of their own.

His Creole antipathy is conveyed with most art in the use of dialect, to which his local audience objected from the beginning. A gentleman does not address his wife or daughter, said the Louisiana historian and man of letters Charles Gayarré, in "the jargon of the Negro."[7] But Cable had theories about the use of dialect and he had a keen ear. What probably offended Gayarré and other Creoles was not so much the kinship to Negro speech as the patronizing air that Cable's phonetics suggest. "Louisiana rif-using to hanter de h-Union!" is the name of a painting by a Creole artist. "If you insist to know who make dat pigshoe—de hartis' stan' bif-ore you!" (p. 114). Whether or not the artist spoke like that, the speech conveys a certain validity, at the same time—and this is important to Cable—that it makes the Creole ridiculous. Though "pigshoe" may be a correct rendering, the orthography is absurd. One recalls Fagin's accomplice Barney in *Oliver Twist*, with his "Biss Dadsy" and "Bister Sikes" and other locutions through which the comedy involved in the young Jewish waiter of Saffron Hill is somehow tinged with race. "OO dad is, 'sieur Frowenfel'?" asks the Creole lady who is the heroine of *The Grandissimes* in a choice of sound and syntax closely akin to Negro speech. Cable has a comic flair with dialect which he can turn to malicious purpose. In *The Cavalier*, he has a Mississippi lady say:

> "Yayse, seh," she was saying to the lieutenant, "and he told us about they comin' in on the freight-kyahs f'om Hazlehurst black with dust and sut and a-smuttyin' him all oveh with they kisses and goin's-on. He tol' me he ain't neveh so enjoyed havin' his face dirty sence he was a boy. He would a-been plumb happy, ef on'y he could a-got his haynds on that clerk o' his'n. And when he tol' us what a gay two-hoss turn-out he'd sekyo'ed for the ladies to travel in, s'I, Majo', that'a all ri-ght! You jest go on whicheveh way you got to go! Husband and me, we'll ride into Brookhaven and bring 'em out to ow place and jest take ca'e of 'em untel yo' clerk is *found*."[8]

The lady's speech has the ring of truth. "Yayse" and "haynds" and "sekyo'ed" are deliberate exaggerations, and yet it is easy to imagine a lady talking in this fashion even today in parts of the South. The stance, as well as the dragged-out vowels, is unmistakably Southern. But to the Southerner the passage is offensive, in precisely the same way Cable's Creole dialect is offensive—or that of Dickens' Jew, for that matter—because it conveys the author's contempt.

Cable made no secret of his views in *The Grandissimes*. Written at a time when passions were high in New Orleans over an attempt to integrate the public schools, the novel as Cable later admitted was intended as a political document. After a mass meeting of segregationists in Lafayette Square, Cable wrote his sentiments to the New Orleans *Bulletin*, which the paper printed, "prefaced by an editorial repudiation as long as itself." A second letter to the paper was ignored, and so he fell to work on his first novel. "It was impossible that a novel written by me then should escape being a study of the fierce struggle going on around me."[9] Thus *The Grandissimes* is allegorical, with Cable's criticism directed actually towards the white South during Reconstruction. Slavery was dead but not the idea of class and caste. Louisiana, says Frowenfeld, will become more and more an illiterate country, "as it persists in the system of social and civil distinctions." The Creoles are "amateurish" in their art, they are provincial in their hostility to the outsider, and any people who contemn physical labor and relegate it to a servile class are degenerate. Moreover, Louisiana is at the disadvantage of being "distant from enlightened centres," and it has "a language and religion different from that of the great people of which it is now called to be a part" (pp. 152–154). Frowenfeld is himself a newcomer, but since they are all Americans now—Louisiana has been under the American flag a matter of weeks—he insists that the old society must be reconstructed to fit the Anglo-Saxon pattern.

Most of Cable's Creole characters subscribe to the prevailing system without giving it much thought. Their attitude towards physical labor, suggests Cable, has affected their mental processes. Lazy and indifferent, they abhor change and distrust the idea of progress. But in spite of racial limitations, they can be charming individuals, like Aurora Nancanou and Raoul Innerarity, the volatile artist. In old Agricola Fusilier, however, the spokesman for the upper class, Cable sums up the Creole qualities that he most dislikes. Fusilier opposes the union with the American government, "the most clap-trap government in the universe, notwithstanding it pretends to be a republic." He resents the introduction of a new language.

> "English is not a language, sir; it is a jargon! And when this young simpleton, Claiborne, attempts to cram it down the public windpipe in the courts, as I understand he intends, he will fail! Hah! sir, I know men in this city who would rather eat a dog than speak English! *I* speak it, but I also speak Choctaw." (p. 48)

Because of loyalty to his tradition, the old man is invariably presented in a bad light. The plot develops from the consequence of a duel with another Creole, after the other man has falsely accused Fusilier of cheating at cards. To settle a gambling debt, he gives Fusilier a clear title to his estate, including slaves. Fusilier kills him in the duel but offers to return the property to the widow if she will affirm that the stakes were fairly won. She refuses; and Fusilier then "puts the laws of humanity aside, and anoints himself from head to foot with Creole punctilio," and keeps the property.

> "Show me any Creole, or any number of Creoles, in any sort of contest, and right down at the foundation of it all, I will find you this same preposterous, apathetic, fantastic, suicidal pride. It is as lethargic and ferocious as an alligator. That is why the Creole almost always is (or thinks he is) on the defensive." (p. 32)

Agricola Fusilier is killed by one of his slaves and from his death bed warns against "the doctrine of equal rights—a bottomless iniquity." "Society has pyramids to build which make menials a necessity, and Nature furnishes the menials all in dark uniform." His last cry is "Patriots! protect the race! . . . Louis—Louisian—a—for—ever!" (pp. 326–328).

"Forever," adds Cable, is a trifle long to confine one's patriotic affection "to a small fraction of a great country" (p. 329). But the Creoles will overcome their faults, or some of them, "under the gentler influence of a higher civilization," by which he means Protestant and Anglo-Saxon. It was the burning passion of Cable's life that the same should happen to the white South in the period of Reconstruction. He looked forward to the time when everything "Southern" should be forgotten, annihilated. In an address at the University of Mississippi in 1882, he attacked Henry W. Grady's concept of the New South. "What we want—what we ought to have in view—is the No South!"[10] His novel *John March, Southerner* is a dramatization of his radical views, which were offensive even to the North, willing at last to let the South settle its own problems. He became a sort of postbellum Abolitionist. In January 1885, after speaking before a Negro high school audience in Louisville, he was addressed by a Negro official as "my hero of heroes." Cable was overcome with emotion. "I thought of the great dead—Lloyd Garrison, Wendel Phillips, and the rest and felt ashamed to let them give such praise to me."[11]

Above all else, Cable was a reformer. He was "fantastically Presbyterian" and as "austerely conscientious and as ardently abolitionist as though he had come into the world at Salem, Massachusetts."[12] The first version of *The Gran-*

dissimes, according to Mr. Turner, was so heavily laden with editorial opinion that his editors persuaded him to tone down the controversy. But the fundamental weakness in Cable as an artist is not in his political or social views. Other Southerners, from Mark Twain to Faulkner, have taken views at variance with those of their region, because, as Faulkner once said, they have both loved and hated it. Cable seems only to have hated it. He cut his children off from "its influence" and looked upon his early life as a period of exile from New England, his natural home. Grace King recalls from her visit to Hartford as the guest of Charles Dudley Warner how often she was reminded of Cable's "oft-repeated assurance that he never felt at home until he came to New England, and had never before felt that he was surrounded by his own people."[13]

Cable lacked the broad tolerance essential to the novelist who deals with a wide spectrum of human affairs. There was little reverence in his nature. He felt nothing of the Southerner's traditional loyalty to person and place—only the humanitarian's zeal and a religious devotion which seems to have abated with age. In Northampton, he forsook Presbyterianism for the milder Congregational Church, and on visits to New York became an avid theatre-goer, who in earlier years had turned down a position on the New Orleans *Picayune* because he refused to write drama review. In spite of their differences in temperament, Cable and Mark Twain had the parallel experience of a self-imposed exile, from which both were articulate concerning the faults of the South. But there the parallel ends. Mark Twain loved the life he knew as a boy in Hannibal, Missouri, and on his uncle's farm in Madison County, and his best work is a nostalgic recreation of "those old simple days."

Cable stands outside and aloof, coldly observant of the rich panorama of his native Louisiana. He feels none of the pathos of the Creole's situation in the early nineteenth century, nor of the white Southerner's after 1865; and in the celebrated story of Bras-Coupé, in which he hoped to dramatize a social evil, he turns to pure romance. The royal slave who told the priest that he was going to Africa when he died was suggested, according to Lafcadio Hearn, by a runaway slave who fled to the swamp and turned robber, "preying on market women and gardeners coming into town by the Gentilly road."[14] Cable's intention is expressed but not felt. His deficiency is a deficiency of the heart. When Mark Twain revisited Hannibal in 1882, the town had changed almost beyond recognition, but "when I reached Third or Fourth street," he said, "the tears burst forth, for I recognized the mud."[15] No detail from his life or his fiction is better testimony to the largeness of his nature, and to that incongruity of heart and head which provides the dramatic tension in his work.

Cable's weakness as an artist is in the affections. In his essay "My Politics" he describes with cold logic the steps that led him away from his native country, apparently without regret. To southerners, it was a betrayal—they liked to quote Browning's line, "Just for a handful of silver he left us"—but he was never one of them in the first place. He drew the surface of their country in exotic colors, but felt only aversion for the life beneath. He calls the dying Agricola Fusilier the "high priest of a doomed civilization," which in his allegory becomes the Old South, fatally wounded by war and Reconstruction. "A doomed civilization"—Cable's inability to comprehend the pathos in that phrase was a necessity to his career as a reformer, but it also marks his failure as an artist.

Notes

1. The Providence *Journal*, February 5, 1925.

2. Arlin Turner, *George W. Cable* (Austin: Steck-Vaughan, 1969), p. 40.

3. Harriet Beecher Stowe, *Uncle Tom's Cabin*, ed. Kenneth S. Lynn (Cambridge, Mass.: Harvard University Press, 1962), p. 168.

4. George Washington Cable, *The Grandissimes* (New York: Sagamore Press, 1957), p. 150. (Subsequent references to this work will appear in the text in parentheses.)

5. Louis D. Rubin, Jr., "The Division of the Heart: Cable's *The Grandissimes*," *Southern Literary Journal*, 1 (Spring, 1969), 44. See also Louis D. Rubin, Jr., *George W. Cable: The Life and Times of a Southern Heretic* (New York: Pegasus, 1969), pp. 77–96.

6. E. F. Harkins, *Little Pilgrimages Among the Men Who Have Written Famous Books* (Boston: L. C. Page, 1902), p. 76.

7. Charles Gayarré, "Mr. Cable's Freedman's Case in Equity," New Orleans *Times-Democrat*, Jan. 11, 1885, p. 8.

8. George Washington Cable, *The Cavaliers* (New York: Charles Scribner's Sons, 1901), pp. 31–32.

9. George Washington Cable, *The Negro Question*, ed. Arlin Turner (Garden City, N.Y.: Doubleday, 1958), p. 14.

10. Ibid., p. 44.

11. Arlin Turner, *Mark Twain and George Washington Cable: The Record of a Literary Friendship* (East Lansing: Michigan State University Press, 1960), p. 85.

12. Edward Larocque Tinker, "Cable and the Creoles," *American Literature*, 5 (Jan. 1934), 314.

13. Grace King, *Memories of a Southern Woman of Letters* (New York: Macmillan, 1932), p. 81.

14. Lafcadio Hearn, *Essays on American Literature*, ed. Sanki Ichikawa (Tokyo: Kanda, Tokyo Hokuseido Press, 1929), p. 58.

15. *Mark Twain's Notebook*, ed. Albert Bigelow Paine (New York: Harper, 1935), p. 163.

George Washington Cable

Daniel Aaron°

*It [the right to secede] was exercised contrary to the belief and advice of
hundreds of thousands of Southern men. That doubtful doctrine was not
our cause; if the gentleman is a young man I pray him to leave the
preaching of that delusion to the venerable ex-President of the Confederate
States. It was the only ground upon which some of our Southern political
advisers cast up the defenses behind which our actual cause lay fortified.
Our real cause—the motive—was no intricate question. A president was
elected lawfully by a party that believed simply what virtually the whole
intelligence of the South now admits, viz., that African slavery—the
existence of which was originally the fault of the whole nation—was an
error in its every aspect, was cursing the whole land. And we chose the risks
of war rather than in any manner to jeopardize an institution which we
have since learned to execrate.*

GEORGE WASHINGTON CABLE, 1884

THE UN-SOUTHERN CONFEDERATE

To many of his Southern critics, George Washington Cable was no Southerner at all but a sort of crypto-Northerner accidentally born in the South who
befouled his birthplace for Yankee gold. Paul Hamilton Hayne was not alone in
stigmatizing Cable (whom he had never met and whose work he disdained to
read) as a renegade and parvenu, a "mongrel cur."[1] As a twice-wounded Confederate veteran, Cable was presumably entitled to speak for his section—"we
of the South," he insisted upon saying[2] —but his opponents never considered
him a bona-fide Southern representative. Neither his father's birth in Winches-
ter, Virginia, nor the presence of Cables in Virginia since before the Revolution
could blot out the taint of his mother's Puritan heritage. It seemed logical
enough to Henry W. Grady, editor of the Atlanta *Constitution*, that Cable

°Reprinted from Daniel Aaron, *The Unwritten War: American Writers and the Civil War* (New
York: Alfred A. Knopf, 1973), pp. 272–82.

229

should end up in New England, for, Grady wrote in 1885, "he appears to have had little sympathy with his Southern environment."[3]

This same Cable in April 1862 watched Farragut's fleet "come slowly round Slaughterhouse Point into full view, silent, so grim, and terrible; black with men, heavy with deadly portent; the long-banished Stars and Stripes flying against the frowning sky."[4] Young Cable formed part of the mob who hurrahed for Jeff Davis and jeered at the two United States naval officers sent to negotiate the surrender of New Orleans. And when General Benjamin F. Butler began his notorious administration of the city in May of that year, the Cable family refused to take the oath of allegiance. In June of 1863, Cable's widowed mother, his two older sisters, and his younger brother were refugees in Confederate Mississippi. Four months later the diminutive eldest son, looking much younger and frailer than his eighteen years, joined Company J of the Fourth Mississippi cavalry.[5]

Unlike the deep-dyed, unreconstructed Rebels or the elegists of the "Lost Cause," Cable gave little thought to the Yankee invaders after he had been paroled as a prisoner of war and returned to New Orleans in the late spring of 1865. So closely, in fact, did his political de-conversion follow on the Confederate capitulation that spiteful antagonists like Hayne and Cable's most eloquent calumniator, the Creole historian Charles Gayarré, doubted whether Cable had ever been sincerely loyal to Dixie. Cable repeatedly testified to the bravery of Southern soldiers, but what rankled in the minds of his critics was his un-Southern appraisal of the War itself. No patriot to the Southern "nation" would dispose of Southern aims and claims in the spirit of a calculating pettifogger. Although not technically an alien, he was "alien" to them "in heart, soul, affection, & principle, while pretending to be 'to the manner born.' "[6]

Such allegations tell us more about the men who made them than about Cable himself, yet as his critics rightly inferred, he did not enlist in the Confederate army to defend Southern civilization against Yankee hordes. Several years of campaigning in Mississippi and Alabama neither seared his spirit nor changed his vision of life. He left the army the same pious, conscientious, and cheerful boy he was when he joined it. The few extant letters Cable wrote during the War years contain reassurances to his mother, admonitions to his brother, and very little about the War. He seems to have fretted about his and his brother's inglorious military record, "one," he reminded his brother, "brought out of a disgraceful skirmish with a slight flesh wound before the fight was done, the other hunted through the swamps, his horse and clothes captured, and himself escaping by precipitate flight."[7] The "slight flesh wound" (a bullet hole in the left armpit) produced no existential reverberations, and in the last months of his military service, when he clerked in the headquarters of General Nathan Bedford Forrest,[8] he found time to study mathematics, Latin grammar, and the Bible.

If his fiction is any test, the War affected Cable much less traumatically than it did De Forest or Bierce or Wendell Holmes, Jr. The few War episodes in his novels, written years after the events described, display some pictorial skill.

At least three of them—*Dr. Sevier* (1884), *The Cavalier* (1901), and *Kincaid's Battery* (1908)—contain bits of realistic observation possibly based on personal experience, but they have less to do with the tragedy of war than with its dreariness and hardship, with "rains, bad food, ill-chosen camps, freshets, terrible roads, horses sick and raw-boned, chills, jaundice, emaciation, barely an occasional bang at the enemy on reconnoissances and picketings, and marches and countermarches through blistering noons and skyless nights, with men, teams, and guns trying to see which could stagger the worst, along with columns of infantry mutinously weary of forever fortifying and never fighting."[9] This unglamorous catalogue probably sums up the War he actually knew, but Cable characteristically skirts military actions in his narratives almost as if they were unpleasant interludes to be suppressed rather than cherished.

CABLE ON THE "LOST CAUSE"

Nothing Cable wrote during or after the War indicates he was ever an enthusiastic partisan of secession. He fought as a citizen-soldier because (as he told some of his army mates), he was "a citizen of this government, a soldier by its laws, sworn into service and ordered not to think, but to fight." Whatever his doubts about the wisdom of secession, at eighteen he did not question slavery as an institution and believed in a "White Man's Government." At the War's end, he felt "not one spark of loyalty to the United States Government."[10]

Two decades later Cable sketched the process by which he changed from a dutiful if lukewarm secessionist into a disbeliever of the Confederate cause and a civil libertarian. First doubts nagged him shortly after 1865 with the South apparently agreeing that the right of secession had been settled by the sword. He could understand why the *power* to secede had been so decided, but why the *right*? Had there ever been a right to secede? He turned to Justice Story's commentary on the Constitution for an answer and discovered no such provision:

> I rose at last from this study indignant against the propagators of that doctrine. I knew it had been believed by thousands of good men, but it seemed, and still seems, to me a perfidious doctrine. How, I queried, could good men—not boys, as I was— ever accept so shallow a piece of pettifogging literalism? What use or need had there been to set up such a doctrine and waste three hundred thousand young men's lives in its defense? There could be but one answer; it was to protect slaveholding.[11]

But granted secession arguments had been compounded of bad logic and bad history, rebellion and revolution were still defensible if slavery was right. This question opened up a new course of investigation for Cable, whose only brush with antislavery ideas had been a cursory reading of *Uncle Tom's Cabin* as a child and an acquaintance with a circumspect German abolitionist. He had no difficulty detecting the sophistry of the biblical sanction of slavery. A harder test was to look with understanding on "the Freedman in all his offensiveness; multitudinous, unclean, stupid, ugly, ignorant, and insolent." Gradually his concern over what white supremacists referred to as "our black peasantry" overcame his revulsion. Someone had to be brave or shameless enough to risk "a complete and ferocious ostracism," lest the old unjust order be preserved under a new name. "Politics" to Cable had come to mean something more than community service; it also required a man to serve his nation and the human race. The black man, he decided, by virtue of his nationality and humanity "must share and enjoy in common with the white race the whole scale of *public* rights and advantages provided under American government."[12]

So at least Cable wrote in 1888 after he had become notorious throughout the South as a renegade who had reaped "golden harvests by haranguing Northern audiences on the fascinating subject of the Southern sins."[13] It was an unjust aspersion. Cable had risked censure in New Orleans long before the North had ever heard of him. He had not deliberately set about offending the South. He wanted Southerners after "calm debate" to settle the "Southern problem" without outside intervention. The South, he thought, "would read from a Southern man patiently what it would only resent from a Northerner."[14]

Cable badly misjudged the audience, or at least underestimated the durability of time-tested Southern dogmas immune to logic and unaffected by even his brand of tactful argumentation. He seems to have anticipated the support of what he called the "Silent South," an inarticulate but substantial segment pleased to be disencumbered of slavery and ready to grant civil rights to Negroes. Speaking for them, he would challenge sincere but misguided "traditionalists" still bewitched by sectional and racial delusions. He would present himself as one who had found it hard to relinquish his antiquated beliefs, whose sympathies had "ranged upon the pro-Southern side of the issue" but whose convictions had been irresistibly drawn by coercive logic to the other side.[15]

Cable's essays and addresses, experiments in persuasion, are as fresh and trenchant today as they were when they first appeared. His tone is invariably conciliatory. He imputes the best of intentions to his adversaries, celebrates Lee and "his ragged grey veterans" in muted rhetoric, exhales love for the South ("I cannot here, yield to any one in pride in our struggle and in all the noble men and women who bore its burdens"),[16] deplores "the dreadful episode of Reconstruction," abjures the social intermingling of the races, insists on Northern complicity in the national tragedy. Nonetheless, these adroit and ingratiating lay-sermons are in essence a devastating arraignment of the Southern ethos, and they must have been all the more infuriating to the "adherents of the old regime" for their sweet reasonableness. Here is Cable's case in brief:

Slavery: Cable denounced it as nothing less than "a deplorable error . . . our crime and our curse." It prevented the emergence of a middle class (for Cable as for Howells the salt of the earth), throttled dissent, stifled culture, isolated the South from the outside world, concentrated and consumed the intellectual energy of the South in its defense, and left it "mired and stuffed with conservatism to the point of absolute rigidity."[17]

The War: Although the Union armies contained a good many abolitionists who enlisted to free the slaves, the majority of Northern soldiers fought for national unity, a cause which, as it turned out, required the destruction of slavery to win. Most Southern whites, on the other hand, would not have supported secession had there been any other way to preserve slavery. In short, the War came because the North and South espoused antipodal principles each held "to be absolutely essential to the safety, order, peace, fortune, and honor of society." The former declared the well-being of society to rest on "the free self-government of all under one common code of civil rights," the other that the highest social development required "the subjugation of the lower mass under the arbitrary protective supremacy of an untitled but hereditary privileged class, a civil caste." Out of the first came the schoolhouse, out of the second the slaveyard. Had the North waived its conviction and compromised with the advocates of caste, the blood of hundreds of thousands might have been spared. It did not. "The freedom of the Negro was bought at a higher price in white man's blood and treasure, than any people ever paid, of their own blood and treasure for their own liberty."[18] Legalized slavery was killed.

Aftermath: But "the ghost of that old heresy"—mass subjugation by a caste—survived. Public servitude replaced private bondage. "The ex-slave was not a free man; he was only a free Negro." The same mentality that trusted to a geological time to solve desperate problems, "the habit of letting error go uncontradicted because it is ours," persisted in the post-War years. The traditionalists learned nothing from the past. They continued to preach black inferiority while refusing to remove the crippling handicaps that kept the Negro from sloughing off "the debasements of slavery and semi-slavery." The reckoning could not be indefinitely postponed, and necessary reform, if too long refused from the inside, would be imposed by the outside.[19]

If these views were widely entertained in the South, then the silent contingent must have held their tongues after the public outcry provoked by Cable's published lectures and articles. Private messages of appreciation and encouragement came from Southern whites and blacks, but no sizable group dared openly to defend him.

Cable's vindictive and scurrilous foes misrepresented his motives and distorted his position on race. He did not, as they kept repeating, preach social equality ("We may reach the moon some day, not social equality"),[20] nor was he by any definition an amalgamationist. But they correctly pegged him as one who had drifted so far from the Southern consensus that even his Confederate war service did not entitle him to speak for the South. Any man who openly expressed his preference for the civilized North, shook hands with Frederick Douglass, numbered Garrison and Phillips among "the great dead," blessed the birthday of Harriet Beecher Stowe, and pronounced the Union cause just could hardly have expected a sympathetic hearing from a people whose cherished prejudices he flouted. "We are just as completely dedicated to God's service," Cable wrote to his wife in 1885, "as though we were Chinese missionaries."[21] That was the year Cable cut his ties with his benighted section and settled permanently in Northampton, Massachusetts—the final disqualification so far as the South was concerned.

The men in charge of the New South wanted none of Cable's evangelism. If he had been of old Southern stock and if he had been more respectful of Southern traditions, they would not have found his plea for social justice to the Negro any more palatable, but they might have given it a more respectful hearing than it got. What made him finally seem alien was his blend of missionary and realist that Southerners had never relished. Cable's friends, Mark Twain and Howells, shared his contempt for the brummagem of pseudochivalry,[22] his conviction that sincere and brave men had nearly wrecked the nation to preserve a shabby barbaric institution, but to survivors of the War and Reconstruction, still spiritually unvanquished and revering the "Lost Cause," Cable's judgment of the War was impious slander and particularly so coming from one reputedly obsessed with Southern blemishes and blind to Northern ones.

THE GRANDISSIMES

A note of pessimism—sometimes close to cynicism—which Cable usually excluded from his public utterances can be heard in his autobiographical essay, "My Politics," written in 1888 as an introduction to a new collection of essays but posthumously published. It was really, as Arlin Turner observed, an apologia, an answer to his critics, and although pacific in tone, it suggests that Cable did not pass through his ordeal unscathed. Experience had taught him some sad truths. Nations fail to live up to their heroic ideas and at best approximate them only after "painful and costly delays." The public is likely to be wrong both as to facts and principles and the "great mass of mankind unconsciously adjust their convictions to the ends they have in view, often to the most short-sighted notions of self-interest or the moment's emergency.[23]

These and other insights that informed his social writing he incorporated into his one enduring work of fiction, *The Grandissimes* (1880), a romantic and often sentimental novel shot through with darkness and terror. The time of the narrative is New Orleans in 1803, the year in which Louisiana passed from France to the United States. Given his state of mind in 1878 when he began his novel for serial publication in *Scribner's Magazine*, it inevitably became, as he said, "a study of the fierce struggle going on around me, regarded in the light of that past history—those beginnings—which had so differentiated the Louisiana civilization from the American scheme of public society."[24]

Like Cable himself, the hero of *The Grandissimes*, Joseph Frowenfeld, is an outsider alternately charmed and appalled by Creole society. He is not unresponsive to those Creole traits—kindliness, generosity, politeness, naïveté—Cable had already affectionately if sometimes satirically rendered in the local-color sketches of New Orleans published a few years before his novel. Yet Frowenfeld's Presbyterian morality cannot condone the Creoles' pleasure-seeking style of life or their grasshopperish irresponsibility. Nor can he abide the rigidity of their social distinctions and the cruel and impulsive acts of some Creole aristocrats. Above all, Cable's hero is sickened by the treatment of the

Negro under Louisiana's *Code Noir* and by the tragic consequences of miscegenation.

Cable wrote his subversive novel to entertain as well as to instruct, but if he had settled for the role of agreeable storyteller he later assumed, an antiquarian delighting in quaint customs, odd forms of dialect, the romantic decor and varied types of exotic New Orleans, he would have remained at best a figure for anthologists, not the author of *The Grandissimes* who looked behind the social façade and described what he saw with a terrible veracity.

The subterfuge of placing the novel in New Orleans around the time of the Louisiana Purchase cannot disguise the obvious parallels between the South of Jefferson's day and the South of the 1870s and 1880s, or better, the South on the eve of secession and the South in Reconstruction. Cable's Creoles talk and think like the post-War die-hards. They hold the same notions of caste, evidence the same dislike and fear of democracy. A harangue by an anti-American Creole patriarch to his retainers might have come from some leader of the Ku Klux Klan or New Orleans White League, and the equivalent of his dying words predicting the recovery of "Old Louisiana's" trampled rights might have been heard in many quarters of Dixie after Appomattox.[25] Frowenfeld is tolerated only so long as he leaves community opinion unchallenged. When he fails, in the words of one Creole, to " 'teh-kyeh 'ow he stir the 'ot blood of Lousyanna!' " a mob wrecks his shop. General Claiborne, the new American Governor of the Territory, is regarded with the same intense hatred later generations in New Orleans reserved for "Beast" Butler and his minions. Cable was not writing allegory, of course, but he capitalized to the hilt on historical analogies and wrote, in effect, a contemporary exposé in the form of a historical romance.

The Grandissimes somewhat resembles *Uncle Tom's Cabin*, a book Cable claims to have read in his ninth year without explaining how it found its way into his family library. Both contain harrowing episodes of violence, play up the misery suffered by Southerners, white and black, as a result of miscegenation, and exploit the romantic (and sexual) associations clustering around the figure of the beautiful quadroon.[26] Repeating a device of Mrs. Stowe, Cable puts the most telling arguments against slavery in the mouth of a slaveowning aristocrat and singles out slavery as the root cause for everything bad that has befallen the South.

What distinguishes Cable's Negro characters from the black cartoon of Mrs. Stowe is the variety and subtlety of his portraiture. The blacks in *The Grandissimes* range from the most primitive servant to the educated f.m.c. (free man of color); collectively they cast "the shadow of the Ethiopian"[27] on a people too enmeshed in the institution to see and judge it. Cable's Negroes may be romantically touched up, but few Southern writers before or later took a harder look at black/white relations. He blurted out what the Silent South dared not say: that never for a minute did the Negro accept the white man's cant about slaves faring better and feeling happier than freed men. He never allowed his readers to forget the murderous war constantly threatening to erupt between the races or the hatred behind the obsequiousness and humor of the servile class. His "bad niggers" have been forged in "fires that do not refine, but that blunt and blast and blacken and char." Clemence, the crafty old *marchande* of calas and ginger cakes, has none of Uncle Tom's immaculacy. She is the heiress of

> starvation, gluttony, drunkenness, thirst, drowning, nakedness, dirt, fetichism, debauchery, slaughter, pestilence and the rest . . . they left her the cinders of human feelings. She remembered her mother. They had been separated in her childhood, in Virginia when it was a province. She remembered, with pride, the price her mother had brought at auction, and remarked, as an additional interesting item, that she had never seen or heard of her since. She had had children, assorted colors—had one with her now, the black boy that brought the basil to Joseph; the others were here and there, some in the Grandissime households or field-gangs, some elsewhere within occasional sight, some dead, some not accounted for. Husbands—like the Samaritan woman's. We know she was a constant singer and laugher.[28]

Throughout the novel, Cable shows how the white man's "criminal benevolence" toward the Negro as well as his rage and ferocity rest on fear. "It seems to be one of the self-punitive characteristics of tyranny," he observes, "whether the tyrant be a man, a community, or a caste, to have a pusillanimous fear of its victim."[29] The response of this community fear is "terrific cruelty," dramatized in *The Grandissimes* by the half-mythic figure of a gigantic African prince, Bras-Coupé, whose presence pervades the entire novel and links all of the main characters. To some of them, he is merely a "pestiferous darky," to others a source of enlightenment, a fearsome portent, a symbol of black revenge. Slavery fails to diminish his manhood and pride. He strikes down his master, ranges the swamps as a fugitive, and is captured only after he leaves his sanctuary to join his fellow slaves who are dancing in Congo Square. The whites lash him, cut off his ears, and hamstring him according to the provisions of Louisiana's Black Code, but his death does not expunge their fears or allay their anxieties.

Cable's powerful statement about a mighty wrong is vitiated by his fits of sentimentality, his tendency to idealize his characters, his weakness for silly mystifications. He sandwiches sugary interludes between the grimmest scenes, perhaps to reassure the same feminine audience De Forest tried but failed to please. Cable succeeded better but at the cost of playing down his sociological bent. He soothed shocked sensibilities by ending his tale of miscegenation, inutilation, and murder with happy marriages. After the crazed black woman Clemence has been savaged by a steel trap and then shot in the back, and after an f.m.c., fathered by the sire of the white Honoré Grandissime, has stabbed a white man to death, Cable can still praise God for "love's young dream."

All the same, such concessions to his editors and to a squeamish public hardly weaken the force of this impressive novel, and not until Faulkner did American writers handle Cable's theme with comparable or greater power. While not specifically about the War, *The Grandissimes* is probably his most consummate statement about the men and ideas that made it come to pass. Implicitly it refuted the wishful thinking of an 1884 editorial in *Century Magazine* that "the passions and prejudices of the Civil War have nearly faded out of politics."[30] Despite the fraternizing of Confederate and Federal soldiers, Cable knew very well they remained.

Cable's experience in the Confederate army and, more important, his subsequent reflections on the War's causes and meaning had turned him into a strong critic of Southern racial prejudice. He sympathized with the woes of the South but not to the extent of pardoning or condoning what he took to be its sins. Had he been content merely to weave fictional tapestries with no hint of social criticism, he would have remained a favorite in the South as well as the North—doubly appreciated because of his trans-Southern reputation.[31] But the Presbyterian moralist drowned out or at least competed with the entertainer, and the South, angered by his allegations and proposals, drummed him out of Louisiana.

For more than a half-century thereafter, no literary renegade of comparable power arose to challenge the Confederate version of the War or Southern assumptions about black subordination. Insiders might be granted the privileges of irony and a degree of levity in treating the past, but sons and daughters of the South were generally more comfortable in the role of hierophants than subverters of Southern traditionalism. This attitude prevailed until the emergence of a new literary generation during or immediately after World War I.

That war, according to Allen Tate, marked the re-entry of the South into the modern world, but the consciousness of an earlier war, far from being obliterated by the newer one, was heightened by it; now his generation had "a double focus, a looking two ways, which gave a special dimension to the writings of our school." Between the two great wars of the twentieth century the long-barren South produced a dazzling literary crop. As before, the past remained an important ingredient in Southern literature, but a past intermingling with the present and stripped of much of its sentimentality and gentility. The Sacred Cause itself, a composite of fact and legend (felt if not mentioned or alluded to even in stories and poems about the contemporary South), smoldered in the Southern imagination.

The men and women writers of the "Renaissance" who returned to the "still visitable past"—the experiences of Southern people during the War and Reconstruction—rejected both the nostalgic fabrication of Thomas Nelson Page and the cheerful boosterism of the New South proponents. In their fiction and nonfiction, they made these years the testing ground of Southern character, manners, and political intelligence, and assessed the value of the Old South's legacy. They did not discount the flaws in the society smashed by the War, but they set the ideals and values of the defeated above those of the victors.

And over their writings the Ethiopian still cast his shadow.

Notes

1. C. R. Anderson, "Charles Gayarré and Paul Hayne: The Last Literary Cavaliers," in *American Studies in Honor of William Kenneth Boyd*, ed. D. K. Jackson (Durham, N.C.: Duke University Press, 1940), p. 247.

2. George Washington Cable, "We of the South," *Century Magazine*, 29 (November, 1884), 152.

3. Henry W. Grady, "In Plain Black and White: A Reply to Mr. Cable," *Century Magazine*, 29 (April, 1885), 917.

4. George Washington Cable, "New Orleans Before the Capture," *Century Magazine*, 29 (April, 1885), 922.

5. Arlin Turner, *George W. Cable: A Biography* (Durham, N.C.: Duke University Press, 1956), pp. 24–26.

6. Anderson, "Gayarré and Hayne," p. 226. See also Charles Duffy, "A Southern Genteelist: Letters of Paul Hamilton Hayne to Julia C. R. Dorr," *South Carolina Historical and Genealogical Society*, 53 (January, 1952), 22.

7. Quoted in Kjell Ekström, *George Washington Cable: A Study of His Early Life and Work* (Uppsala, Sweden, and Cambridge, Mass.: Harvard University Press, 1950), p. 27.

8. Cable claimed to have made out the manumission forms for Forrest's Negro teamsters. How this experience may have influenced his views on slavery is a matter for speculation. See Arlin Turner, "George W. Cable's Recollections of General Forrest," *Journal of Southern History*, 21 (May, 1955), 222–28.

9. George Washington Cable, *Kincaid's Battery* (New York: Charles Scribner's Sons, 1908), p. 163.

10. George Washington Cable, *The Negro Question: A Selection of Writings on Civil Rights*, ed. Arlin Turner (New York: Doubleday, 1958), p. 4.

11. Cable, *The Negro Question*, p. 5.

12. Cable, *The Negro Question*, pp. 6–9.

13. Cable, *The Negro Question*, p. 21.

14. Cable, *The Negro Question*. p. 15.

15. Cable, *The Negro Question*, p. 81.

16. Cable, "We of the South," p. 151.

17. Cable, *The Negro Question*, pp. 39, 41.

18. Cable, *The Negro Question*, pp. 134, 135, 155.

19. Cable, *The Negro Question*, pp. 139, 116, 63.

20 Cable, *The Negro Question*, p. 71.

21. For the reference to Douglass, see Guy A. Cardwell, *Twins of Genius* (Lansing: Michigan State University Press, 1953), p. 22. The tribute to Garrison and Phillips is quoted in Arlin Turner, *Mark Twain and George W. Cable. The Record of a Literary Friendship* (Lansing: Michigan State University Press, 1960), p. 85. Turner's *George W. Cable*, pp. 22, 206, is my source for the birthday letter to Mrs. Stowe and Mrs. Cable.

22. "But I believe the time is not very far away," he told a graduating class at the University of Mississippi in 1882, "when anyone who rises before you and addresses you as 'Southrons' shall be stared at as the veriest Rip Van Winkle that the time can show" (Cable, *The Negro Question*, p. 44).

23. Cable, *The Negro Question*, pp. 2–5.

24. Cable, *The Negro Question*, p. 14.

25. George Washington Cable, *The Grandissimes*, ed. Newton Arvin (New York: Sagamore Press, 1957), pp. 282–84, 326–27.

26. Lafcadio Hearn, an admirer of *The Grandissimes*, argued that abolitionists would never have won over the racist-minded to their position without the presence of the "colored race," his name for the people of mixed blood: "In the first place, they formed as a body the great living testimony to slavery's worst sin; and that testimony . . . more than any other, brought in the courts of human conscience, and in the courts of governments, the conviction and condemnation of the sin itself. Their very existence tended above all else to kindle the world's shame of slavery as a vice;

while the force, beauty, and intelligence of the race conquered the sympathy of humanity. There are many evidences in the pages of anti-slavery literature to show that the writer was thinking of the man of color while pleading for the negro, whose nature he never clearly understood." Albert Mordell, ed., *An American Miscellany* (New York: Dodd, Mead, 1924), pp. 225–26. In another comment applicable to Cable's novel, Hearn suggested that the denial of race equality on the part of whites forced "men of color" into an alliance with Negroes. The latter were used to slavery and had known it in Africa. But the mixed-blooded Negro taught the blacks the injustice of their bondage and inculcated into them the moral power to rebel.

27. Cable, *The Grandissimes*, p. 197.

28. Cable, *The Grandissimes*, p. 251.

29. Cable, *The Grandissimes*, p. 315.

30. *Century Magazine*, 28 (October, 1884), 943.

31. In the interests of sectional harmony, Cable occasionally honored Confederate heroes. "The Gentler Side of Two Great Southerners" (*Century Magazine*, 49 [December, 1893], 292–94) reports two anecdotes. In one, General Lee speaks kindly to an urchin who interrupts a conversation with President Davis; in the other, General Jackson worries about his colored Sunday School: The noble gentleness of character that distinguished some of our Southern generals in the Civil War—I think the 'our' may rightly be offered in a national sense—will still, I venture to say, be a pleasant theme when the generation that fought that war has passed away."

INDEX